D1356661

Chalk Stream Salmon and Trout Fishing

Charles Bingham

SWAN·HILL
PRESS

DEDICATION
For my nephew, Robert Bingham (1961-82). He fished the Avon
and the Itchen for a while

ACKNOWLEDGEMENTS
The author wishes to record his grateful appreciation to the
following for assistance: Ian Abbot, Capt Donald McEwen RN,
Hugo Wood Homer, Dick Houghton, Bill Humphreys, Stephen
Jones, Peter Lyne, Cdr Bryan O'Neil RN, and Chris Rothwell.
Special thanks are due to the owners of The Bossington Estate
and Brian Parker for grayling fishing, and to Bill Heller who
allowed Lara and me to deceive his trout. The open hospitality
of Tony and Frances Allen, Lindsay Parker and Bill and Jean
Waldron sustained my travels.

Copyright © 1993 by Charles Bingham

First published in the UK in 1993 by
Swan Hill Press an imprint of Airlife Publishing Ltd

British Library Cataloguing in Publication Data
A catalogue record of this book
is available from the British Library

ISBN 1 85310 224 5

All rights reserved. No part of this book may be reproduced or
transmitted in any form or by any means, electronic or mechanical
including photocopying, recording or by any information storage and
retrieval system, without permission from the Publisher in writing.

Printed by Kyodo Printing Co (S'pore Pte Ltd)

Swan Hill Press
an imprint of Airlife Publishing Ltd
101 Longden Road, Shrewsbury, SY3 9EB

Contents

Introduction

There are four purposes in the writing of this book. The first is to describe a number of representative game fishing locations on each of the chalk-based rivers of the South of England. Salmon, trout, sea trout and grayling waters receive attention. The river descriptions, locations of the different fish, the methods of fishing — all to be described — will enable an angler searching for water to make an informed choice. He will not lose days in travel and research.

The second purpose is to present angling methods of proven success, in many places, which will enable the different species of fish to be caught. For this, knowledgeable anglers and river keepers of today have contributed their experiences on the waters which they fish. No single author is able to inform *in detail* how to fish the Itchen, Frome, Allen, Hampshire Avon and other chalk streams. If he or she tried to do so, and include in the account the four game fish, the effect would be too general to carry conviction. One person may make regular salmon catches on the lower Test, but his methods may differ from those of an angler with a rod on the Hampshire Avon at Somerley. Both of them might be at a loss if sent out to take trout from the clear waters of the Allen in Dorset.

I have therefore sought out anglers and keepers on each river who are experienced fishers on their waters and innovative in their methods. They are not all as young as they might wish: the octogenarians and a nonagenarian spoke finely sieved words of wisdom into my pocket tape recorder at the waterside; other contributors have the energy and application of youth. All have laid many fish upon the grass and I am privileged to present to you their methods.

Times change: many rivers have reduced in flow in recent years; some scenes have altered. Those of us who are over the top of the hill knew streams and ponds and muddy places now replaced by houses. For 15 years, commencing in 1963, I lived close to the river Allen in Dorset. It was a delightful stream, full of water and wild brown trout. In the evenings of those summers of memory I relieved the trout of freedom in the company of my friend Bill Humphreys who still lives nearby. We spoke on the telephone in 1990: 'I don't go down so often now. There is little water, and what there is could pass through a 9-inch pipe'.

There is the third purpose of this book: to record the present beauty of these rivers. It is clear that the flow, and thus the condition, of many has deteriorated over the last 30 years. Will they now be protected and improved by the newly formed National Rivers Authority? We must hope so and give support. But whether improvement or deterioration unfold over the coming years, times change. And so, as we kneel in the evening light beside these rivers and the rod is bent into a fish, my contributors and I have endeavoured to make a record in words and photographs for those who follow our generation.

The fourth purpose is to set before the reader my own methods of catching trout and salmon on the chalk streams. There are many who have caught more fish than myself — opportunity and desire play their part. But I have caught sufficient to know that delicate casting, the circumspect approach, and being 'tuned in' to the ways of fish will ensure an enjoyable day. Trout willing, this combination usually provides a brace for the pan. To catch a trout one does not need to know the Latin name of the lesser knobbly-kneed greenfly. One does need the alertness to see that the greenfly was eaten, and that it was small. A small fly wi!l then take that trout — probably!

So, sit with me beside the river whilst I talk. Watch the water. Mark a rolling salmon or a rising trout and, when my discourse is complete, creep forward on hands and knees to catch him.

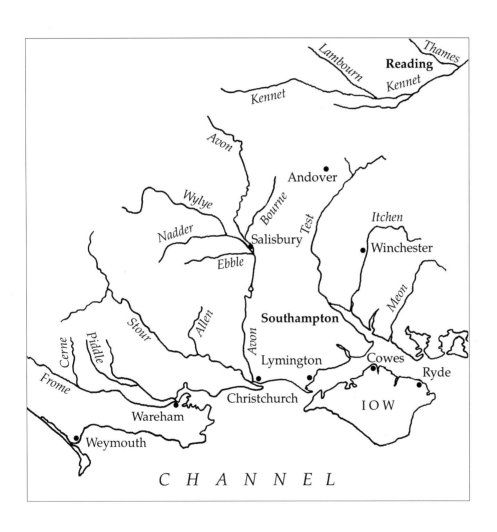

Chalk Stream
Salmon and
Trout Fishing

Part 1: Salmon and Trout Fishing Techniques

Part 2: The Rivers and the Angling Experts

The Characteristics of Chalk Streams

Many would-be trout anglers come to my home county, Devon, each season to be taught to catch game fish. On the first day of their visit they are instructed on a lake where the water is conveniently static. The second day is more demanding, casting a dry fly upstream on the West Dart, Teign or Lyd. Many difficulties arise on the second day: the fly is swept downstream before they can say 'Jack Robinson', and the Red Sedge may drag or sink. The wind often blows downstream, and their shadow precedes them up the river, scattering trout, before they have learned to wade below the bank.

Then, to their astonishment and joy, after much effort, the fly alights just right. The first rise is missed. Prepared for the second, the trout is hooked, persuaded to the bank, beached, admired and released — all six inches of him. Half a foot of golden fish, red spotted and shaped in perfect symmetry. Then they want to catch another. They succeed. Questions have been darted at me throughout the day, but as we wend our way to the car I anticipate the next:

> 'Where can we catch a larger trout in a river?'
> 'Not here. On the Devon moors they don't exist.
> You'll have to go to the chalk streams.'

The Lie of the Land

To explain myself to the pupils, attention is drawn to the surrounding hills and tors, some of which rise to over 2000 ft above sea level. The river Dart falls 1,250 ft from a number of streams on the moor to sea level, a course of roughly 20 miles. The river Test flows 35 miles from its source at Ashe to Southampton Water, falling 300 ft on the way. The Frome drops 450 ft over 28 miles to the estuary at Wareham. The Dart thus drops 62 ft per mile, the Frome 16 ft, and the Test 8 ft. In slow water silt settles; in fast water it is scoured away, if any were present in the first place. Water plants need mud in which to grow. There is little mud in a moorland river, but plenty, often too much, in the slower flowing chalk streams. Water weeds are sparse on the moors; in the rivers of Hampshire, Wiltshire and Dorset they have to be controlled by cutting.

The position of the moorland rivers would not be so adverse if the flow, fast as it may be, were constant. Instead, spates — those floods rushing down the valley following heavy rain in the hills — often followed by dry weather and long spells of low flow, provide unstable conditions. Plants and fish do not thrive where one week there is too much water and the next too little. A spate arises because the rock beneath the moorland peat is impervious; rain is not absorbed, and is thus shed straight down the watercourse. This happens where the bedrock is slate or granite.

Contrast this physical construction with a chalk-based river. The fall is not so great, the surrounding hills are gentle, and the underlying rock — chalk — absorbs water, as do water meadows on each side if still present and not ploughed. In these rivers, which flood infrequently, water plants and fish have a stable environment in respect of water level and rate of flow.

The key to the stability of the chalk stream is the aquifer, that sponge of chalk which underlies the surrounding hills, absorbs rain and discharges it into the river in the valley through springs. Chalk streams are spring-fed. After a winter of rain (of which there has been too little in recent seasons) the sponge is replenished, and the springs 'break' after Christmas. Rain is of little use if falling in summer, being taken up by trees and vegetation, and lost through evaporation. Lower than desirable rates of water flow have been causing deterioration in chalk streams in recent years. Reduced flows have allowed increased deposition of silt on trout and salmon spawning beds. This has resulted in fewer wild brown trout in some areas, and contributed to the steady decline in the numbers of salmon spawning in these rivers, often due to silt-covered ova failing to hatch. The lowering of the aquifer water table is due to a combination of lack of rain and increased abstraction through boreholes sunk into the chalk.

A factor in favour of the chalk streams over rivers rising on the moors is altitude. The closer to sea level the warmer the air and the water; the higher the altitude the colder the situation. In addition, the keeper hatching trout ova, and salmon too, has a supply of spring water rising out of the ground at a constant 10°C, an advantage of perhaps 5°C over the Highland hatchery. In hatcheries utilizing spring water, ova hatch in roughly 50 days, half the time taken in the uplands. Latitude also plays a part. The farther north one travels the colder will be the average temperature — Aberdeen, therefore, being colder than Southampton. The chalk streams in this book flow out along the south coast of England. These temperature factors improve conditions for trout growth. The warmer the water (up to about 60°F) the greater the appetite and rate of digestion of a trout, and the more constant the growth of water plants and the attendant availability of trout food.

pH (Hydrogenion concentration) of water

Water which is neither acid nor alkaline, being neutral, has a pH of 7.0. If less than 7.0 it is acid, if more, alkaline. Large trout are rarely produced in acid waters, but small trout may be present in large numbers. This is because the gravel on the beds of many acid streams is an admirable base for spawning, but there is then little food on which trout could thrive.

Alkaline waters are more likely to grow large trout. Chalk streams are alkaline, having a pH in the region of 7.5. Water weeds, like most farm crops and grass, other than potatoes, grow best in alkaline waters, and weeds are, for reasons to be disclosed, desirable for trout growth.

I do not possess the laboratory equipment to test pH accurately to within 1/10th of a point. Instead, I rely for my personal interest, on litmus papers. These papers change colour to indicate the acidity, or alkalinity, of water. Dipped into the river Dart, close to my house, or the Lyd, a tributary of the river Tamar, the papers indicate a pH of 6.0. The river Test is mid-way on the shade key between pH 7.0 and pH 8.0.

Hardness of water

Hard waters, usually alkaline, produce large trout; soft waters, generally acid, do not, unless it be small numbers of large cannibal trout such as are found in a Highland loch. Total hardness may be expressed as parts per million (ppm) of calcium carbonate. A Dartmoor stream will have up to 50 ppm, whilst the rivers of the chalk possess 150 to 250 ppm. We are made aware of this if we look inside an immersion heater or kettle; in a chalk area they soon have a white layer on the element. In my home there is no white layer due to an absence of calcium, and the element just dissolves due to a low pH!

The hardness, and thus alkalinity, of river water interests us to the fullest extent, for it largely controls plant life which is one of the keys to the growth of trout.

Additionally, calcium salts are necessary for the shell coverings of crayfish and freshwater shrimp, these forming part of the diet of trout.

Water plants and trout food

In agricultural terms a weed is a plant out of place, ie: a thistle in a field of barley. The term 'weed' has a much looser meaning in a river.

George Maich, head keeper to The Piscatorial Society, looks with the greatest favour upon ranunculus and starwort for, amongst other qualities, they provide cover for trout. Watercress protects insect life at the edge of a river, and water parsley is also desirable.

Laurie Stokes, head keeper to The Salisbury & District Angling Club, told me that his favourite weeds are ranunculus, water celery and starwort, 'but any weed is better than none'. That is true. Weeds are essential. In chalk streams they are present, often in profusion, having to be kept in check by 'cutting'. In times of drought keepers may desist from cutting, for heavy weed growth holds back water flow and assists in maintaining depth.

The plant is the basis of chalk stream life and, through silting at their roots, provide the habitat of many invertebrates on which trout feed. Through the presence of chlorophyll in their leaves they are able to use the energy of the sun to manufacture starch and sugar from carbon dioxide and water. The plants grow, and on them feed zooplankton which, in turn sustain larger forms of life on which trout feed. Associated with the weeds I have mentioned are midge larvae, mayfly nymphs, beetle larvae, shrimp, and caddis larvae. Partially silted areas (and weeds collect silt) are favoured not only by the above invertebrates but by dragonfly nymphs (the carnivores of the river insect world), alderfly larvae, water boatmen and snails. The more the merrier, the fatter the trout, and the faster their rate of growth. There is a dragonfly larvae case on my desk as I write, it is $1^1/_2$ in long, and thus the original occupant was a sustaining mouthful for any fish.

Over a span of three years wild brown trout will reach the following lengths:

Chalk, alkaline: River Test — 13 inches
                      River Kennet — 13 inches
Moorland, acid: River Dart — 7 inches
                      River Lyd — 7 inches

Natural spawning and stocking — trout

Ron Holloway at Martyr Worthy on the upper Itchen relies on natural spawning to keep his river stocked with wild brown trout. He has a suitable environment: the river not too deep, a shallow sidestream created by himself and his employer, and he keeps the spawning areas free from silt. Trout redds in winter are visible in profusion.

Fred Kemp and Dave Walford, at Whitchurch and Laverstoke at the top of the Test rely, as the basis of their stock, on planting out trout fry. These provide takeable fish after two or three seasons.

Terry Snelgrove of Govett's estate at Newton Stacey on the Test and its tributary the Dever, relies on both wild spawning and stocking with keepable trout. He has shown me his river at the end of October, commenting that by mid-November the river bed in places will be pitted with redds.

As we proceed down the river the trout fishing, superb as it may be, becomes less the pursuit of wild spawned brown than of stocked brown and rainbow trout. Nature and man force stocking upon the keepers.

The natural environment in the lower reaches of a chalk stream is rarely noted for wild spawned trout. This is because the river is usually deeper, there are few shallows on which redds could be cut, and the water becomes increasingly suited to coarse fish. If the lower areas of a chalk stream are neglected, it is likely that there would be a reversion to pike, perch, roach and chub. They would gobble up the fry of trout, as well as feeding on their own offspring. In these areas, therefore, both the removal of coarse fish and the introduction of keepable trout must take place.

The demands of man govern stocking policies. Even chalk streams are unable to generate the food necessary to produce the weight of trout flesh called for by the financial expectations of some estates. In other words, if 10 season rods are let on a beat which is only naturally capable of meeting the catch expectations of five season rods, the water must be stocked with keepable fish.

So, if my pupils ask: 'Where can we catch large trout in a river?', my answer could be: 'Almost anywhere if stocked'. This reply disregards the fact that a trout stocked at 1lb in the river Lyd in spring, will become a skinny 12oz specimen in three months, if not eaten by the herons! In chalk streams, if 1lb trout are stocked in the season, when food is plentiful, their weight will be maintained until the majority have been caught by the end of September.

But, if the question is more specific: 'Where can I catch large *wild* trout in a river?', my reply must be accurate. I would point them to the headwaters of the chalk streams, reduce expectations to an average keepable weight of 1lb, with the occasional two-pounder. I would warn that trout might still be stocked as fry, and suggest they search for an under-fished water. The truth of the matter is, that in these days when fishing pressure on our rivers is great, such Elysian places are hard to find on earth and may only be expected when we have passed the examination at St Peter's gate.

Trout Fishing

In my library is a book of 431 pages on trout fishing. I have another of over 200 pages on natural flies, and two more, each of over 250 pages, on artificial flies. Halford, Skues and the *Trout Fishing* volume of The Lonsdale Library are on my shelves. To dip into those volumes is enjoyable, but the detail of those instruction and reference tomes need not be absorbed in order to catch trout. Fish don't read. They take small flies, and large flies, and beetles and bugs and nymphs regardless of their names. I have met many celebrated and successful anglers who present dry flies in equal blissful ignorance.

Octogenarian Sir Michael Hordern:

'I am not an entomologist. I might be if the flies called out their names as they landed on the water.'

Ninety-one year-old Sir Owen Aisher on the Test:

'We're not all that fussy. We try to do what the clever chaps do. Collins (the keeper) has a look at the river, and I have a look. We fish either a fly we think is there, or a nymph. We believe in Mr Halford and in Mr Skues! We enjoy ourselves. What was that horrible thing we used last week? That was a nymph, wasn't it?'

Find a rising trout. Observe the size of the natural on which he is feeding. Tie on an artificial of the same size; it does not have to be an imitation. Present this offering with skill and he will usually gulp it down. Quiet motionless observation; the stalked unseen approach; the gossamer presentation of a correctly sized fly in pristine condition — these are the keys.

Be not overawed by the names Itchen and Test. Trout in those rivers have not attended an underwater university. They feed and make mistakes. Follow the suggestions in this book and you will take your share. Delving into detail may come later on your own if you become intimately involved. The pages of this book are limited. They will not be wasted teaching you to cast by diagrams, and explanations of how to tie knots. For the former go to a casting school, there is a list at the back of the book. For the latter study the booklet which comes with each new Scientific Anglers' fly line.

Insect Life and the Trout Angler

The belief is common, and is evident from the interviews with trout anglers in this book, that exact identification and imitation of insects are less important than placing before a trout a dry fly of the same size as the natural on which he is feeding. We thus arm ourselves with general purpose flies in different sizes: Kite's Imperial, Grey Wulff, Red Sedge and hackled Black Gnat amongst others. We also carry a few exact imitations, or as near to exact as may be dressed. These are needed to represent flies which are notably different from any members of the common Orders which appear during the season, ie: the crane fly, commonly known as the daddy long-legs.

Whether or not our successful artificial flies and nymphs resemble the natural in appearance as well as size, an understanding of basic entomology enhances riverside enjoyment. We are able to discuss fly life with fellow fishermen and appreciate the meanings of the terms in use: nymph, dun, spinner and other descriptions. Hatches of duns and falls of spinners may then be anticipated. The fluttering and dancing in the air, and whirling on the water, of sedge flies at dusk may be looked forward to throughout the day. Pleasure is enhanced and self confidence increases.

As we go through the season on chalk streams we are likely to see flies of the following Orders:

EPHEMEROPTERA — Olives and Mayfly
These are the up-winged flies. They have two large upright wings, two small hind wings and two or three tails. Their life cycle is as follows:
● **Egg**
Deposited by the female, after being mated in flight, on the surface of the water from which it sinks to the bottom of the river. Some members crawl down to the river bed to deposit their eggs on the chalk or silt. The eggs hatch after days, weeks or months, depending on the species and the temperature of the water.

● **Nymph**

The egg hatches and a nymph emerges, to live in the water for weeks, months or a year, or longer. It grows through stages which increase in size, moulting its body case at each size.

● **Dun**

The mature nymph swims to the surface, struggles through the water skin, the nymphal case splits and is trodden down. The dun, now supported by the surface tension of the water, unfolds its wings, which dry, and flies away.

● **Spinner**

The dun, whilst resting on land, splits its back casing and moults. The skin is sloughed off the body, wings and tails, and the bright spinner becomes airborne. It mates on the wing, the males die, and the females descend to the river to lay their eggs, unless blown away by a strong wind.

The observable stages above the water surface are the sudden appearance of duns as a hatch commences, and a 'fall' of spinners as the males die and the females drop to the water to lay their eggs. If the reader will refer to 'A Grayling Day' (page 166, 5 October 1991, later in this book) a sudden hatch of iron blue duns is described. When a mayfly nymph hatches it is easy for the angler to see the large transparent nymphal case left behind on the water surface. The only underwater stage of interest to the angler is the nymph. If a trout is observed, one or two feet down, clearly feeding and yet not rising to the surface, he may be 'nymphing'. Such fish are often tempted by the copper wired Pheasant Tail Nymph.

TRICHOPTERA — Caddis or Sedge flies

These flies have four roof-shaped wings which are folded back over the body. The wings are covered with tiny, virtually invisible, hairs. The members have two long antennae and no tails. The life cycle is in four stages:

● **Egg**

The female lays these on or under the water.

● **Larva, pupal case, adult fly**

I look upon this as the angler's equivalent of the schoolboy's caterpillar. Beneath the surface, on the river bed, creeping about on the sides of stones and on river plants, the larva builds a case of vegetable matter, gravel or sand. This small cylinder may be up to one inch in length, depending on the species, and is open at one end from which the head and legs are free to emerge for feeding purposes and movement. The larva grows inside the case until mature, seals the open end, pupates (changes into a fly) emerges, and swims or crawls to the river surface to hatch. There is thus only one aerial stage.

DIPTERA

These flies usually have two flat wings, no antennae and no tails. Included in the Order are the smuts, house flies, hawthorn, crane fly (daddy long-legs), black gnat and midges. Of these, the smuts are very small and barely possible to imitate. Their early life cycle takes place in water: egg, larva, pupa and the adult fly above water.

The midge life cycle commences when the female lays eggs on the water surface. The eggs hatch and the larvae descend to the river bed. Often of a red colour, they are sometimes known as blood worms. The larvae pupate and after some time swim to the water surface to hatch into the adult winged fly.

The black gnat, crane fly (daddy long-legs) and hawthorn are land-based members of *Diptera,* but interest us as they are often blown on to the river.

SIALIDAE

The alder-fly has a life cycle which, unlike the other flies described, I have been unable to observe, except in witnessing the adult fly. Eric Taverner in *Trout Fishing From all Angles,* (Seeley, Service & Co Ltd, 1929) describes the sequence as follows: 'The eggs are laid on bankside vegetation, hatch and the larvae descend to the river bed. After a period the larvae crawl out of the water, burrow into the bank and pupate. When the fly is ready to emerge from the pupa it creeps to the surface and takes wing.'

PLECOPTERA

The common name is stonefly. They possess four hard wings, often pointed, leading to the name needlefly for one member. They are usually found in fast stony-bedded rivers of the North, and in cold upland waters. The flies of this group are common on my home river, the Dart, in those areas which are often 1,000 ft above sea level. I shall not describe the Order, for the flies are of little interest to the chalk stream angler in the warmer rivers of the South.

Beetles, water lice, grasshoppers etc

There are, of course, many of these species which form part of the diet of trout. Fishing the chalk streams we are limited to dry fly and may, at times, present a nymph. There is thus no point in describing these additional forms of sub-surface prey as the methods required to represent them are not allowed, but a word on the shrimp may be of interest.

GAMMARUS PULEX — Freshwater Shrimp

Is common in most of the chalk streams. Trout may be seen feeding close to the bottom, sometimes 'tailing', ie: grubbing with the nose in shallow water whilst the tail waves above the water surface. These fish, often of large size, may be eating shrimp, caddis larvae or snails. A copper wired Pheasant Tail Nymph or a Grayling Bug should be tried, but don't waste too much time on these tantalizers — they seldom finish in the creel!

A Calendar of natural flies

Set out below, month by month, are the natural flies as they emerge. Adjacent are their Orders by which their life cycles, given above, may be anticipated. General or specific dry fly imitations follow.

The two aerial stages of *Ephemeroptera,* being dun and spinner, may often be represented with the dun pattern (if winged) by flattening the wings to lie outstretched on the water surface. Midges (*Chironomidae*), caenis (*Caenis*) and reed smut (*Simulium*) — all *Diptera* — appear in summer. Some people dress artificials on No 20 or even No 22 hooks. I do not follow their example, having no faith in my ability to land trout hooked on so small a pattern, or the strength of mind to control my temper whilst attempting to dress so fiddly an object. Instead I fish a No 18 Black Gnat.

April
- Large Dark Olive (*Baetis rhodani*). *Ephemeroptera.* Kite's Imperial No 14 with a dark hackle. The natural hatches between luncheon and tea-time.
- Hawthorn (*Bibio marci*). *Diptera.* Hawthorn No 16 or, if refused, a Black Gnat No 18.
- Grannom (*Brachycercus subnubilus*). *Trichoptera.* Grannom No 14. This fly hatches early in the month and may be absent by the time the season starts, if this is on 1 May.

May
- Iron Blue (*Baetis pumilus*). *Ephemeroptera.* Dun — Iron Blue No 18; Spinner — Houghton Ruby No 18.
- Alder (*Sialis*). *Sialidae.* Alder No 14.
- Black Gnat (*Bibio johannis*). *Diptera.* Black Gnat No 18.
- Medium Olive (*Baetis vernus*). *Ephemeroptera.* Dun — Kite's Imperial No 16; Spinner — Lunn's particular No 16.
- Mayfly (*Ephemera danica*). *Ephemeroptera.* Dun — Grey Wulff No 12; Spinner (Spent Gnat) — squash flat the Grey Wulff wings.

June
- Mayfly — as above.
- Medium Olive — as above.
- Black Gnat — as above.
- Pale Watery (*Baetis bioculatus*). *Ephemeroptera.* Kite's Imperial No 16 with a pale hackle.
- Blue Winged Olive (*Ephemerella ignita*). *Ephemeroptera.* Dun — Greenwell's Glory No 14; Spinner — Sherry Spinner No 14.
- Cinnamon Sedge (*Limnephilus lunatus*). *Trichoptera.* Red Sedge No 14.

July
- Blue Winged Olive — as above.
- Black Gnat — as above.
- Cinnamon Sedge — as above.
  There will also appear brown, black, red and grey sedges of mixed size. Many hatch at dusk, and I do not believe trout appreciate their colours when the trout is below, and the fly above, the water surface. One will take one's share whilst relying on a Red Sedge No 14 or No 12.
- Small Dark Olive (*Baetis scambus*). *Ephemeroptera.* Kite's Imperial No 16 with a dark hackle.

August
- Blue Winged Olive — as above.
- Black Gnat — as above.
- Sedges — as above.
- Caperer (*Halesus radiatus*). *Trichoptera.* Caperer No 14.

September
- Iron Blue — as above.
- Medium Olive — as above.
- Blue Winged Olive — as above.
- Caperer — as above.
- Crane Fly (*Tipula*). *Diptera.* Daddy Long-Legs No 12 long shank hook.

Trout Fishing on the Middle River Test

I decided to take it upon myself to write about fishing on the river Test, both for trout and salmon, because I have greater knowledge of that river than the other chalk streams, with the possible exception of the river Allen in Dorset. For salmon, for a number of years, I had a rod at Broadlands. For trout, I have paid visits to almost every section, although not always fishing. Three times in three seasons Bill Heller has allowed me to fish his water at Compton, based upon The Thatched Hut which I described in an earlier book. My first visit to the Test was in 1951, to Leckford, where I caught a trout on an 8ft Ogden Smith's split cane rod under the guidance of head keeper Ernie Mott. There have been visits to Bossington where head keeper Brian Parker assists my efforts and allows me to share his knowledge. It is to Compton that I ask you to accompany me and my daughter Lara on 27 June 1991. I will analyse the tackle and tactics which brought us the success recorded in my fishing diary:

> '4 brown trout. Total weight 9lb 11oz. Best fish 3lb 1oz. Flies: three on No 18 Iron Blue, one on No 14 Red Sedge. Started 11.30am; finished 4.30pm. Lunched in Thatched Hut. An exceptional five hours. Rises to small gnats and smuts. Windy rough day, with sunshine. Sat, watched and waited. Then, over the hours, and one by one, we picked them off with a shared rod. I took the first three, then Lara had her first Test brown of 3lb. He was taking gnats and smuts and rising from deep down. Ignored our Iron Blue, but came up with a swirl to swallow the Red Sedge first chuck. A thick, heavily spotted fish. With Bill's permission we recorded our catch on the wooden wall of the hut.'

The tackle
The rod
The rod in use on that day was a two-piece 9ft 3in Bruce & Walker tubular carbon Multi-Trout, rated for an AFTM No 6 or No 7 line. This rod is no longer in their catalogue, but has been replaced by the improved models in their Merlin series of Stream Kings.

For a narrow river overhung with trees an 8ft rod is necessary to cast within the canopy. On a medium river, such as the Wylye or the upper Frome, an 8ft 6in rod will cover the water. The middle Test calls for a rod of between 9ft and 9ft 6in, although a good caster can manage with 8ft 6in. Distance casting is not required — one may creep along the bank towards a fish. In consequence a stiff rod and heavy line are out of place, and are likely to snap fine nylon on the strike. The requirement is for a rod of 'all-through' action, one which flexes throughout its length and will bend and accommodate the stress of the strike. It must not snap a fine tippet.

To select such a rod is simple. Flex the rod in the casting hand. A stiff rod will bend only at the tip; one suitable for dry fly will bend right down to the hand grip. A further guide to suitability is the manufacturer's suggested line weight. For an 8ft rod this should be AFTM No 4 or No 5; for 8ft 6in AFTM No 5 or No 6; for 9ft AFTM No 6 or No 7. If a 9ft rod is rated AFTM No 8 it is likely to be too stiff and of a design suited to distance casting on still waters.

It is a fact that the lightest and most efficient material for fly rods is carbon or boron. Such rods do not have to be maintained, other than by an occasional rub of candle wax to the spigot, and a coat of varnish to the silk wrappings of the rings. Rods to a maximum length of 9ft in split cane have a place in river trouting for those to whom an item of fine workmanship and beauty imparts satisfaction. These rods are slower in the action, and heavier. They need tender loving care but, in the shorter lengths, will do all that is required other than cast a long distance.

Reels and lines
The reel on that day was a Hardy Marquis No 7. It accommodated a Scientific Anglers light green Aircel DT6F line (DT6F = double taper No 6 floating) and 75yds of 20lb monofilament backing.

Go for simplicity in fly reels. Avoid the multiplier — there are more moving parts to go wrong and the only advantage is rapid line recovery. This can be achieved by using a single action reel one size larger in the diameter than the manufacturer recommends for a particular weight of line. It is the diameter that counts in the initial speed of line recovery, not the width of the spool. Make certain the spool is full by putting on the fly line first, filling with backing to capacity, and then reversing the whole. More backing will be required than a trout ever pulled from my reel — but that does not matter.

There is no doubt in my mind that the finest fly reels are made by The House of Hardy. They are expensive, but there is a broad range and they last forever. An excellent low cost reel is the Leeda graphite Dragonfly. I have used one for years. The Dragonfly Regular 80 is just right for a No 6 line and backing. The Kingsize 100 suits a No 7 line and a 9ft rod.

I am not in favour of reels for rods of 8ft 6in and above, being less than $3^{1}/_{2}$ in in diameter, and $3^{1}/_{4}$ in for an 8ft weapon. Reels should have an adjustable drag, not that I use this to control the fish, but so that it may be set to a light resistance. The drag on the fish is provided with greater sensitivity by the forefinger of the hand on the reel. Fixed drag reels may be set too hard by the manufacturer and cause breakage in the point of a fine leader.

The AFTM (Association of Fishing Tackle Manufacturers) Scale of line weights is based on the weight of the first 30ft of the line, excluding the 2ft parallel tip. This length includes all the tapered part of the line and some of the belly. The Scale is based upon the ability of a rod to aerialize outside the tip 10yds of line. This length is chosen on the supposition that most anglers false cast that length before shooting and delivering the final throw. If a rod is rated No 6/7 and I am making long casts on a wide river I use a No 6 line. If the river is narrow, and a shorter length of line is being cast, the extra weight per unit of length of a No 7 would be chosen. If one only possesses a light rod of 8ft and is invited to fish a wide river, the ability to change the line from No 5 to No 4 is desirable. This may be achieved by carrying a spare reel spool holding the alternative line. Quite recently I was sea trout fishing in the dark. Only short casts were being made with a No 7/8 rod. In consequence, to balance the rod, and have sufficient line weight outside the tip, a No 8 line was in use.

In general, for chalk stream fishing, a double tapered No 6 floating line is all that is required. It will float because it is lighter (less dense) than water. It should not be greased as this may damage the plastic coating, causing it to crack, let in water and sink.

Do not purchase a cheap fly line. They may lack suppleness and have a rough finish which will inhibit easy shooting through the rings of the rod. Before making a purchase, run the line between your fingers — it should be perfectly smooth.

Weight-forward lines and shooting heads do not find a place in chalk stream trouting, distance casting being unnecessary. The double taper is the best choice, being reversible when one end is worn and cracked. Sinking, and sink-tip lines, are not used when fishing a floating fly.

I have caught trout on white floating lines and those of a green colour. On the whole I suggest a green coloured line. White lines flash in the sky when false cast, and I have read that underwater photography has shown them to be more visible on the water surface when viewed from below. The backing should be of 20lb monofilament needle knotted to the end of the fly line. Braided backing should be avoided. It has greater water drag when playing a fish far off, and has to be joined to the fly line with a bulky Albright knot or with a whipping which could possibly rot. Monofilament and the needle knot junction will run smoothly through the rod rings — the Albright knot could jam in the corner of a snake-type intermediate line guide.

The leader
The leader in use was a 5X Leeda Platil knotless taper of 9ft in length. The tip diameter of this cast is .006in and the breaking strain 3lb.

For the dry fly a knotless tapered leader is better than a cast made at home by joining lengths of nylon together with blood knots. These knots show on the water surface. A made-up leader is suited to sub-surface wet fly fishing, being less visible when sunk. If you wish to make leaders for dry fly use, to save expense, knot sections of Maxima Chameleon together as follows:

    3ft butt of 25lb with Blood Bight Loop at end
    1ft section of 18lb Blood Knotted to
    1ft section of 10lb Blood Knotted to
    1ft section of 6lb Blood Knotted to
    3ft point of 3lb or 4lb
    or other suitable combination.

The leader strength should match the size of the fly. A No 18 or No 20 hook is well presented by a 5X or 6X leader; 5X is also suitable for hook sizes as large as, but not larger than, No 14. To turn over a No 10 mayfly against the wind, and present it at the cast extremity, a 3X point is desirable. Always one has to consider that the finer the point the less is it visible to trout. If feeding fish constantly refuse the fly on 4X try 5X, and make sure the leader is fully 9ft long — if many flies have been changed or replaced it will be shorter and thus thicker.

Before selecting my leader strength I take into account certain variable factors in addition to the size of the fly: the size of the trout in the river, the clarity of the water and whether the surface is ruffled by current or wind, and the presence of weed. One is unlikely to land a 5lb trout on a 5X leader if it can take refuge in a weed bed, but if 3X had been used the trout might have refused to take the fly. Risks have to be taken. In general I fish a 5X leader, but increase the strength to 4X if large fish are present (over 4lb) and there is much weed.

Join the loop at the end of the leader to the fly line with a double Sheet Bend. This knot is easily undone at the end of the day, or to change to a heavier or finer leader. It is only when fishing in the dark that it is advisable to join the fly line to the leader via a short section, about 9in, of 25lb nylon monofilament needle knotted into the end of the fly line. This line extension, which used to be called a collar, is then joined to the leader by a Blood Knot. The advantage of the collar arrangement is that the line/leader junction will travel through the tip ring of the rod without jamming. This is a necessity at night when playing a fish, but not by day when one can see the line/leader junction knot and prevent winding it into the top ring on the rod. The disadvantage is that the line and leader may slide down through the rings of the rod when it is in the vertical position, leaving the fly hooked up at the tip.

When fishing a floating fly I apply a line grease, such as Mucilin, to the 6ft of leader closest to the fly line. Take a smear of grease on forefinger and thumb and run the leader through this dressing. Do not apply the grease to the 3ft point of the leader for two reasons. The first is that greased nylon floats high and is more visible. Many anglers apply 'sink mix' (Fuller's Earth and Fairy Liquid on a damp cloth) to the leader point in order that it fishes under the water surface film, and is thus almost invisible. The ideal is a high floating fly, sunk tippet of 3ft and a floating greased leader butt. The second reason for not greasing the point is that if one changes to a nymph it will at once sink a foot or two below the surface if so required.

Artificial flies and nymphs for trout and grayling

If there is not a noticeable hatch of an easily seen fly, and yet a trout is rising in the same lie every four or five minutes, it must be feeding on a very small insect. This will either have hatched from a sub-surface nymph, larva or creeper or, if land-based, been blown on to the water. This was the case on 27 June 1991 as recorded in my diary and noted earlier in this book. In the morning mayfly, pale olives, sedges and other worthwhile mouthfuls were absent. Tiny reed smuts and gnats could be discerned at the edge of the river. My smallest flies are No 18 Iron Blue and No 18 Black Gnat, both hackled (dressed without wings). The first three trout took the Iron Blue. This was a clear example that exact imitation is not, except on rare occasions, a necessity, whilst correct size is crucial to success.

A few years ago I was fishing in the autumn below Stockbridge. Two natural flies were hatching: blue winged olive and iron blue. It would be correct to imitate these with No 14 and No 18 hooked artificials respectively. By lunchtime one of my companions, John Jacobs, who had observed trout eating the iron blue, had taken three on a No 18 hooked imitation of that fly. I had caught nothing, having fished a large No 14 hooked fly, not having observed that it was the tiny iron blue on which the fish were feeding, and not the blue winged olive. Now, the point of this account. I had no Iron Blues, but my box had plenty of No 18 Black Gnats to which the trout raised no objection. It was of the same size. Catches followed at once.

Consider the fourth trout in the diary entry, Lara's first three-pounder from the Test. He fell in the afternoon at a time when sedges hatch at that period of the season, and they appeared, dancing at the edge of the river. That trout refused the small fly but gulped down the No 14 Red Sedge. Perhaps it was the food he expected at that time of day, and hoped for, even though he was taking smuts and gnats. But there could be another fact behind his downfall to the large artificial — he was deep in the water. The other three trout could be seen — they were on the fin, just below the surface. They took small flies. A trout which is deep will often refuse a small artificial, but come up to a large offering banged down just behind his head and slightly to one side.

Artificial dry flies may be winged or hackled. With the exception of the spent (spinner) pattern, Lunn's Particular, I prefer hackled flies. They cannot land upside-down or on their sides.

There have been many drawings made to illustrate the fact that as a dun drifts down river, and arrives at the circumference of the trout's window, the first things he sees are the tips of the upright wings of members of the Order *Ephemeroptera*. No doubt this is true. It is also true that trout will eat a hackled artificial having been precluded, by their absence, from seeing advancing wingtips. Additionally, the wings of *Diptera* and *Trichoptera* are not vertical but are flat in the first case and folded over the body in the second. Yet trout eat them. Once a fly has drifted into a position vertically above a trout I doubt that he sees the wings, for they are shielded by the legs and body. This is as true for the down and flat-winged naturals, the sedges, hawthorn and alder, as it is for the up-winged olive duns. To imitate a down, or roof-shaped winged natural, just knot on a fly with a more substantial body. The hackled Caperer and hackled Red Sedge meet this need.

Critical attention must be paid to the quality of the hackle. As a dun drifts along on the mirror-like surface of the water film, its legs form pin-pricks on the water skin when seen from below. So, also, must the individual fibres of the cock hackle. I have about 1,000 trout and salmon flies dressed annually to my own patterns by one man in Kenya. For 10 years he has attended to my whims. I send him top quality Partridge hooks and some of the materials. He returns the finished patterns and they are superb.

If purchasing dry flies in a shop it is as well to hold the fly against the light — reject those which have soft fluffy hackle fibres. In addition to insisting on fine quality I only use a fly to catch one trout. The fly is then taken home and thrown away, for the hackle fibres will, almost certainly, be slightly bent.

Dry flies ought to be carried in a compartment box; they will be squashed if held on clips or flat on foam. Suitable boxes are made by Richard Wheatley, Century Works, Midland Road, Walsall. I have had mine for 45 years, it has 10 compartments and a flat area in the lid for leaders. When ceasing to fish, in order to walk up the river or take a short break, do not hook the fly on to the keeper ring just above the cork butt of the rod. In this position the hackles will be flattened against the tube of the rod. Hook the fly away from the rod tube on a bridge ring line guide.

To waterproof the patterns, tie them to the leader and then dip them into a bottle of Supafloat. The fly must be given two or three minutes to dry before being used. When dry it will not feel cold when brushed against the angler's lips.

The patterns
These are few, but sufficient to bring success. All are hackled, with the exception of Lunn's Particular as previously mentioned, and the Grey Wulff which has forward-sloping wings of bucktail

• No 18 Iron Blue

This, my smallest fly, represents the natural of that name which hatches in spring and autumn on rough days. It may also be fished when gnats and smuts are on the water in summer.

• No 14 and No 16 Kite's Imperial

Oliver Kite invented the fly in the 1960s. It is an excellent imitation of the large dark (spring) olive when on a No 14 hook. The smaller No 16 pattern forms the basis of my summer *Ephemeridae* dun patterns when the hackle is of honey dun or very pale ginger cock.

• No 16 Lunn's Particular

Invented by William Lunn, head keeper of The Houghton Club at Stockbridge on the Test from 1887 to 1932. To be fished when trout are taking small spinners.

• No 12 Grey Wulff

Lee Wulff produced his series of flies with bodies, tail and wings of hair in the 1930s. The Grey Wulff is an excellent representation of a mayfly. This is my largest pattern, and at any time of the season may be used to tempt up a trout which is not feeding and is lying close to the river bed.

• No 16 Hawthorn

This large natural is blown from the land on to the water at the end of April and in early May for about a fortnight. It is a stark black fly with two long trailing legs and a prominent cased thorax. Correct imitation would require a No 12 or No 14 hook, but I suggest No 16, for larger sizes are usually rejected. Trout take three or four days to lose fear of the Mayfly, which is also large. It takes some time for trout to accept Hawthorn, but a small pattern is readily eaten.

• No 14 Greenwell

This fly kills well as an imitation of the blue winged olive which is present from June until the end of the season. The fly was produced by Canon William Greenwell of Durham who dressed his pattern with wings. I prefer a hackled Greenwell, such as that given by Freddie Rice in his book *Fly-Tying Illustrated* (Batsford).

• No 14 Red Sedge

This fly comes into its own from June until the end of the season. The pattern takes trout whether the hatching natural is black, brown or red.

• No 14 Caperer

In his book *River Keeper — the Life of William James Lunn,* the author John Waller Hills wrote: 'Let me name the three patterns which he found the most successful at Houghton in 1932, his last year there'. They are the following, in this order:

　　1. Hackle Caperer; 2. Lunn's Particular; 3. Houghton Ruby.

　　I have used the Caperer at summer sedge time in the evening. It kills well. In addition it is noted as a pattern which takes trout on hot bright summer days. Hills again, in his book *A Summer on the Test,* writing about a difficult trout. 'What to do?' Why, try a Caperer — the invaluable Caperer — the greatest of the summer flies. Many and many are the fish it has yielded to me in burning, still weather, under a cloudless sky, in transparent water.'

　　Finally a fly for grayling, a fish which will have a go at most of the flies listed above. This fly is his downfall.

• No 14 Red Tag

If dressed with an orange tag it is known as the Treacle Parkin.

Artificial nymphs

In some waters the nymph is not permitted. On other sections of the same river it is allowed throughout the season. Some suggest it be withheld until 1 July or 1 August.

I carry one pattern for trout in two forms: the Pheasant Tail Nymph with, and without, the addition of fine copper wire. The lightweight pattern on a No 16 hook to fish in the surface film. The weighted nymph is dressed on a No 14 hook for trout which lie deep, swinging in the current from side to side to take passing food.

For grayling one cannot do better than find a place in your box for Frank Sawyer's Grayling Bug on a No 12 hook.

Hooks

'Catch and Release' is a requirement on some fisheries; on others it is voluntary but recommended. On all rivers one will wish to return undersized trout. Removal of the hook from the mouth of the fish is easy if Partridge CS20 or CS27 down eye barbless hooks are used. Provided constant pressure is maintained on the trout during play it is unlikely that hook-hold will be lost. If one is equipped solely with flies having barbed hooks, the barb may be squeezed down before use with a pair of fine snipe-nosed pliers. To us all, the time will come when we wish to release a trout taken on a barbed hook. This is readily accomplished if a pair of artery forceps are carried in the pocket. Proceed as follows: net the fish and place upon the bank, wet one hand and hold the fish through the mesh, with the other hand push the hook back and out with the forceps. The net may then be turned inside out under water to release the trout.

Nets

The net we used on 27 June — and which is carried clipped to a ring below my belt — was a **Hardy telescopic Favourite Trout Fisher's net.** Details are:
Width of bowframe: 15$\frac{1}{2}$ in
Length of bowframe: 13$\frac{1}{2}$ in
This product may be purchased with a knotted or knotless net.

I recommend two other nets to the angler:
The Leeda Bowframe trout
Width of bowframe: 16in
Length of bowframe: 19in
This net is sturdy, and marketed at a low price. A telescopic model is also available.

The telescopic Hay net (The Rod Box, King's Worthy, Winchester)
Width of bowframe: 13$\frac{1}{2}$ in
Length of bowframe: 15in
The Hay net is the best I have seen. It is a trifle more expensive than the Hardy Favourite.

All these nets have a clip which is not readily attached to, or disengaged from, one's belt. I suspend a 1$\frac{1}{2}$ in split ring on a leather strap 4in below my belt, and on this hangs the net. Nets should have a bowframe. With this one may poke into weed where a trout has taken refuge. In addition, a trout almost into the net — but balanced across the front of the bow — may be shaken into the bag. Avoid nets that have two 'Y' shaped arms which fold down parallel to the handle. The arms are joined by a cord at the front. Such a net cannot be used to probe into weed, the cord will sag if a fish is being shaken into the bag, and sometimes the arms fail to open, being jammed in the meshes of the net.

Additional equipment

The priest
Mine is a 6in length of $\frac{1}{2}$ in steam pipe with a hole drilled at one end. A split ring is fitted to the hole; a cord passed through this and around my neck prevents loss in the river. The priest is then stored in the right-hand pocket of my trousers. My daughter's priest is an 8in garden gate latch, and we have given the *coup-de-grace* to trout with a tractor drawbar pin. Many small trout have passed out of this world following a rap on the skull from the business end of the artery forceps.

Marrow spoon
Having killed a trout it is instructional to examine his diet. The stomach contents may be removed by a marrow spoon, or a sample drawn out by thrusting a doubled stem of twisted grass down the throat of the fish. Nymphs, creepers and bugs so withdrawn are more readily examined when washed apart in a small quantity of water held in the cupped hand or a thermos top.

Scissors
The smallest Swiss army knife incorporates a pair of scissors. Purchase the model with a lanyard split ring and hang it on a tape about the neck. I use the scissors to clip short the nylon end before tightening a Turle knot about the neck of the fly, and in clipping short the ends of Blood and other knots. The Swiss knife also incorporates small tweezers, and the blade is useful for cleaning fish.

Clothes
Doubtless the colour of one's clothes makes little impact on trout, for one is seen in silhouette, but garish garments reveal the lack of the stalking instinct and care of concealment in the fisherman. 'Dressed to kill' in trout fishing should mean that the angler blends with the river bank. A dull-coloured hat with a brim not only keeps the rain from the neck and off the lenses of polarized spectacles, it also intercepts the rays of the sun. Green Barbour and Grenfell jackets are subdued in shade, and Grenfell market a jacket which allows the outward passage of perspiration, whilst remaining waterproof. A jacket should always be long enough to cover the top of thigh boots. Many jackets are too short and channel rain into the tops of the wearer's boots.

The fishing waistcoat has numerous pockets. It is an ideal summer garment, being cool and allowing free movement and ventilation of the arms. Those marketed by Barbour and The House of Hardy have a pocket at the back of sufficient size to hold a folded lightweight waterproof jacket.

Throughout the season there is stowed in the back of my car a bag of spare clothes. It is a rarity to sit down in the river, but it has happened. Recently my 87-year-old father-in-law was nudged into the water from behind by a cow! My fishing bag also holds a tube of midge cream — often a necessity when fishing the evening rise.

Thigh boots are only needed on those rivers where wading is allowed and a necessity. Wading disturbs the river, but the need arises at times to take up a position in the water below the bank. The bed of a chalk stream is soft, often muddy, and thus is not slippery. Studded thigh boots are unnecessary and should be avoided, often being excessively heavy. In summer, thigh boots can be hot and sticky to wear. My own practice is to purchase a pair of cheap thigh boots and cut them off level with the knee cap. This provides a boot 6in taller than the normal Wellington and allows free ventilation to the lower leg.

Polarized spectacles
These cut out glare and enable one to see trout in the water, particularly those not rising, but lying deep, and which have to be persuaded by a weighted nymph. Spectacles ought not to have dark lenses but should let through as much light as possible. My own polaroids are Optex HLT (high light transmission). These allow 33% more filtered light to pass through, and the lenses are available in the colours grey and amber. I like grey, but Jim Haddrell, who instructs for the Orvis Co on the Test at Kimbridge, prefers amber. We both catch trout.

Catching Trout

On the majority of chalk streams we are only allowed to cast our floating fly or nymph upstream. Our aim, in the case of the fly, is that it drifts back on the surface, passing within the circular circumference of the trout's window, at the same speed as the water flow — in other words, without being dragged by the leader and fly line. This definition of presentation also applies to the nymph, with the following exception: it is permitted to 'induce a take'. I would define an induced take as follows: spot a trout, cast the copper wired Pheasant Tail Nymph 2-3yds upstream of his position and allow it to drift down to him, sinking as it goes. Then, when just to his front, give the nymph a tweak towards the surface to induce the trout to take. A nymph about to hatch would also move to the surface. An unweighted, Skues-type, nymph should drift downstream in the same manner as the dry fly but in, not on, the water surface skin. To put these descriptions into a nutshell, we are, in addition to imitating an insect, ensuring that our rendering moves naturally. If I were asked the most important matters to which to pay attention in catching trout on a chalk stream they would be, after choosing the right fly:

- To see a takeable trout without being seen
- To observe his action, if any, and plot his downfall
- To present the offering with gossamer delicacy without frightening the trout
- To time the strike correctly
- To play and net him as quickly as possible, and thus without exhausting the fish.

It will be noted that the first two stages require only that the angler keep still and use his eyes and brain. Let us examine these suggestions.

Observing the takeable trout

On arriving at your beat or reach, walk to the lower end and be seated. It is always easier to spot trout whilst moving up the river than moving down. In addition, a trout cannot see directly to his rear and, in any case, you have to cast upstream. So, there you are, sitting down at the bottom of your beat. Watch and wait. Rises are not always voluptuous affairs. The tiniest sip may betray a trout of ample size, and he is just as likely to be below your bank as on the far side. Then, you turn to see that a trout has risen mid-stream. He would be mid-stream where it is more difficult to present a naturally moving fly than to a fish under your bank! Watch for the second rise to pin-point his position. Almost always one sees the first rise a second or two after it has taken place, and when the rings have drifted down 2yds. The second rise fixes the position.

Plotting, presenting and striking

Is he takeable? Are there smaller trout between you and the quarry which, being scared, will run up and frighten him when you cast? How may drag be eliminated? Which fly? Tie on a fly of the same size as the natural he has eaten. Approach with care to the casting position — this could be standing whilst keeping 2-3yds back from the bank, or kneeling close to the waters edge. Keep low. Stalk that trout. Now the cast. You have noted that the fish is rising in slow moving water mid-river, and that the flow is faster between you and the fish. If you cast a straight line, to alight the fly a yard or two in front of the trout, the fast water will take hold of the line and drag the fly out of the window of the trout. He will be frightened by the skidding of the line and leader, and if a made-up knotted leader, each knot will create a tiny wake. He will be 'put down'. That will be that. No. You must cast a crooked line which, before it is straightened by the current, has allowed the fly time to drift over the trout before drag commences. To cast a crooked line check it in the air just as it is about to alight — it will fall in curves like a swimming grass snake. The time taken for the line to be straightened, and drag commence, will be delayed if the tip of the rod is moved downstream in line with the drifting line and leader. John Waller Hills in his book *A Summer on The Test* (Philip Allan, 1924) describes with satisfaction:

> 'The cast was made, and by the mercy of fate the fly for once landed just right. There it was, floating gaily in the slack water, cocked, and the line behind it was beautifully crooked to absorb the drag. And there too was the trout, slowly turning himself out to look at it. He came out, raised his nose to it, and for what seemed an eternity backed down behind it as the stream carried it along; then he broke the water and took. Once more I had the fortitude to wait until his head was well down again, indeed until he had turned to go back, before striking. I knew then I had him firm.'

The trout which rises directly above the angler, below his bank, or mid-river if he is wading, is an easier proposition. Easier, that is, if the trout can be seen, on the fin, moving from side to side, swallowing his flies, and his position is exactly marked. Allowance need not be made for cross-current drag, but the fish must not be 'lined' by casting too far ahead. He must not see the line, and as little as possible of the leader. In other words, precisely, the fly ought to land on, or a trifle behind, or slightly to one side of his head. Only a few inches of nylon will then be in his window and he will not have time to consider them, just time to turn and take.

The window of a trout is circular. The closer the fish to the surface the smaller the circle; the deeper the wider. A trout lying 6in below the surface sees through a window 1ft 2in in diameter. The trout which is 2ft deep has a window 4ft 6in in diameter. An accurate cast is necessary for a trout close to the surface, or lying in shallow water. It may be that if it is more than 2ft from a spot vertically above his nose it is beyond his window and cannot be seen. Being struck from behind, that trout is usually firmly hooked in the scissors.

When you go for your casting lesson, ask to be taught 'The Shepherd's Crook Cast'. This enables one to place the fly in front of a trout lying close to your bank without the nylon passing over him. It is also useful to reach a trout above you but in front of a bank protrusion.

The larger the trout the more dignified will be his rise. Your response, the strike or — a preferable description — the raising of the rod and gentle tightening, need not be hurried. The smaller the trout the quicker the rise and the angler's response. For the alderman, the wild brown trout of 3lb 14oz taken before the days of stocking at Broadlands, on 5 May 1976, striking was superfluous. He hooked himself. This portly fellow was rising mid-river, on a bend, to mayfly, which by then were hatching. A large trout taking large natural fly is a memorable sight: the black snout which encloses the insect, the rolling back and dorsal fin, the wide tail which slides away. Several times the rod dropped the Mayfly ahead of his position; it drifted over the leviathan; he did not stir. 'He has gone down; he saw me; that last throw was splashy; he's been "lined".' All these depressing thoughts flitted, shadow-like, through my mind. Then, when I looked again the fly had gone. There was nothing there. Just flat river. 'It's sunk,' I thought, and raised the rod to find him on the end!

The larger the trout, the wiser it is to treat them on the rise as salmon — slowly. Raise the rod as the surface smooths. Timing the strike to the sunken nymph being taken by a deep trout is different. I watch my trout, pitch the nymph upstream, let it wash down, sink, then give life by lifting the rod. The response is usually rapid: he swings up and across, the mouth opens and, as soon as the white rim of the lower jaw is visible, the rod tip is lifted high. The delay between sight, brain, hand, rod, line and leader allows sufficient time for the trout to take and turn.

When searching the water for deep unseen trout or grayling, if this practice is acceptable on the water instead of addressing visible fish, the greased yard of leader closest to the line acts as a tell-tale. Cast upstream, allow the nymph to sink a little and then retrieve the line a fraction faster than the flow of the water. The slightest pause or check on the greased nylon should prompt an immediate response. In calm mill or hatch pools the nylon will slide forward 'into the black hole'. I will never forget a trout from the Dun, a stream which runs parallel to the Kennet below Hungerford. Slight movements were apparent below the surface, close to the blackness of the river bed. I could not discern the fish. Out went the Pheasant Tail Nymph to sink, slowly. All was dark, mysterious, still. I held my breath. The nylon then slid down 'into the black hole'. He weighed a ton.

Playing and netting

When a trout is hooked he doesn't know what has happened. He is unaware of the angler and ignorant of what is pulling at his jaw. Be sure he remains in ignorance for as long as possible. The fish which sees the enemy fights harder and may dash into weed. So, remain kneeling behind the cover of the bankside sedges, peer through the vegetation, keep low, but hold the rod tip high. A rod held close to the vertical acts as a spring to absorb shocks which might snap the leader or break out the hook hold; it also keeps line out of the water. As short a length of line as possible should be allowed to become submerged. This reduces both drag on the hook and the chance that the line or leader may pass around an obstruction.

As the trout tires the net should be extended, sunk below the surface and placed close to hand. When the moment arrives, the fish is drawn over the submerged net which is then lifted. At the point of netting, one must recommend the Hay net, the metal of which is anodised black. If your bowframe is polished aluminium, paint it black or green. Shining net rims scare trout to further exertion when all would otherwise be accomplished. A further point — when the net is extended the bag may float when the requirement is for submersion. A pebble held in the bag will solve the problem, or a strip of copper clamped in the lowest meshes.

How should the danger of a jumping trout loosening the hook, or snapping the nylon, be reduced? I drop the rod point to slacken the line whilst the trout is in the air. There is the small risk of a barbless hook coming away, but almost always the fish is still on when the rod is lifted as soon as the trout hits the water. There are arguments for and against dropping the rod tip. I am in favour of the practice, particularly with fine nylon.

The trout which dash into weed present a problem, but they nearly always enter the weed bed from downstream, and a pull from below will usually draw them out. The pull is more effective if made by hand rather than the rod, for the fingers may feel for an informative wriggle. In weedy places always try to keep a hooked trout as high in the water as possible, in fact a fish may sometimes be skidded over the top of growing weed towards the angler by a rod held high in the air.

Weather and time of day
I do not pay much regard to the weather. It cannot be altered. The day is ahead, perhaps the only day that month, so one does one's best and rarely fails.

If it is rough and cold, perhaps the iron blue will hatch. If it is mayfly time, but cold, there will still be one or two determined flies, and if it is too warm too many. The great thing is to fish, not stay at home or shelter in the hut.

The same applies to the hour. Most of us start after breakfast, and return home to dine. During those intervening hours we would be extraordinarily unlucky not to be presented with several targets. My father-in-law, fishing on the Kennet, invites me for a July day each season. 'It will be no good arriving at the bridge before 9am, and little happens between noon and 4pm'. This observation may be accurate, but happily the mid-day quiet time coincides with the opening hours of The Three Swans in Hungerford and the afternoon snooze!

Salmon Fishing

Catches by salmon rods on the chalk streams have reduced steadily since the mid-1950s. At the same time, in many places, fishing pressure has increased. The inference must be drawn, and is being confirmed by electric counters, that the runs of fish have decreased. In the early 1970s, up to 1975, the Broadlands catches were between 250 and 350 salmon. Recent seasons have produced in the region of 20 salmon, and much of the four miles of the Estate river, formerly reserved for salmon anglers, has been changed to stocked trout beats.

The average salmon catch at Nursling in the 37 years from 1932 to 1968 was 434 per annum. To the time of writing this account at the end of September 1991, the catch is 53 for the season. The Itchen salmon take is falling, and the general chalk stream picture is of reducing runs.

The result of this depressing scene is that many rods have given up, taken to trout, or switched their salmon fishing to Scotland, Iceland and Norway. In writing of salmon fishing on the chalk streams one must have personal experience of catching salmon in the rivers described, and draw on the knowledge of others who have grassed many fish from these alkaline rivers. Due to the present reduction in catches our accounts are largely of historical events, but the methods described will again prove effective if salmon return in substantial numbers. It is hard for me to write 'How to do it' whilst knowing, at present, that the opportunity has largely been lost. Perhaps not lost forever.

I put forward my methods in the hope, indeed in the expectation, that the picture will be restored. Knowledge of the numbers of salmon is being acquired through fish counters; passes have been installed to ensure free passage to salmon and sea trout to the spawning beds; the gravel areas where redds are cut are being raked clear of silt.

Salmon parr in hundreds of thousands are being raised in the Highlands by Alan Mann of Kings Somborne from Test fish, and transferred south to the river. 620,000 were planted out in 1991.

The use of the worm as a bait has been banned. All is thus not gloom, but time must pass before the success of these steps can be measured. In the meantime I put before you the life history of this courageous and fascinating fish.

Salmon life history

The spawning weeks vary from river to river, but December may be taken as the mean. The hen fish digs a redd in gravel and small stones with her tail, excavating a trough about 6-9in in depth. The redd itself may be as long as her body, in the region of 18in wide, and is usually cut in water 2-3ft deep. Sometimes the river will barely cover the back of the fish, and an exposed tail or dorsal fin waving in the air will draw attention to the scene. Creep to the river's edge on hands and knees, look over, and there she is in the redd. Sometimes a cock fish lies with her, or he may wait to the rear behind the ridge of piled up gravel. At intervals of half an hour, or thereabouts, the hen will turn on her side, quiver and thrash. This muscular spasm expels ova from the vent, numbering about 700 eggs per 1lb liveweight of the hen. The cock fish also convulses to eject milt from his vent over the ova which are thus fertilized.

During these happenings the cock fish expends much energy chasing rivals from his chosen hen. He rushes and butts them, and surges of water are displaced as he arrows beneath the surface. On returning next day it is likely that you would find the bed of the river had been smoothed, the eggs covered, their presence betrayed solely by a patch of light coloured disturbed stones and gravel from which green algae has been washed. The hen usually moves on to cut second and third redds to spread the risk.

A hen which enters the river weighing 10lb in April might weigh only 6lb after spawning. She, and the cock, are then thin in shape, debilitated and with soft white flesh. The cock fish will have a hook — the kype — at the end of his lower jaw, and this fits into a socket beneath the nose. Many of these fish, known as kelts, die on the spawning beds or on their way back to the sea. Very few, a minute percentage, reach the salt water, feed, recover, and make a second spawning entry. The life history of a mature salmon, the number of river and sea years, may be discovered by examination of the growth rings on scales taken from the flank of the fish.

The time taken by the eggs to hatch depends upon the temperature of the water, but one would not be far wrong in considering three months under natural river conditions. An alevin emerges from the egg, complete with a sustaining yolk sac suspended beneath his chin. This sac is absorbed over the next few weeks. He then starts to feed, being called a fry. At 3-4in in length the fishlet becomes known as a parr, and is so described until, after one or two years, he changes to a silver colour in April and May. Then called a smolt he migrates down the river to the sea. The time spent in the river until the fish 'smoltifies', at 6-7in in length, varies, depending on the food available. In alkaline rivers, where food is abundant, the one year smolt is more common than in more barren acid waters.

We now lose track of the fish, but know it has been imprinted by the taste and smell of the parent river. The majority return to the river of their birth to spawn in their turn, and thus complete the cycle of life. The minimum time spent at sea is in the region of 15 months. A fish returning between June and spawning time of the following year is known as a one sea-winter fish or grilse. They weigh between 3lb and 7lb or 8lb in weight, or even more, are slim and have no knuckle of gristle at the tail wrist as has the two sea-winter fish. This slimness affects the methods by which a grilse may be landed, as will be seen. If salmon stay at sea until the second spring, summer or autumn, returning in the region of two years after their seaward journey, they are known as two sea-winter salmon. Three and four sea-winter fish, the heavyweights, are much less common than was the case 20 or 30 years ago; this may be due to high seas netting, for the longer they are at sea the greater the chance of capture. In recent years the run of two sea-winter fish has greatly reduced, being replaced by a preponderance (if it may be so described in these scant seasons) of grilse.

A salmon does not feed in fresh water, having to increase the size and maturity of its roe by transference from the fat and muscle of the parent body. It is therefore careful to expend as little energy as possible, only occupying certain places in the river. A salmon will not remain static in rushing water, it would have to work too hard to maintain position, and would thus lose stored energy. This will be seen when salmon lies are discussed in the fly fishing section which follows.

As salmon do not feed in fresh water I am often asked why they take an artificial fly, spinning bait, worm or prawn. Nobody knows the answer to this question. My own view is that a salmon takes a lure due to aggression, curiosity, a feeding memory, or for the relief of boredom. A salmon spending 9 months in a river in a state of torpor must lead an incredibly boring life — suddenly a red General Practitioner fly goes by. This is a startling event, and if a shower of rain has provided further excitement the fish may be stimulated to take the lure. But it is as well to remember that only one in five or 10 salmon will be interested in your bait — the majority will ignore your offering, or swim away to hide under the bank or in the weeds. Rod angling is very inefficient!

Methods of salmon fishing

Unless otherwise regulated on an estate we are allowed to fish with fly, spinner, prawn and shrimp. The worm has been banned on the river Test to conserve salmon, and will not be included in my instructions. I am not 100% against worm fishing, having used the method myself with success in the past when there were plenty of fish. Skill is required to cast a worm upstream with a fly rod, for a sensitive touch is needed and penetrating observation. But, almost without exception, salmon populations in the chalk streams are reducing. Many and varied steps have to be taken to halt the downward curve on the salmon numbers graph. If anglers cease using the worm they will save the lives of some fish, and be seen to be doing their bit to assist salmon recovery.

Some methods of fishing may bring success throughout the season, and thus in both cold and warm water. I define cold water as being below 45-50°F, and thus confined to February, March and April. In those months deep fishing, with downstream casts, by prawn and spinning bait provide the best chance. By the end of April the river temperature is likely to be 50°F. Fly fishing, upstream spinning, prawn and shrimp are all now productive. Why this division of methods based upon water temperature? It is because salmon take their body temperature from the surrounding water. If the water is at 40°F, the body of the fish will assume this temperature, or perhaps half of one degree higher. A cold fish is lethargic. Not only does he have to be stirred to action by a large lure, but the lure must be sunk to his level — close to the river bed. This is done with ease by spinning downstream with a weighted minnow or other artificial lure, or by a prawn in conjunction with a weighted trace.

The flow of a chalk stream in the full cold water of early spring is strong. It is thus difficult to fish an artificial fly close to the river bed because the current will continually raise the fly towards the surface. In a river where 'fly only' is the rule this difficulty is overcome, so far as this is possible, by the use of a fast sinking fly line. The Test, Itchen, Frome and other rivers are not 'fly only'. In their waters low-temperature fishing is more productively undertaken by deep downstream spinning or the use of a well sunk prawn. Nothing I have written precludes the use of the fly in cold water, and I have taken fish on fly at 45°F when using a floating fly line. To me, fly fishing is the most pleasurable method but, under the circumstances described, is not the most effective.

In my section on salmon fly fishing, sinking line is not included because I do not use that method when fishing on the Test. At present, when runs of salmon are largely of grilse, arriving from July onwards, the choice between floating and sinking fly lines is almost academic — the fish are just not in the river until the floating line temperature has been with us for some weeks. Once the river has warmed salmon are more active, leaping from time to time, and they will rise from the river depths to take a fly fished off a floating line. They will also chase, and sometimes take, a spinning bait thrown upstream and retrieved at high speed. Smaller prawns may be fished, and the shrimp takes its share.

Salmon Fly Fishing on the Lower River Test

I caught my first salmon in 1954 on the river Findhorn. It was not a vast fish, it weighed 9lbs, but it was silver-bellied, black-backed and supported many sea lice. This was followed by salmon from the Helmsdale in June at Kilphedir. Those fish fell in warm clear water to a No 6 Low Water Hairy Mary single and a Lady Caroline of the same size fished off 10lb Fog camouflage nylon. The river Dart yielded fish to the same combination. Contrast those fine hooked flies and thread-like leader to the size of fly and strength of nylon which brought about the downfall of my first Broadlands salmon. My diary records:

> '9 September. The Grove. In big pool by cattle drink on left bank above White's Island. Noon. No 1 Thunder & Lightning. 9lb.'

That fly would have been traditionally dressed on a heavy single iron. The wing was of mallard flank feathers. The nylon leader, 17.6lb Platil Strong, came straight off a spool in my pocket.

The Test is different from other rivers — one needs large flies. Strong nylon is also a necessity to match the weight of the fly and give the angler a chance when the fish dashes into one of the many weed beds. Not only are salmon likely to take refuge in growing weed, drifting cut weed floating down the river may become entangled on the leader whilst the fish is being played. The following year my second Test fish arrived:

> '23 September. Moorcourt. The Flats. 11lb. No 4 Thunder & Lightning (hair wing). 11.45am.'

As a further example of the need for a large fly:

> '28 September. Rookery. River high after much rain. Water coloured. 2.00pm. Rookery Pool $8^1/_2$ lb. No 1/0 Hairy Mary single. 6.00pm Ash Tree 7lb. Same fly. Tony one on prawn.'

All those flies were dressed on single hooks. Today I use a hair wing tube fly and an outpoint treble hook. Let us start at the beginning by looking at tackle needs for salmon fly fishing on the Test.

Tackle
There is little to be said for using a short salmon fly rod on a medium sized river. The Test is not heavily treed or overgrown with bushes — it is too well keepered. Fields usually line the banks. There is thus plenty of room on most stretches for a carbon fibre double-handed rod of 13ft, taking an AFTM No 8 or No 9 line. A shorter rod than this limits the ability to cover the full width of the river, manoeuvre the fly and play fish with good control. A longer weapon is not necessary. The rod ought to have authority, being stiff rather than soft in the action. Power is needed to project a fly into the wind; the open Test valley is a rough place when gales come up from the Solent.

Soft rods render breakages of fine wire Low Water hooks and 8-10lb nylon unlikely on the strike because the rod bends and accommodates the stress, but on the Test strong nylon is in use and tough trebles in the large tube flies. Go for a rod which will transmit your wishes, both in casting the fly and controlling the fish. The reel should accommodate the floating fly line and 100yds of 20lb monofilament backing which should be needle knotted to the line. The Hardy St John reel of $3^7/_8$ in diameter is ideal, and so is the less expensive Leeda Dragonfly Imperial.

Due to later runs in recent seasons few salmon are taken before the water warms to 50°F. This temperature level is normally reached in April. In fact, fly fishing with a chance of meeting a fish is concentrated into June, July, August and September. These are months when salmon will rise to take a fly fished close to the surface off a floating line. Purchase a green floater. As already noted, white lines flash in the air, and underwater photography has shown them to be more visible on the water surface when viewed from below. A sinking fly line is not necessary in summer, and in March and April, when the water is cold, one would be better advised to fish a prawn or spin an artificial bait close to the level of salmon on the river bed.

The nylon leader should be of 15lb breaking strain. I use Maxima Chameleon and ensure the leader sinks below the water surface where it becomes almost invisible. Skating leaders are a problem on the smooth, sometimes rather oily, surface of the Test. Wiping the nylon with mud may cause it to sink, but the nylon is roughened in the process and becomes more visible. The problem may be overcome by making certain that the fly has sufficient weight to cut through the water skin and, secondly, by wiping down the leader from time to time with 'sink mix'. Purchase a 100g tub of Fuller's Earth from the chemist, sprinkle this onto a small piece of wet cloth, add two or three drops of Fairy Liquid and place in a 35mm film spool plastic container.

Keeping the fly and leader below the surface may also be achieved by using a sink-tip fly line. The greater density of the tip over the floating belly of the line causes the tip to splash down on the water when cast. This disturbance is of little consequence in rough turbulent runs, but cannot be tolerated on smooth surfaces.

To land salmon and grilse one could not choose a better device than the 25in Gye net. In the carrying position, held on the back by a peel sling, the shaft slides across the mouth of the net. Release is achieved by a sharp tug on the Velcro and leather tab when the net will fall into one's hand. Bearing in mind that the other hand is occupied with the fly rod, the shaft may be pulled out by drawing against one foot placed in the net ring.

Do not use a tailer; the wire noose is likely to slide over the slim tail of a grilse. The gaff is an outmoded instrument which will damage gravid hens in autumn, when they ought to be returned, as must kelts in spring.

The fly
The General Practitioner (GP), an orange fly dressed on a treble hook, is the invention of the late Lt-Col Esmond Drury. Tied on an up-eyed No 2 or No 6 long-shanked treble hook, the fly specifically imitates a prawn. Of orange feather, silk and bucktail, it is in the cooked colour! Drury designed the fly for the Test where the prawn is probably the most common lure. The GP is heavy, particularly in the No 2 size, and fished off a sinking line may be encouraged to go down to the level of a fish. It is a fly for the deep slow manoeuvre. I mention the GP because the orange colour is attractive to salmon which are able to appreciate colour at the red end of the spectrum more readily than blue shades. In addition, the slow deep style of fishing this fly is in contrast, and provides an alternative to my preferred, more rapid, fly movement, as will be seen. My style employs a floating line and two flies which were my own design:

● **The Black Dart**
Tube: Type B Slipstream socketed $1^{1}/_{4}$ in
Hook: Partridge No 8 black X1 outpoint treble
Tag: No 16 oval gold tinsel

Body: Black floss over close turns of fine lead wire. The lead is stopped short of the head where the bucktail wing is to be tied in
Rib: No 16 oval gold tinsel
Wing: Orange bucktail
Cheeks: Jungle cock. A long feather, three-quarters the length of the tube, one on each side
Head: Black varnish
Silk: Black Naples

● **The Copper Dart**
Tube: Type B slipstream socketed 1in
Hook: Partridge No 8 black X1 outpoint treble
Body: Side-by-side turns of 0.40mm copper wire over a single layer of black Naples silk
Wing: Orange bucktail
Cheeks: Jungle cock. A feather three-quarters the length of the tube, one on each side
Head: Black varnish
Silk: Black Naples

There is another tube which I throw to salmon which rise to the Dart tubes, but fail to take.

● **The Hairy Mary**
Tube: Type B Slipstream socketed 1¼ in
Hook: Partridge No 8 black X1 outpoint treble
Tag: No 16 oval silver tinsel, three turns next to the socket, and three turns of yellow floss above
Body: Black floss over close turns of fine lead wire
Rib: No 16 oval silver tinsel
Wing: Natural brown bucktail
Head: Black varnish
Silk: Black Naples

These three tubes are heavy, large in size and well suited to the peculiarity that Test salmon go for a substantial mouthful. If the reader refers to Tony Allen's discourse on salmon fishing at Lower Itchen (see page 75), it will be noted that these three flies fulfil his needs with the addition of the Thunder & Lightning. Bernard Aldrich, head keeper at Broadlands where he has fished for over 35 years, tried the Black Dart with success when I first produced the pattern.

Salmon lies
Salmon lies are revealed slowly to those who understand the salmon's needs. Where will fish be found? Because salmon do not feed in fresh water their energy requirements are met from their own body material. The development of ova and milt take place by transference from muscle and fat. The body is thus slowly depleted from the time of entry into the river from the sea. A salmon can control the rate of depletion

to a limited extent by selecting lies which allow the fish to maintain station without the profligate expenditure of energy.

A lie will be used by many fish, one after the other and, if the river bed remains unchanged, over many seasons. There will be provided: security, oxygen and a position in which the fish does not have to work to maintain station. Such places are usually in front of obstructions, which break down the pressure of water flow, rather than in the turbulence behind a concrete block or boulder on the river bed. Search with Polaroids in front of weed beds rather than in the weed. Just ahead of the bed rise at the tail of a pool, before the water spills over into a fast run, is always worth a cast. Pay attention to the front of a wooden groyne, or just off the end of the boards. Do not expect to find a salmon tucked in behind the wooden strut supporting the groyne. The flat water in front of the lip of a weir, or before the water is drawn through a set of hatches, are always likely places, and far more productive than the boiling water down below.

Then there are the banks. Salmon cannot be seen when tucked below a bank. The river wall may be undercut and this gives hidden refuge, as do the washed-out roots of trees. Fish press themselves against the flanks of the river, you cannot see them, you can only cast, swim the fly and tempt them out, whilst remembering the place for your next visit.

Slowly a map of lies will be recorded in your mind. Learning never ceases, for lies alter with the height of water, which itself changes almost daily, and the bed of the Test alters as the seasons pass.

Fishing the fly
There are anglers who fish the fly slowly, mending the line upstream to retard the passage of the lure as it crosses the river. Such fishing has a place on fast turbulent waters where the whirls and rushes of the river give life to the fly. Steady movement, sink and draw, hanging the fly deep in the current have a place, particularly in cold water below 50°F. But we are considering floating line fishing in a warm summer river of many smooth glides. In such conditions salmon are not lethargic, sunk in torpor, for they will seize the fleeting opportunity to rush and grab a passing lure. I sometimes throw a match box to a pupil I am teaching to fish for salmon. Whilst the box is in the air I shout 'Catch' — he grabs in instantaneous reaction. Such response may be that of a summer salmon. They act in this speedy manner when chasing the upstream Mepp, and will shoot up from the river bed to take a swiftly moving fly with equal verve.

I like to swim my fly across the river in a wide curve. A curving swim is always more attractive than a straight retrieve. This is commenced by casting almost straight across to the far bank from a kneeling position. You must keep out of sight. Kneel, hold back from the bank, fish from behind a bush, or in front of one, but don't stand silhouetted against the sky. 'He's a hands and knees man' is a compliment, and a long rod is an asset in the art of concealment if it enables the angler to remain back from the bank when casting, and 20yds away from the lie as he makes his throw.

Now, what to do when the salmon which was resting off the groyne on the other side surges forward? Nothing! Do nothing or, putting it another way, continue what you were doing in fishing the fly across the river. Whatever you do don't lift the rod when the water skin bulges with the lift of the fish; instead watch the line/leader junction knot. If the knot moves off in a steady sliding submersion, raise the rod slowly and the chances are he'll be hooked. If the bulge subsides, the fly continues its progress and the knot remains unchecked, fish out the cast and try again. Lack of a second response, to two or three more casts, leads me to wind in, sit down, change the fly and fish down on him again after a 10-minute wait. Do not change the size of fly, just the pattern. It is my experience that a salmon, having risen to a fly, if ultimately caught, usually falls to the original size offered, if not the same pattern.

Playing and landing

A salmon does not know what has happened when he is hooked, just that something mysterious is pulling at his jaw. But he will recognize the enemy if he sees you standing on the bank, and will then fight even more valiantly. So, move down opposite the fish, keep low and out of sight, and hold the rod tip high to act as a shock absorber. In addition to acting as a shock absorbing spring, a near vertical rod keeps line out of the water, reducing the risk of sunk line being wrapped about an obstruction, or the drag of drowned line pulling out the hook.

Should the rod point be dropped when a salmon jumps? I believe so. The movements of a fish in the air are violent and sharp, much more so than actions slowed by the enveloping resistance of water. A dramatic display of aerial gymnastics may slash at the leader and jerk out the fly — this will not happen if the rod point is dropped and the line is slack. But, what relief when the tip is raised and the top curves down once more.

A two sea-winter salmon gives two seconds notice of a jump, sudden underwater acceleration warning the angler to be ready. Not so the little grilse of one sea-winter, he pops out at any time and is known as a 'hopper' by West Country netsmen. Pools tend to be less clearly defined in a steadily flowing chalk stream than in a rocky river. All the same, one will be faced, sooner or later, with checking a salmon which starts to run downstream out of an open water area. A small grilse may be stopped by rod pressure, but this is not possible without risking loss of hook-hold in a two sea-winter salmon — the hook may bend open or just pull out. Stop the fish by guile. Lower the point of the rod, strip two yards of line from the reel and release all pressure. Do this in time, before he reaches the end of the pool. In four cases out of five the fish will swing around to face upstream, for he has to have his head into the current in order to breathe. The same ruse may be employed when spinning with a fixed spool reel — open the bail arm for two seconds to allow the line to run free. In both cases contact should then be regained, the rod lowered over the water, a slight and then increased upstream draw applied and the salmon 'walked up' away from danger.

About the netting. A salmon should go in head first. If it is possible, crouch unseen below the bank, swim the fish upstream, turn him and draw him down head first into the net. He may then be dragged ashore, or the net lifted by holding the rim. A Gye net should not be raised by the aluminium shaft which is soft and will bend. It is unwise to attempt to pull a salmon up the river to the net against the current. The hook may pull out or, if exposed, a single hook of a treble may catch in the net meshes and pull out the other two. Neither is it advisable to attempt to scoop a salmon up from the tail end — he only has to swim forward to escape.

Many anglers land their fish by hand. A good grip with the thumb and forefinger ring may be taken above the tail of a two sea-winter salmon. This is due to the presence of a knuckle comprised of two knobs of gristle where the tail starts to spread behind the wrist. Grilse tails are slim, lacking these swellings, and the hand will slide over the tail and the grip be lost. To land a grilse by hand, place the palm across the top of the head with the fish tail towards your elbow. Then, with thumb on one side and fingers on the other, press in the gill flaps. A firm hold will be obtained beneath the skull and the fish may be lifted. Salmon may be beached if a chalk stream shelves gently at the edge. Play out the salmon, draw him to the edge, keep his head raised, and any flapping will be ineffective. Then nip behind and push the fish up the bank. It is a sad fact that beaches are seldom where one would wish, and with that in mind I always carry a Gye net.

Carry a priest. Mine is the same as that described in the section of trout fishing. Thump the fish on the back of the head and then stand back and wonder. Satisfaction will mingle with sorrow.

Spinning For Salmon

As we have seen in the discourse on methods, different tactics are used in cold and warm water. Much the same tackle may be used under both conditions.

Tackle
The rod
If one is to purchase a single double-handed rod for both spinning and fishing the prawn, 10ft is the ideal length. A shorter rod of 9ft is suitable for spinning, but when fishing the prawn or shrimp the extra length assists placing and holding the bait in front of a visible fish. As in fly fishing, a long rod controls a salmon being played better than a short one. The House of Hardy produce two 10ft spinning rods, both capable of casting $1^3/_4$ oz (combined weight of bait and any additional weight). The Favourite is of carbon fibre and weighs $8^1/_4$ oz; the Fibalite, of glass fibre, weighs $12^1/_2$ oz and is less expensive by one-third. I fish with the Fibalite. Both are suited to fixed spool and multiplying reels. If purchasing a different make, be sure that the butt line guide above the reel is at least 1in in diameter. If it is smaller, the coils of line coming off a fixed spool reel may be held up at this point.

The reel
Two types of reel are available: the fixed spool and the multiplier. The former is versatile and may be used for heavy and light spinning, and to fish a prawn. The multiplier is suited almost solely to casting heavy baits in places where there is room to swing the rod to build up momentum in the bait. This momentum is required to overcome the inertia of the drum, causing it to revolve. Once revolving, if the bait stops in mid-flight due to hitting a tree, the revolutions may continue and the line forms a birds nest. Most multipliers have an adjustable centrifugal brake designed to prevent over-runs. This should be set before fishing. To do so, feed the line through the rings of the rod and suspend weight and bait from the top ring. Their hanging weight should just cause the drum to revolve. Even this arrangement does not remove the risk of an over-run and the resultant tangle. Lubrication of the reel should take place daily as instructed.

The multiplier is not suited to flicking out a lightweight bait beneath the overhanging branches of trees. Other than the ability to cast heavy baits in spring, the sole advantage of a multiplier over a fixed spool reel is the variable braking pressure that may be applied by the thumb to the revolving drum when playing a fish.

The Mitchell 300 left-hand wind, and 301 right-hand wind, fixed spool reels are ideal for general purpose fishing. They have three advantages over the multiplier: the first is the ability to cast light and heavy baits because the spool does not revolve, and thus inertia does not have to be overcome; the second is the ease with which lightweight baits may be flicked out from restricted positions where the rod cannot be swung through a wide arc; and the third is the infrequency of line tangles if the reel is correctly filled. This is because a bait stopped by the branch of a tree in mid-flight, or overcast onto the far bank, no longer pulls line off the spool, and as the spool is static a tangle does not result.

The reel should be lubricated daily with light oil. A single drop should be placed on the bail arm return spring, the bearings at each end of the bail arm, and at the point where the winding arm enters the housing. The interior gears need lubrication once a year through the screw at the end of the housing.

The variable drag of the Mitchell 300, being a slipping clutch against which a salmon has to pull, should be set before fishing. This may be done by hooking the bait onto a fence, raising the rod and adjusting the clutch by the finger knob on the front so that it slips just before the rod applies maximum pressure. Drag may be increased or reduced as required when playing a salmon by turning this knob.

It is not possible to reel in a salmon when using a fixed spool reel because a correctly set clutch will slip if excessive pressure is applied to the fish. Instead, place the forefinger of the hand holding the rod onto the edge of the line spool so that it cannot unwind, raise the rod to draw the salmon closer, and then reel in as the rod tip is lowered. The process, known as pumping, may be repeated.

Lines for spinning reels

Tangles on the multiplier are less likely to arise if braided line is used, rather than monofilament. I have found 20lb pale green Sea Ranger by Milward to be suitable. This firm also produces a 15lb braided line known as the Black Spider.

On my own Mitchell 300 reels are 110yds of 17lb Platil soft Universal. The word 'soft' should be included when purchasing, as other Platil monofilaments are on the market. The spool should be filled to within 1/10th of an inch of the front lip; 110yds, which is the length on the purchased spool, is not quite sufficient in volume and must be backed-up underneath by some additional line, or a length of old nylon. If overfilled, coils of nylon will come off the reel when casting a bait, and tangles will result. If underfilled, casting distance is reduced.

A second popular monofilament is Stren. This nylon is available in fluorescent blue, white and gold. These colours are helpful to the angler who wishes to see the exact course being followed in the water by his bait. Breaking strains of 14lb and 17lb are suitable.

When purchased, a Mitchell 300 or 301 is supplied with two spools, one being of greater depth and capacity than the other. For cold water spinning with heavy baits, the deep spool should be filled with 17lb nylon. In summer, when lighter baits are often cast, 14lb nylon on the shallower spool provides a balanced outfit.

When filling the reel from a spool of nylon, do not place the new nylon spool on a pencil and wind on to the reel, as one would with a fly line and reel. This is because each turn of the bail arm will make one twist in the nylon being loaded. Instead, place the new spool flat on the ground, stand above and wind on to the reel. In this position, if the spool is placed on the ground with the correct side on top, the coils coming off the spool in one direction will be matched by the opposite turn going on to the reel. If the spool of new nylon is placed on the ground with the wrong side on top, many twists will be seen to form between the spool and the reel. The new spool should then be turned over. Even when correctly filled, a new line is under some twisting tension on the reel. Before fishing, this tension and any twists should be removed. This may be done by making a few casts into the river with the line tied to the swivel of a Wye weight and without a bait attached. This swivel would, of course, have to be reversed before fishing, and the reel line tied to the brass ring on the other end of the Wye.

Weights, swivels and traces
At the end of the reel line it is normal to attach a weight and/or swivel by a tucked Half Blood knot. It will be found, when discussing spinning baits and methods, that some baits do not require additional weight. In such cases the line and trace may be joined by a barrel swivel. Personally I prefer the ball-bearing 'BB' swivel, although it is more expensive. If additional weight is required, the likely position in cold water, a lead-free Wye weight should be tied by the brass ring at one end of the weight to the reel-line. The trace being attached to the swivel at the other end of the Wye, from which swivel the bait may revolve.

It should be mentioned that it is not legal to use lead weights of between 0.06g and 28.35g. In practice this excludes all lead Wye weights of 1oz or less (1oz = 28g). It will be found adequate to carry lead-free Wye weights of 8g, 11g and 17g.

If the reel line is of 17lb breaking strain, a 1yd trace of 15lb should join the bait to the swivel or weight at the end of the reel line. If the reel line is of 14lb the trace ought to be of 12lb. If the bait becomes stuck on the river bed and cannot be released, so that a break must be made by pulling, the trace will snap before the reel-line. A trace longer than one yard should not be used. This is because the rod will have to be held too high to keep the bait off the ground when commencing to cast.

Traces and monofilament reel lines should not be of fine double-strength nylons. Even if of 15lb, they are liable to break under shock conditions when casting heavy terminal tackle. I have found Maxima Chameleon to be suitable for traces.

Mention should be made at this point of the Paternoster or ledger system of fishing a bait slowly, close to the river bed. The line/trace junction is made by a three-way swivel, about a No 8 in size. From the eye at right angles to the barrel one attaches 8in of 8lb nylon, at the end of which is a pear-shaped weight of about 30g. To the two eyes, one at each end of the barrel, the line and trace are attached in the normal manner. When cast, the weight sinks to the bottom, and the bait swims a few inches above the bed of the river. The most suitable weights are of the Pear or Arlesley Bomb type.

Whilst on the subject of lines and traces, consider the matter of personal safety. One may pull and break the trace of a bait and weight snagged underwater with safety — the weight will not fly back into your face. A bait which has been cast too far and is hooked onto the far bank, or even worse into the branch of a tree, creates a dangerous situation. The nylon line is elastic, and the branch of the tree bends under tension like a long bow at the battle of Crecy. You have set up a catapult, and you are the target! There is no alternative other than to pull and break if you are unable to cross the river. The line must not be cut, or many yards of line will trail in the water. Proceed as follows: wrap a handkerchief about your hand to prevent the nylon cutting the skin, take two turns of the reel line about this insulation, turn your back, put down your head and walk away until the line breaks. If you are hit by the flying weight it will be on the backside!

Artificial baits for downstream casting

As already stated, salmon are lethargic in cold water. They have to be tempted to take. Large lures fished slowly and deep in the water are the order of the day. As the river warms, if still casting downstream, the same type of baits may be reduced in size, fished closer to the surface and at a faster speed across the river.

● The Devon minnow

This may be of metal, wood or plastic. My preference is for metal or plastic if using a Wye weight. A wooden minnow fishes well in conjunction with the Paternoster system, for it will rise slightly from the river bed to sway downstream and above the level of the three-way swivel. The Paternoster method is particularly suited to fishing slowly down the side of metal or wood vertical piling, so often used to protect the bank of a chalk stream from erosion. Salmon frequently lie against these vertical supports.

Devons are available in lengths of about 1-3in. As I only use the Devon in cold water I carry 2in and $2^1/_2$ in lengths, using the larger size if the river is full and slightly cloudy. Many colour combinations are available, but one will not go far wrong by carrying two: Yellow Belly for discoloured river conditions, and Blue & Silver for clear water.

When purchasing Devons inspect the mount (swivel, wire and treble hook) with care. The mount is sometimes called a 'flight'. This should be of plastic-covered steel wire passed through an eyed hook, the swivel, and the ends of the wire crimped together in a metal sleeve. Plain steel wire may rust. Do not purchase flights where the treble hook has a spade end, the wire being passed over the division between the hooks and whipped down on the shank with silk. The silk may rot or be cut by the teeth on the edge of a salmon's mouth. Particularly good plastic Devons with excellent mounts are called Spey minnows. These are available from Fog Fishing Tackle of Ross-on-Wye. If unable to obtain a good flight, make your own. Necessities are a spool of 30lb Berkley Steelon plastic-covered wire, No 4 sleeves, red plastic tulip beads and No 4 or No 6 Partridge X1 outbend trebles. With care, the cutting grip of a pair of pliers may be used to crimp the sleeve.

● The Mepps spoon

This is available in various shapes, colours and sizes. Only two types need be carried: the Aglia and the streamlined Aglia Longue. The Longue spins more slowly than the Aglia. It may be fished in fast water in which the Aglia, in large sizes, would offer considerable resistance to retrieval. In the early part of the year, with a water temperature in the mid-forties, a No 2 or No 3 Aglia is suitable, but a No 4 would be hard to recover against the current. A No 3 Aglia Longue also fishes well at this time in the season. In summer, if one wishes to spin downstream, a No 1 or No 2 Aglia or a No 1 Aglia Longue would be correct. As to colour, these spoons are available in silver, gold and copper. All these colours are effective, and so is black if one cares to purchase a pot of paint.

● **The plug**

A plug starts to wiggle as soon as it hits the water. No 'start-up' room is wasted before it entices fish, as is the case with a Devon minnow before it starts to revolve and, in slow water, the Mepps. Plugs are therefore particularly suited to the smaller stream with a limited fishing width.

Makes, models and colours are legion. One does not want to become a tackle fiddler, carrying boxes and tins of clanking baits along the bank, half of which will never enjoy the freedom of a swim. Confine yourself to the Rapala. Black back and silver belly, and fluorescent red back and gold belly are, I believe, the best. They are obtainable jointed in the middle or as a single body. Suitable sizes are 5cm, 7cm and 9cm, but 7cm is the smallest in the jointed style. Rapalas are made to float or sink. For downstream work in spring purchase the sinking type.

● **The Flying 'C'**

This weighted lure has a latex body with two tapered tails which extend beyond the single treble hook at the tail. At the head is a revolving Mepps-type spoon. It is available with a red or brown body and a gold or silver spoon. Length is standard — about 3in. It comes in three weights: 9.5g, 12g and 16g — 12g is suitable for general fishing.

The Flying 'C' is a new bait, untried by myself other than to test the different weights for a few throws. I put it forward for you as a hope stimulator, and due to a record of astonishing success, one-third of which I witnessed.

In September a novice came to be instructed on my beat on the river Dart. He had fished on one other river, the Wye, for two days. These were the first two days of salmon fishing of his life and on each he caught a salmon, and this, on very secondary water. On the third day, with me, I fished a No 4 Mepps upstream, it being September. He followed with a Flying 'C' and took a rather stale 7lb fish. So — three days, three salmon! He used the red colour latex, silver spoon at the head, and the 9.5g body.

Artificial baits for upstream casting

If in the mood a salmon will take almost anything: a slice of orange peel, a carrot shaped with a pocket knife, a table spoon with the handle removed, and wobbling broken-backed baits intended for pike. Put forward for your consideration are just two: a No 4 gold Mepps Aglia, and a gold or silver 28g Toby. Nothing else is needed.

The hooking and landing qualities of the Toby are suspect; the long body sometimes levers out the hook. As an attractor it is unbeaten. Most anglers use the bait as purchased; others improve the hook-holding powers in one of two ways. The simplest is the addition of a second split ring joining the treble to the end of the body. This rather waggly method of treble attachment almost certainly prevents the hook being levered free. The second is the use of a flying treble at the end of a steel wire the length of the body of the Toby. The wire is passed through the swivel at the head of the bait, and through the eye of the treble which is positioned just behind the tail. The treble is held in place by a single strand of fuse wire which breaks when a salmon takes — the hook then swings free at the end of the wire and is unhampered by the Toby body.

Casting and fishing spinning baits

As with fly casting, be taught by a professional, but bear the following in mind. The flight of the bait across the river, or straight upstream, may be parallel to the water surface or in a rising and then falling curve. Let the trajectory be almost flat unless the river is entirely free of trees. The rising and falling bait may pass through the branches of a tree overhanging the water; a flat flight will pass beneath the hanging claws of twigs.

The normal, cold water, cast is downstream and across the river, moving down the bank a pace or two after each throw. Do not continue to cast from one stand or the surprise/automatic response reaction of a salmon will be lost if he sees the bait advancing many times within his range of vision. It is better to fish down a pool with 20 casts rather than 40 then, at the bottom of the pool, change the bait, walk back to the top and work down with another 20 throws.

In spring the bait should be retrieved slowly and encouraged to descend to the depths. Few turns will be required on the handle of the reel. I once met Lt-Col S.H. Crow who managed the Somerley water of Lord Normanton on the Hampshire Avon, and wrote a book about his methods in 1966 entitled *Hampshire Avon Salmon* (Angling Times). He described his early season anglers to me as 'Fishers or winders. The fishers catch the fish and the handle turners get nothing.' There was some truth in this observation! Those who turn the handle at speed in spring, particularly in a deep fast river, such as that under his control, are liable to fish too quickly with the bait swimming too close to the surface.

As the water warms, smaller baits may be fished downstream closer to the water surface, and at quicker rates of retrieve. It might be wondered why the fly is not in use throughout the summer — some small streams are overgrown and lack the room for a fly rod to cast.

Upstream fishing in late spring, summer and autumn is quite different. As already described, a large Mepps Aglia or Toby is the lure. The cast is made up-river, a long throw is best, and only a swivel is needed at the line/trace junction. On hitting the water the bait is allowed to sink for one or two feet, and is then reeled back at a speed which prevents any further increase in the depth of fishing — in other words, quite fast. If the bait passes over the head of a salmon the fish may turn and give chase. One pursuit in 10 will terminate in a take, or some similar percentage. A salmon will often follow and then turn away at the feet of the angler, whom he probably sees. For this reason make your upstream cast whilst kneeling to cut your silhouette against the sky. Do not slow down the bait to a following fish — keep going. There is nothing to be done if you run out of river room as the bait approaches your bank, other than to cast again. Upstream spinning reveals fish. If they do not take they can be tried later, perhaps with a different bait or method. There is little that the angler can do to ensure a good hook hold by a spinning bait. In fly fishing with a floating line, one allows a salmon to turn down and away before tightening. When a fish takes a spinning bait, in or out of sight, I respond to his pull by raising the rod sharply to set the hooks.

Prawn and Shrimp Fishing for Salmon

Prawn fishing can be the most exacting of methods, or suited to the armchair somnolist. Exacting and pulse quickening when an alert hunting angler tempts a visible salmon swaying on the river bed. Fished off a static Paternoster, out of sight, for invisible fish in deep stained water, line tied to the toe of the dozing fisherman, it is a method deserving contempt and an insult to this superb fish.

First find your bait

When I started to fish the prawn at Broadlands the bait came from the fishmonger's tray. This was not popular with the apron-clad fishmonger who watched me sorting through his specimens. Specimens they were: large, fat and soft, with broken legs and whiskers. A few casts on the river bank and many fell to pieces. They were smelly, oily and ancient. My dog disdained them.

In those early days, if one was lucky, head keeper Bernard Aldrich would pay us a visit in his Land Rover. Alerted by the noise of this vehicle, which sometimes worked and sometimes did not, thundering up the bank in a cloud of dust, one put on a helpless forlorn expression: 'Bernard, these prawns are hopeless. You couldn't . . .'. Out of his pocket would be drawn one or, if favoured, two fresh little bewhiskered English prawns.

The finest rod, a reel of gold, an angler with laser eyes, all count for nothing unless the prawn is tough and fresh. Hard to locate and expensive to purchase, you should buy them uncooked and straight off the boat as it enters harbour. Don't stint yourself. Purchase three or four pounds in August or September, for they only come from the sea in summer. Pop them into boiling salted water until they just turn pink — no longer or they will soften. Now drain, spread out on a towel and dry with a hair dryer. Packaged in half-dozens of the same size, they should then be frozen. Large prawns will be used in spring; small ones when the river is warm in summer. They should be taken to the river packed on ice in a wide-necked soup or stew Thermos flask. If unused, the packages may be returned to the deep freeze at the end of the day.

Unless you have a shrimping net and know where to go on the coast, shrimps have to be purchased from the fishmonger. One in 10 will be unbroken — choose those, freeze and care for them in the same manner as their larger brethren. The best shrimp is uncooked, fresh, rubbery and in the natural brown colour.

Mounting the bait

The simplest method of mounting a small prawn is to thread a Partridge 50mm T2 prawn pin onto the trace before knotting on a No 8 or No 10 Partridge X1 round-eye outbend treble hook. T2 pins, which have an eye at one end and a barb at the other, are available in three lengths: 64mm, 50mm and 38mm. The short pin, with No 10 or No 12 treble being suitable for a shrimp.

The pin is inserted under the tail of the prawn and pushed down the full length of the body. Following this, one hook of the treble is pressed into the head below the whiskers of the prawn, and the whole bait is wrapped about with fine fuse wire. A cooked prawn is pink, and thus pink wire from an unravelled flex would be less visible if sufficiently fine. Between the tail and head, the nylon trace should pass along the belly between the legs which should not be damaged or displaced when the body is wire-wrapped. The tail vanes of the prawn may cause it to revolve unnaturally in the current — they should be pinched off. The spear on the head should also be snapped away, for this sharp spike might deter a salmon from gripping the bait in the area of the treble. Salmon frequently avoid the single treble in the head by gripping the prawn across the middle. This is evident from inspection of crushed bodies. A second small treble hidden in the legs is an asset. Nonspinning, sink-and-draw mounts of this type may be obtained from Leeda Group PLC stockists (see list of suppliers on p 175).

A prawn may be spun. Purpose-made flights with celluloid fins, a swivel, a spike to insert through the body from the tail, and two trebles are available. The end treble is placed in the whiskers of the prawn; the middle treble has one hook straightened, and this is thrust into the body. These mounts, when in use, are more firmly held into the prawn if wrapped about with red bait elastic. These items may also be purchased from retailers dealing with the wholesalers Leeda Group PLC. Personally, I consider a spun prawn appears so unnatural that I rely entirely on the sink-and-draw method to be described.

There is a lethal way of mounting a shrimp. Two No 12 Partridge Code 'P' double-fly hooks with down eyes are joined, one behind the other, by heavy nylon. The overall length of this 'in-line' mount being approximately 1in. In conjunction with a T2 shrimp pin inserted forward under the tail, the joined doubles are fuse wire or silk-wrapped under the belly of the shrimp with their points facing the tail. The trace is then knotted to the eye of the tail hook. If the width of the mouth of a grilse is measured, it will be found to exceed the length of this mount. As the doubles are at the head and tail of the shrimp there is no way in which it can be taken without the mouth of the grilse coming into contact with at least one of the doubles. A salmon's mouth is wider and may well enclose the lot!

Before mounting a prawn or shrimp I rub my hands in earth or mud. A salmon often mouths a prawn, rather than taking it at speed. The take may be delicate, as though the fish is tasting the bait or appraising the aroma. If it doesn't like the taste or smell it will eject the prawn before you are able to strike. I cannot write that this rejection is due to the aroma of male hands — which are offensive to salmon, whilst female fingers are not — neither can anyone gainsay me with authority, but the risk is not worth taking. Other than the mounts, prawn and shrimp fishing is accomplished with the same tackle used for spinning artificial baits with a fixed spool reel.

Fishing shrimps and prawns
Different methods are required when tempting a visible salmon, than when searching the river for hidden fish. Let us try for a salmon we have sighted.

Clear water allows us to discern salmon and grilse as they rest on the river bed, between growths of weed, swaying just off and to the rear of a wooden groyne and in other lies. Spotting fish through polarized spectacles is a knack which has to be acquired. Practice will enable one to look into, rather than at, water. Shadowy forms take on substance; the white rim of a momentarily open mouth; the out of place vertical line of a tail when all else is streamlined; the sun shadow outlining a fish resting on gravel.

Start at the bottom of your beat and walk up the river — slowly. Sooner or later a salmon will be seen. What to do? Move back from the river bank and work your way to a kneeling position upstream of the fish, and as far back from the river edge as the length of rod allows. Swing out the Paternoster outfit beyond the fish and do your best to drift the prawn across his bows, at his depth, 1ft before his nose. A tall order? Yes, but achievable with practice. Sometimes the Arlesley Bomb or pear weight may rest on the bottom and the prawn sway steadily in front of his nose. At other times the current sweeps the bait across, and the angler has to keep repeating the process.

Now, the salmon. His reaction is unpredictable: he may move forward and take at once; he may flee in alarm; the prawn may be regarded as it rests on the river bed before his nose for five minutes, and then be taken with decision. One never knows, and therein lie suspense and excitement — the reason why we fish! But one thing is certain, if your prawn swings behind his tail, or to a position to the rear of the dorsal fin, he will swim away. Fear, I suppose, of something outside his area of vision, for a salmon is unable to see directly to the rear due to the bulk of his body. If a salmon flees, that is not the end of the matter. He will probably return, if not in five minutes, then in half-an-hour, because the lie suits him, but a nervous fish is seldom caught.

If the river is turbid, or a fish cannot be found, one has to fish the water. With the Paternoster system this is accomplished by touch. Cast out the bait, the weight sinks to the river bed and the fingers of your free hand on the monofilament feel the bump as the weight hits the chalk. The prawn or shrimp is now swaying, downstream of the three-way swivel, a few inches above the bed. Raise the rod tip, the current swings the outfit one yard closer to your bank, and 'bump', the weight again thumps down as the rod tip is lowered. All the while the free hand fingers act as eyes and ears, transmitting underwater activity. Touches there will be: eels, trout and salmon all touch and tweak the bait. At each message I strike at once. There are those who say 'Wait a while. Let the fiddling continue. Allow him time.' They may be right — but not always. There is no sure way, unlike the worm when a lunch-break of eating time should be allowed.

There are open, shallow and wide areas where prawn and shrimp are fished to better advantage by a Wye weight at the line/trace junction. Cast down and across to the far side of the river and the current will sweep the bait back to your bank. The weight should be sufficient to tap constantly on the river bed.

Prawn and shrimp may be fished, weighted, beneath a float. A wine bottle or pike cork are suitable. This is not a choice way. The deck chair sleepers are well suited by the method.

Prawn fishing has its fascinations, it can be skilled, and much will be learned of fish behaviour by watching visible salmon. It is a sad fact that, where allowed, prawn fishing is almost always overdone. Bait anglers pester salmon which become scared, nervous and ultimately uncatchable. Offering a prawn may decline into a habit, not only detrimental to the fishery but the hooked angler loses the pleasure of fishing the fly. He may be unaware, through dedication to this one approach, of the stirring joy when a salmon boils up to the fly, goes down and the rod arcs.

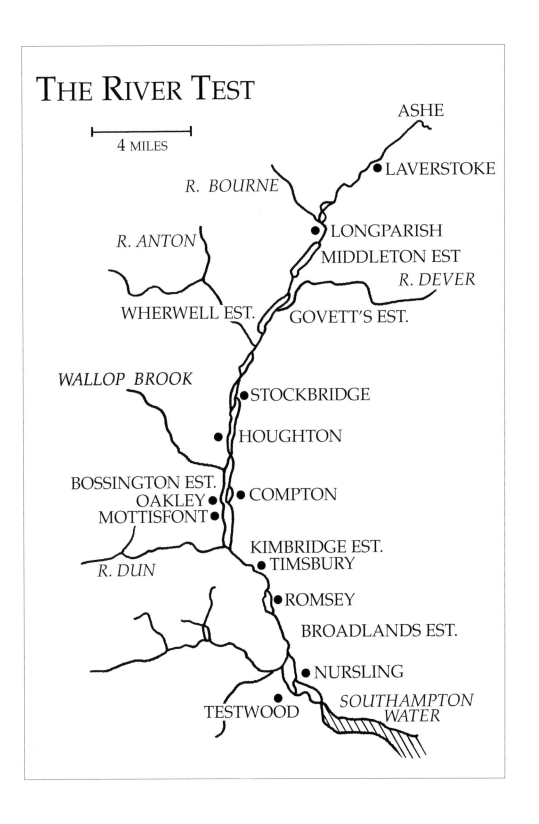

THE RIVER TEST

4 MILES

ASHE

LAVERSTOKE

R. BOURNE

R. ANTON

LONGPARISH

MIDDLETON EST

R. DEVER

WHERWELL EST.

GOVETT'S EST.

WALLOP BROOK

STOCKBRIDGE

HOUGHTON

BOSSINGTON EST.
OAKLEY
MOTTISFONT

COMPTON

KIMBRIDGE EST.

R. DUN

TIMSBURY

ROMSEY

BROADLANDS EST.

NURSLING

SOUTHAMPTON WATER

TESTWOOD

The River Test

The Test is the most famous chalk stream in the British Isles. She is also amongst the most beautiful. For centuries her waters have yielded trout, salmon and other fish beyond the capacity of lesser streams.

For generations there was a gentleman's agreement that salmon stopped at Romsey on their upstream migration. It was averred that salmon disturbed brown trout. Like weeds in a flower garden they were out of place. The trout interest prevailed. In the 19th and early 20th centuries Halford and Skues, Col Peter Hawker and John Waller Hills fished her waters and wrote their classics of her charms. The Houghton Club was founded at Stockbridge in 1822 and continues to hold and fish many miles of the middle river.

In addition, in the 1880s, the salmon angling potential of the Test began to be appreciated. G.R. Kendle, agent to the then owner of the Broadlands Estate, Lord Mount Temple, arranged the first rod lets on the estate below Romsey. The rod catches at the Nursling and Testwood fisheries, which are tidal in their lower reaches, and at Broadlands, were prolific until the 1970s, but are now in decline.

Today, trout predominate above Romsey and salmon at Nursling and Testwood. In between are the four Broadlands miles where trout and salmon mingle.

The river rises at Ashe, between Overton and Basingstoke. It flows by or through Laverstoke, Whitchurch and Hurstbourne Priors where it is joined by the river Bourne, celebrated in the writings of Harry Plunket Greene. Below Longparish House, home of Col Peter Hawker in the Napoleonic era, it is joined at Wherwell by the river Dever on the left bank, and the river Anton is added at Fullerton on the right.

The river now arrives at the centre of trout fishing in England: Leckford, Longstock, Stockbridge, Houghton and Bossington. The Test is then augmented by the Wallop brook in winter and spring; in recent years the brook has shrivelled in summer to a trickle. At Mottisfont is the Oakley stream, and before Kimbridge the river is joined by the Dun.

And so the waterway comes to Romsey to enter the salmon fisheries described. The total length is in the region of 34 miles, but there are, in addition, many miles of flanking streams and carriers.

Trout Fishing

Sir Owen Aisher — Fishing Tenant, Mottisfont Estate
Ralph Collins — Head Keeper

We met after lunch at The Oakley Hut on the Oakley Stream, which is part of a divided Test at Mottisfont. I questioned Sir Owen about his water:

'The Meinertzhagen family had the river in the old days. They were bankers; there is a village named after them on the Rhine. They only came for the mayfly, and in

September. Two of them, as boys, played up an oak tree on Duck Island which is on the main river. Thirty years later they returned and found some tins up the tree.'

'What were the tins there for?'

'Well, for food, of course. Tins had only just started. It was early days for tins.'

Sir Owen continued:

'The Barker-Mills family had the river at one time, and the Russell family for a while. The Oakley Stream is named after part of the Bedford Estate near Woburn. Halford fished here; he had a cottage nearby at Brook. There is a photograph of him having lunch with Robert Coxen, our first keeper, who died last year aged 94 years.'

The Oakley Hut, where Sir Owen has lunch, was built over 100 years ago by Ralph's wife's great-grandfather. His name was Billacombe. For a time the hut was known as Billacombe's Cottage.

'When Coxen was a boy he came across the fields towards old Halford, who was kneeling down addressing a fish. The boy was wearing a white collar. Halford yelled at him "Get down, you'll frighten the fish." They crept about on hands and knees in those days. Things have changed. We walk up and down the bank, and drive motor cars along the river, and still expect to take trout on the fly.'

Sir Owen was born on 28 May 1900 and started his fishing career by going for chub on the Hampshire Avon. A single trout came next from the Dove in Derbyshire, and that expedition was followed by a visit to the Dart.

'It was a small river, and so were the trout. You needed two or three for breakfast. I was fishing there in blazing sunshine when two ladies came by. They obviously knew more about it than me, for one of them observed "I don't think you'll catch much today. It's much too sunny." She was right, of course. Not that you catch much there on any day!'

Sir Owen fishes once a week, on Fridays, starting at the beginning of May. He drives to the river by himself from his home near Godstone. The day is spent with Ralph who cooks a lunch of beans, sausage and cheese in the hut. I asked about their trout fishing methods.

'What flies do you use?'

'We're not all that fussy. We try to do what the clever chaps do. Collins has a look at the river, and I have a look. We fish either a fly we think is there, or a nymph. We believe in Mr Halford and in Mr Skues! We enjoy ourselves.'

He looked at Ralph.

'What was that horrible thing we used last week? That was a nymph, wasn't it?'

Ralph described The Mottisfont Ruby:

'When rainbows are about they can't resist the colour. Someone makes our nymph in the village of silver-ribbed orange wool on a No 14 hook, a bit of weight, a yellow hood and a red Ibis tail. You can always take them on the Ruby.'

Sir Owen lamented the passing of the early years of the Lunn family who did much for the insect life of the river, and spread grannom on fly boards. Alfie Lunn taught him to fish.

'Last week, by the grace of God, I caught one fish, but not on a grannom. Where are they? I haven't seen one for eight years. Mayfly come and go as the years pass, but the absence of grannom worries me. They brought the fish on the rise, ready for the mayfly. Today, it's no good sitting down with a pipe in your mouth and a box of Swan Vestas, watching for a rise because they don't come up as they used to.'

Ralph observed that the 1991 season had started with wonderful hatches of alder, on which many trout had been caught, and that mayfly had just started to appear. This was true, for on my way to Oakley I had looked over Main Bridge, at the lower end of the Mottisfont water, and seen several duns emerging from the river.

In 1990 a seat was placed upstream of the Oakley Hut in memory of Ann, Sir Owen's wife. On the backrest is the inscription: *ANN AISHER 1893–1989.*

'She learned to fish when she was nearly 60. She enjoyed it. She sat on a seat in that place looking up the river. If a fish rose it was as good as dead. She was the best of us all. She got five salmon one day at the age of 89 years from our water in Ireland on the river Slaney. Her best weighed 27lb, and my brother's wife, Jean, had one of 28lb. We have caught salmon here on the Test. My daughter Clare had one. They don't appear now, and neither do the wild trout spawn in the river as used to be the case.'

Lack of natural spawning, and increased fishing pressure has led to regular stocking. When Sir Owen kept the water to himself and his brother, trout were introduced twice a year. Marley Tiles now send down many anglers, and Ralph stocks six times during the season. In 1990 the catch of brown and rainbow trout totalled over 600 fish.

I examined Sir Owen's tackle. The rod was a 9ft No 6/7 Hardy Graphite on which was mounted an LRH Lightweight reel and white floating line. The reserve rod, kept in the hut, is a Hardy fibreglass 9ft Jet with a Marquis No 8/9 reel.

'I caught two trout on the Graphite rod this morning. Rainbows of 3lb and $2^1/_4$lb. There was little movement in the river, but we saw these two dimpling and took them on a nymph. You say there are mayfly hatching on the main river? We'll go there. Collins will lead the way in his van, then me, then you.'

Before we left the Oakley Stream I told him of my father-in-law, aged 86 years, who farmed and fished in Patagonia and on Tierra del Fuego.

'The Land of Fire. He's 86 you say. Well, he's coming on well.'

Knowing a little of Sir Owen's ocean yacht racing prowess I asked if he had sailed to Cape Horn.

'Me? No. Not bloody likely. I'm much cleverer than that! I wouldn't go there. Australia, the States, South Africa, the Baltic; I've sailed to those places. But I never wanted to go around the world or do anything dangerous.'

At the main river Ralph assisted Sir Owen across a footbridge, set up the rod, knotted on a hackled mayfly and pointed out rises. They were generous rises, full and round and taking time to smooth. The mayfly were clearly 'up'. Sir Owen cast with decision and power. Out shot the fly to plomp down on the river in front of a trout. One or two fish were scared and bow-waved off. One or two leaves went missing from the bushes to the rear. If the fly remained in the bush as the line flew forward Ralph murmured 'I think I'll change the fly, Sir' and attached a replacement. But a trout, a brown of 2lb, withstood the onslaught and, with a head and tail roll, took down Sir Owen's fly.

'You going back to Devon?'

'Yes.'

'Then take that fellow with you.'

17 May 1991

Salmon Spinning

Brian Parker — for 12 years Under-Keeper on the Broadlands Estate. Since 1986 Head Keeper on the Bossington Estate.

Reduction of salmon runs and rod catches

Before the drought year of 1976 it is likely that between 3,000 and 5,000 salmon ran the Test each season. Of the run in those years it was always assumed that 10% would be caught on rod and line, but the catch was probably a much higher percentage. In the 1950s the rod catch was usually over 1,000 salmon.

The drought season of 1976 saw the start of a drastic decline in the run. It was unfortunate that this decline coincided with the drought because this masked the real reason for the decline. The true reason is largely the deterioration in the quality of the river and the silting of spawning beds. In 1990 fish counters on the lower river showed that 800 salmon ran the river, of which number in the region of 40% was taken by the rods.

Measures are being taken by the National Rivers Authority to reverse this decline. Fish passes and counters have been installed, a fish micro-tagging scheme is in operation in conjunction with stocking, and radio tracking of salmon returning from the sea is taking place. Gravel raking is essential in the spawning areas to provide silt-free redds, and work in this direction is in hand.

Cold water and warm water spinning

Brian considers that there are two distinct methods of spinning for salmon on the Test. The first, in the early season, is by casting downstream and allowing the bait to track deep and slow across the river. By the middle of May the water has warmed and casting upstream becomes the most successful method. For downstream fishing he favours the Mepp spoon, and for upstream casting a Toby. The changeover is governed not only by increased water temperature, but by improved clarity.

'It is no good chucking a bait upstream and spinning it back 1ft below the surface if a salmon on the river bed cannot see it through the murk.'

Rods and reels

He uses two spinning rods. For the early season, when casting heavy baits, a stiff 9ft 6in fibreglass rod by Fosters of Ashbourne is used. For the upstream casts, when less weight is thrown, a 10ft Hardy fibreglass rod is employed.

When spinning downstream in spring Brian uses an Abu multiplying reel with a 15lb or 18lb monofilament line. Casting the Toby upstream is accomplished with a Mitchell 300 fixed-spool reel and 15lb monofilament.

Terminal tackle and baits

When spinning downstream with a large Mepp, additional weight is usually added by a Wye weight. If really slow fishing is required he fishes with a weight on a dropper — the paternoster system — which keeps the bait just off the river bed and prevents snagging. This weight is changed frequently as progress is made from pool to pool.

'If you use a $^1/_2$ oz weight in a fast spool your Mepp will fish at mid-level where your chances are slim — you must fish near the bottom. Use 1 oz in such places, and $^1/_2$ oz in the slower pools.'

The spoon is a gold No 4 Mepp Aglia.

The Toby for upstream casts is usually silver in colour on both sides and, being available in a variety of weights and lengths, additional weight is not required, although a swivel is tied in 3ft above the bait. The length of his Toby is $2^1/_2$ ins at a weight of 28g.

'Most people cast their Toby straight up the river and reel back too fast. I like to cast up at 45° and retrieve more slowly. In this way the bait flips over and changes direction to move slightly upstream when opposite my position. This change in direction, simulating an escape attempt, often causes an impulsive grab by the predatory salmon. Mind you, only one in six follows turns into a take. You experience more follows in the autumn and fewer takes — this may be due to the aggression of cock fish in spawning colours. Fresh salmon, earlier in the season, are more likely to take hold, and not sheer off at the final moment.'

If a Mepp Aglia is cast upstream Brian will tie in a swivel 3ft above the bait and add a sliding bullet weight. This additional weight keeps the bait 2-3ft below the surface on the fast retrieve.

He does not use Devon minnows, but sometimes fishes a plug such as a Flopy or Rapala. He retrieves the Flopy slowly because that plug fishes on its side if drawn quickly through the water. 'Fished steadily the Flopy has a beautiful action.'

Landing tackle

'Do you use a gaff or a net?'

'I usually forget both, and am stuck with trying to hoick out salmon with my hands.'

He told me of an unusual incident whilst fishing from North Bridge on the Broadlands House Beat.

'I cast a Toby up the river and it was taken. I was on the bridge without a net or gaff. It was impossible to come off the bridge due to brambles at each end, and so I played the fish to a standstill until it rested in the water 4ft below my position. I grabbed the line and held on to the bridge with one hand, nipped over the rails and stretched down with the other. The fish was just within reach. I put my hand over his head, pressed in the gill flaps and lifted him out onto the planks. He weighed 15lb.'

Brian never uses a tailer.

'Few people these days carry a gaff. Many of the fish coming in during recent seasons are grilse. It is a shame to disfigure such small salmon with a gaff. Most anglers use a net.'

Salmon lies

Brian knows that many salmon lie just behind the point of a groyne and one or two feet downstream. In this position fish will be scared if the angler stands on the groyne platform. The correct method is to fish the area from a position a few paces upstream of the groyne, and thus remain out of sight. If casting from this place, the weight at the top of the trace will be level with the end wooden pile of the groyne, and the bait will revolve 3ft downstream. Subsequent casts should extend further downstream about one pace at a time.

If the groyne is at a shallow angle, fish will rest at the distance of the point from the bank. If the boards are at a steep angle, throwing the water out to the middle of the river, salmon will rest beyond the end of the groyne and some way out into the river.

Brian recommends care in spotting salmon where the water shallows out at the tail of a pool. If fish see the angler first they will move up into the security of deep water. Sometimes they are seen in channels between weed beds, or resting with their tails in front of a clump of ranunculus which breaks the current. A similar resting place is in front of a bridge support pile.

'If you watch a piece of floating weed drifting down towards a bridge pile, the weed will move to one side before it reaches the pile. It is pushed aside by the cushion of water in front of that support. Salmon also take advantage of this break in the flow by resting with their tails in front of the bridge pile.'

If the outside bend of a river is reinforced by wood or metal piling, salmon may lie tight alongside these vertical bank supports.

Brian fishes throughout the day, but prefers the middle hours. This preference is based upon the fact that the Test flows due south and thus, at noon, the sun is shining up the river and assists the visual search for salmon. This search has become more difficult in recent seasons due to increased water turbidity.

'What type of polaroids do you use?'

'It all depends on the make I find on the river bank!'

The weather

He agrees that fishing is poor when the air is colder than the water.

'There is a lot of truth in the old saying "When the wind is in the east, you'll catch the least".'

When water temperatures reach 70°F, as in the summers of 1989 and 1990, fishing is poor, even by upstream spinning.

'How about thunderstorms and rain. Are they helpful?'

'I'm normally in the hut!'

Brian's largest fish weighed 16½ lb and was caught in May. The following week he had another of 16lb. One fell to a Toby and the other took a prawn. Both came from Lord Brabourne's Platform on the Broadlands House Beat. This place was the scene of a student's training in the art of a salmon keeper.

'I was standing on Lord Brabourne's Platform with my student Robert. On the opposite bank was a thick bed of weed which we had left to push the water over to the platform side of the river. I hooked a salmon on a Toby, and the fish dived into the weed. I sent the student off to run across North Bridge and up the far bank to free the fish. He arrived, removed his clothes and waded in up to his neck. He saved the Toby, but I never told him the fish had gone long before he got there.'

17 May 1991

Prawn and Shrimp Fishing

Dick Haston — Salmon Rod, Broadlands Estate

Dick caught the first salmon of his life on the river Test in 1951. He was fishing by a wooden groyne on the left bank of that placid stretch of water known as Long Reach on the Lea Park beat. The fish weighed 8lb and fell to an un-dyed natural bait, a silver sprat.

'Sprats were a common bait in those days. We fished them on a spinning mount; known as an Archer Tackle it is little used today. The mount has fins and a long needle which is inserted down the centre of the sprat. Archer's were also used to spin a prawn.'

He fished at Broadlands for 25 years, and in 1963 took his largest fish which weighed 35lb.

'It came from The Grove, which is the bottom beat on the estate. It was the largest fish of my life. At that time I used to fish with a friend, Harry Cook. The following week he hooked a great salmon on Kendle's Corner on the Lea Park beat. That fish was also 35lb, and I took some of the steam out of it for him because he had arthritic elbows.'

'Where did you hook yours on The Grove?'

'I was fishing at the top of the beat, on the metal piles. It took a prawn. From then on I became a fanatical prawn man, and I also love the shrimp.'

At one time Dick and a companion took 11 salmon averaging 12lb in weight in one morning.

'Did you take those on a prawn or a shrimp?'

'On a medium prawn. The shrimp is now more popular. It is small and probably better suited to the lower flows of water in recent years. You have to decide yourself which to use; trial and error on the day are essential. Sometimes they go for little ones. On other days they won't take any notice of the small ones, but gobble up the biggest in the box. You've just got to try them out as you fish.'

Purchasing and preparing prawns

Dick used to buy English prawns in Poole Harbour.

'The finest bait you could have would be to go down and catch the prawns alive, then cook them on the river bank. If you could do that, and put one on, that would be perfection. The staler the prawn, the smaller the chance. If you see a salmon at a prawn you will notice that he mouths it; if there's the least bit of staleness he doesn't help himself.'

In past years Dick purchased several pounds weight of lightly cooked fresh English prawns in July, August or September. They were then packaged in various sizes, frozen, and kept for the following season. Prawns are unobtainable in spring and early summer when one starts to fish.

'For the last five years fresh prawns have been unobtainable. I almost ran out, but I have just managed to buy 35lb of them at £5 per pound. They are in the freezer, graded in sizes. I use large ones in the cold water of the early season, and then reduce the size as the water becomes warmer.'

He does not dye his shrimps a magenta shade — which is a common practice — for he considers that the dark natural colour is best.

'Sometimes you can buy them in the market, but only a small percentage would be any good.'

In his early years prawns were fished on Berrie mounts. These had a spear to pierce the body and a flat vane at the tail. Mounted in this way they wobbled, rose and fell in the current.

'Berrie's became expensive. For years I then used a paper clip. I bent this with a pair of snipe-nosed pliers, forming an eye at one end and pushing the other in under the tail and up the length of the body. The eye was then bent down slightly below the tail, the nylon fed through and tied to the treble which was placed in the whiskers. The whole should then be bound with 5 amp fuse wire, or wire unravelled from an electric cable.'

Today, Dick buys a length of steel wire which is stiffer than the paper clip metal. His trebles are Partridge outpoints of a size to match the bait — usually No 4 or No 6. Shrimps are mounted in the same manner, but the hook size is reduced to No 8.

Fishing the prawn

When fishing, Dick holds the rod in one hand and his line, in front of the reel, in the other. Each touch and tremble from below is transmitted to his fingers.

'I fish a particular lie where I think there will be a fish. The weight has to be adjusted to suit the depth and flow. You must know the river bed and get the bait down to the fish. Many anglers swim their prawns 2ft above the river bed — that is no good. They also fish their bait off the top of the rod; you can see them cast out and reel in — that is no good either. The line must be in your fingers. You hold out the prawn into the lie, and you annoy the fish. If I'm bumping the bottom with my weight I know I'm somewhere near the fish.'

To conclude our meeting Dick produced three letters from Broadlands House. The following is one of them.

Broadlands
Romsey
Hampshire

Dear Mr Haston,   *29 December 1959*
The biggest surprise, and quite the nicest present I have had for Christmas, was that delightful salmon spinning rod which you so kindly sent to me. I am sure that if anything will help me to kill a few more salmon than last year it is this rod, not only because it is such a nice one, but because it will be an added inducement for me to go down to the river, 'though I can hardly expect to emulate your success.
With all good wishes for the coming year,
Yours sincerely
Mountbatten of Burma
P.S. I am sending a rather belated Christmas card because it shows a rather nice view of the house.

6 February 1991

Top: The river Test at Longparish.
Bottom: Mick Lunn, head keeper (1963 to 1990), The Houghton Club, the river Test.

Top: Sir Owen Aisher and head keeper Ralph Collins on the river Test at Mottisfont.
Bottom: The river Test – stocking trout at Bossington.

Top: The river Test – weed cutting at Bossington.
Bottom: The river Test – salmon fly fishing at Broadlands Estate. (Tony Allen)

Top: The Long Bridges at Wherwell on the Test.
Bottom: The river Test – Broadlands Estate – spinning for salmon.

Sea Trout Fishing

David Train — Rod

Graham Purbrick — Head Keeper, Testwood Fishery

Testwood is the most southerly salmon and sea trout fishery on the river Test, and is owned by the Barker-Mills estate. It is divided into two beats: the Upper Water and Testwood Pool. From the top of the Upper Water the M27 motorway may be seen at the lower end of the Broadlands fishery. This upper section is joined on the right bank by the river Blackwater which rises in the New Forest. Many more sea trout spawn in the Blackwater than in the Test. Sea trout fishing does not take place at Broadlands because the majority have swum into the Blackwater, although I have myself caught a four-pounder in the Broadlands Boundary Pool.

Rods reach the fishery by car over a bridge, to the right of which, and upstream, is Testwood Pool, with the Fishing Lodge beside the pool on the right bank. Sea trout and salmon used to be caught downstream of the bridge, but due to alterations to the river bed this section now is rarely fished.

Testwood Pool is tidal, not to the extent that salt water enters, but high tides push back the river, causing the fresh water level to rise. The pool is in the region of 150yds in length, and perhaps 60yds wide at the centre opposite the eel grids. If one walked up the west, or right, bank, one would pass the Fishing Lodge where Graham lives, continue over the eel traps, the main sluices, a pipe and the new fish pass, to reach the electrically operated flood relief hatches at the top of the pool. To complete the circuit one would then walk down the left bank, passing a fishing hut, to the bridge over which one arrived.

The legal, open, fishing seasons are:

Salmon —   18 January – 2 October

Sea trout —   1 May – 31 October

In the 1991 season Testwood opened its sea trout season one month later on 1 June.

Timing of sea trout runs

There is no defining name at Testwood for those little fish which return in the summer, three or four months after going to sea in the spring as smolts. In Scotland they are known as finnock; we decided to use the West Country name of 'school peal' or 'schoolies'. These little chaps of 12oz — or at the most 1lb — enter in late July and August, continuing their run into the autumn. At one time, in past seasons, there might be 30, 40 or 50 schoolies in a shoal; today only half-a-dozen.

Before the season opens, large sea trout enter in April. In the past Rods rarely fished at night in May, but David sometimes took the first sea trout of the season in that month. Such fish ranged up to $7^{1}/_{2}$ lb. A 3lb sea trout is considered small, a four-pounder, average.

As the summer arrived smaller fish of 2lb entered. A fresh entrant could be distinguished by the silver colour and, sometimes, the presence of sea lice. The fish are of superb quality, being very thick and almost resembling bream in their shape. David:

'Sometimes, in the water, one misjudged the size. A fish which looked like 3lb would be found to weigh 6lb when on the bank. Mind you, they don't fight as well as salmon, at least, not here. People always say a sea trout is violent, but I have found salmon to be the hardest fighters.'

During July, and thereafter, the runs are of mixed sizes: schoolies, two-pounders, those of four pounds, the occasional specimen of 10lb and, once or twice a season, a submarine! By October some of the fish in the pool will be dark in colour, having been in fresh water for some weeks. Others, in that month, carry sea lice.

In West Country rivers a spate will cause peal to run upstream, vacating a pool in which they had been present in low water for two or three weeks. That is not the case at Testwood. In the steadier flowing spring-fed Test, sea trout may remain in Testwood Pool for several weeks.

The runs of sea trout into the Test have seriously diminished. David no longer fishes for them at night, and if he catches one by day he returns it to the water. However, he agreed to fish on my visit to show me his style, and we had hope! In the autumn of 1991 there appeared to be a resurgence of the population.

David Train

His game fishing career started as a youth, catching small wild brown trout in tributaries of the river Thames. Interest in salmon and sea trout was stimulated by a visit to the Royalty Fishery on the lower Hampshire Avon. A day came his way in 1972 on the Lea Park beat of the Broadlands water on the Test. Head Keeper, Bernard Aldrich, later allocated him a season rod on the estate.

In 1975 he seized the chance to share a rod at Testwood through the good offices of Col 'Scrappy' Hay of The Rod Box letting agency. One year later he obtained a full rod. Two seasons after this a second rod was taken out of the total of 28 rods on the water. He has now fished Testwood for 15 seasons.

A rod is entitled to fish one specified day a month in the Pool, and one day on the Upper Water. Only two people are entitled to fish at any time in the Pool, and two on the Upper Water above the hatches.

The tides and the moon

A high tide will push up the level of the water in the Pool by 3-4ft. Although he is unable to offer an explanation, David has found a high tide, and full pool, are detrimental to fishing in the early season. In summer it has less effect. In May and June he ceases fishing when the tide raises the Pool. When he sees the water going away there are greater expectations. In full summer he fishes right through the rise and fall of the water. If the tide was so high that it turned the Pool into a pond, with no visible current, fishing would be useless. It follows that spring tides, at new and full moons, are by no means ideal. As to the light of the moon — this is detrimental. It is rarely pitch dark at Testwood, even on a cloudy night, due to the background glow against the sky of the lights of Southampton. In fact, a cloudless night is darker than a cloudy one, there being no cloud to reflect these lights. The best fishing experienced by David was in a fog!

Temperatures of air and water at Testwood do not control the quality of fishing to the same extent as on other rivers. He has not found that a cold night is unproductive: 'On one excellent night I returned to my car to find it frozen over, it was so frosty'. It may have been that the special quality of the Testwood sea trout fishing was primarily due, in the past, to exceptional numbers of fish overriding adverse weather.

Taking times

'The longer you fish the more you catch — here. When I started to cast in nights gone by, I used to brace myself or the rod might be snatched out of my hand.'

Testwood is, again, abnormal on taking times. There is no first and second half to the night as on other rivers. Neither does daytime disturbance reduce the night-time chance. Salmon may be hooked and played several times during the day, Mepps and Tobies may fly about, and sea trout will still be caught with the arrival of the night. David has also taken four salmon in the dark on sea trout flies.

Some years ago his total for one season was 49 salmon. On the final day he wanted one more to round off the score at the half-century. In daylight, he failed. At night, fly fishing for sea trout on the Upper Water, he had a pull under some alders, but the fish was not hooked. He cast again to the same place and was taken, at 2.00am in mist and fog. It was the 50th, a 6lb grilse. A 14lb salmon has also taken his $1\frac{1}{2}$in tube fly at night.

Tackle and flies

He is not fussy about tackle. A 10ft rod, two No 8 or No 9 fast and medium sinking fly lines on Hardy Marquis reels, and a 22in Gye net. David always fishes a sinking line because the water is deep, being 7ft or 8ft in places. If casting to a shallow area, the cast is retrieved at a faster speed, rather than changing to a floating line. The leader is home-made, being tapered through 15lb and 12lb sections to an 8lb point.

Great care is taken with the fly, which he dresses himself. The body is a long shanked No 6 streamer hook cut off at the bend; this leaves just the shank and eye. Articulated to the rear is a Partridge No 14 needle-eyed outpoint treble. The articulation is arranged by 18lb nylon as follows. The hook shank is mounted in the vice and varnished. The nylon is then whipped down tightly along the whole length of the shank with black silk. Every effort is made to ensure that this nylon cannot slip. This forms the body, to which nothing more is added. The nylon, after a gap of $\frac{1}{4}$ in at the end of the streamer shank, is passed through the treble eye, between the hooks of the treble, turned back and whipped down on the treble shank. There is thus a gap, as stated, between the treble eye and the end of the streamer shank. This gap removes any risk that the hook could be levered out of the mouth of a fish by the shank. The hair dressing is simple: squirrel tail dyed black. The fly is between $1\frac{1}{4}$ in and $1\frac{1}{2}$ in in total length.

One night, after catching salmon by day, David took, amongst other sea trout, three outstanding fish of 11lb, $10\frac{1}{2}$ lb and 6lb — all on the black fly.

The advantage of using a single pattern, in which one has absolute trust, is that if nothing is being caught one accepts that fish are not in a taking mood, and not that one is fishing incorrectly.

Graham Purbrick joined us as we talked in the Fishing Lodge. He started fishing for trout as a schoolboy, and always had a river keepers position as his ambition. Amongst the many letters of application he wrote was one to Mick Lunn of The Houghton Club. Mick was one of the very few to reply. He sent detailed advice.

On this Graham acted, taking a course with the Institute of Fisheries Management. After other employment he was offered the Testwood position, and started to manage the fishery on 4 March 1991.

There are, as stated already, a limited number of Rods at Testwood. Anyone wishing to join the waiting list should, in the first instance, approach Graham. His address is in the directory at the back of this book.

To the date of my visit on 9 October 1991 the sea trout catch was 85 fish at an average weight of just under 4lb. This average included undersized fish returned to the water. Amongst this total are two fish of over 10lb and four of approximately 8lb each. A high average weight is not desirable if a river is in decline, for it is evidence of a reduction in young fish. In 1991, a hopeful sign is that entrants to the river have included a considerable number of schoolies.

I asked Graham his favourite sea trout fly. He brought out a slim lure 2in in length. This resemblance of an elver is called The Snake. It is dressed on a No 10 low water double hook at the head, a flexible body of silver Mylon-covered nylon terminating in a No 12 outpoint treble hook. The wing is squirrel tail dyed black, with a few strands of lureflash.

An hour on the river

Before I arrived at 5.00pm there had been heavy rain for some hours. The road had been flooded near Southampton. Although the Test remains clear after rain above the Blackwater junction, that river will soon become dirty and the Test at Testwood will follow suit.

As soon as it became dark David put up two rods in the hope that the river would remain fishable for an hour. Both rods carried the same 1¼in black fly, but one had a faster sinking line than the other.

The fishing took place from the east bank where some of the water flows in back eddies. David was thus casting up the river in places, although down the current, and moving the fly by a steady figure-of-eight retrieve. During this hour on the water he had a number of plucks and pulls, but not a solid take. His system was to keep moving about the pool to find a taking fish, and one of the plucks was experienced in front of the bridge.

It soon became apparent that drifting weed was coming down, shifted by rising water and the rain. The fly was repeatedly clogged with debris, and the fishing had to stop. Activity, with the glimmer of a lantern, now started on the far bank. Graham was diverting the flow through his eel grids. Eels run to the sea when there is heavy rain and increased flow on dark nights. We crossed to the far side, and there they were, many eels, stranded on the grid. Raked up, they are retained alive and ultimately sold.

Salmon

Although this account had not included, by design, the major Testwood activity, salmon fishing, I set out below some salmon catch figures. These are of the present and of 40 years ago. During both of these periods the river was in decline. After the 1940s the catch recovered. All efforts must be made to repeat the process.

Year	Total	Best fish	Rod
1986	368	24lb	D. Train
1987	238	15lb	W. Gardner
1988	327	23lb	W. Gardner
1989	294	19lb	G. Purbrick
1990	167	23lb	W. Gardner
1991	69	$23^1/_2$ lb	G. Purbrick
1945	88	35lb	
1946	63	29lb	
1947	27	–	
1948	170	30lb	
1949	201	$42^1/_2$ lb	

9 October 1991

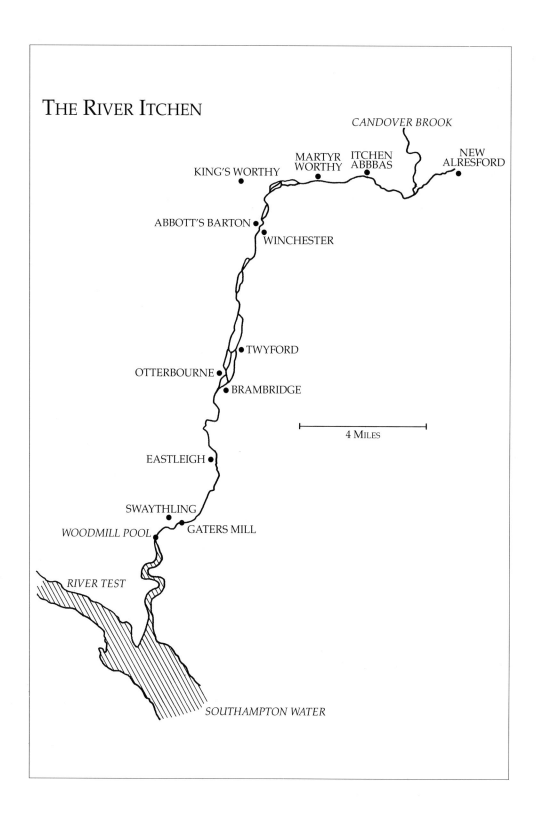

THE RIVER ITCHEN

CANDOVER BROOK

NEW
ALRESFORD

MARTYR   ITCHEN
WORTHY   ABBBAS

KING'S WORTHY

ABBOTT'S BARTON

WINCHESTER

TWYFORD

OTTERBOURNE

BRAMBRIDGE

4 MILES

EASTLEIGH

SWAYTHLING

WOODMILL POOL   GATERS MILL

RIVER TEST

SOUTHAMPTON WATER

The River Itchen

The Itchen could be described as the small sister of the Test. Both offer salmon and trout fishing: salmon in the lower reaches and brown trout above. In the Itchen, in addition, are grayling, pike, perch and other fish, and a few sea trout of good size are caught each season. It is a beautiful winding chalk stream of medium size, rightly famous in the upper reaches for wild brown trout.

The river has a long pedigree: Isaac Walton (1593–1683) is buried in Winchester Cathedral; G.E.M. Skues fished the Abbot's Barton water for 56 seasons, and there pursued the theory and developed the practice of fishing the nymph. The river rises south of Alresford to pass through or by Itchen Abbas, Easton, Winchester and Eastleigh, before entering Southampton Water at Swaythling.

Trout Fishing

Ron Holloway — Head Keeper, Martyr Worthy Fishery

A morning river walk

We met at the narrow wooden Martyr Worthy footbridge which spans the river a few hundred yards below Ron's house. If one looks upstream it is at once apparent that the river has been reduced in width on both banks. The left bank, having been brought towards the centre of the river by about 10ft, is now lined with horizontal tree trunks. The right bank has also been brought forward by 15ft from the willows which previously lined the water's edge. Narrowing chalk streams to increase the speed of flow is becoming a common practice. It takes account of the reduced volume of water going down a river due to increased abstraction and lower rainfall.

I thought it best that Ron confirm his reasons for the work:

'The original width of the river was fine when we had plenty of water. We haven't had high consistent water since the early 1970s. Two years ago we had to do something to increase the speed of flow and keep silt on the move. Wild trout need a clean gravel bed on which to spawn. That has been achieved.'

I looked downstream onto a fine fast-flowing water, not particularly deep but with desirable weed growth on the gravel bed. Close inspection of the bottom revealed the true worth of Ron's expert management: large healthy trout redds.

'I dig, rake and prepare the gravel after the autumn weed cut in October. You can now see 40 or 50 redds. Look at that large one: that will be the work of three pairs spawning, one after the other. The pile of gravel below the trench is the incubation area. There are probably three lots of eggs inside: the first will be at the downstream end, the second in the middle, and the final spawning at the front. Our trout didn't start shifting any gravel until mid-November. In December they are busier, with a peak between the last week of that month and the first week of January.'

'Isn't that late for trout to spawn?'

Ron thought for a moment.

'Not really. You see, in many rivers there is a great mix of trout, with a fair sprinkling of inter-bred stock brownies. They don't know when to begin. This water was last stocked in 1926; all our brownies are truly wild and they have always spawned late.'

'Do salmon spawn on your water?'

'We always have a few pairs. Seven years ago I counted 17 fish by the wooden bridge above the Easton Road. This year there were three couples in the last week of December. They don't stay long, just two or three days for a quick redd cutting. There are not as many as there used to be. I have only known two caught on our stretch during the trout season; both fell to a fly. There may be one or two sea trout, but they cannot be vouched for amongst all the trout.'

'Any other fish?'

'No chub. No dace. Would you believe I have 13 roach? They live in one particular hole, and the group ranges from half-a-dozen to 15 in number. They are of all ages, and weigh from 4oz to 2lb. They have been in the same place since I arrived.'

'Eels?'

'Masses of eels. There is no commercial trapping upstream. There are two eel grids which are set from time to time to provide a few for the owners above our water.'

There are no grayling at Martyr Worthy.

'Any pike?'

'Yes. You show me a length of chalk stream in England where there are no pike. It doesn't worry me. The water is shallow. I can see them. If there are too many and they grow too big I wage war on them and use my keepering skills: wire them, spear them, shoot them. Every three years I have an electric fish to clear out anything we don't want such as rainbow trout; they come down from the trout farms. This also gives me a chance to check my stock.'

I asked about his weed growth:

'For some reason the ranunculus dies right back in the winter, far more than used to be the case. The roots are still there, but growth is now later in the spring. I haven't cut weed in April for the last seven or eight years. Still, in the summer, there will be a mass of ranunculus. We have different weed cutting dates to those on the Test. If both rivers were the same the weed cutting contractors couldn't cope. We organize our dates to suit our river. They don't cut weed during the mayfly, but we do on the Itchen.'

We walked up the right bank above Martyr Worthy bridge. A young jack of about 1lb glided off from beneath our bank to safety in mid-river. The morning was cold and dull; typical February conditions. I wrapped my scarf tightly around my neck and thrust my hands into my pockets. Yet there was life. A rise commenced to large dark olives, which Ron calls winter olives. Grey wings erect, the duns floated around the corner into view, and the trout were feeding, picking them off, steadily and continuously. Generous rises by purposeful fish. Who would say that spring was far away?

'Look there — masses of caddis on the bottom. Thousands of them. We have a whole range of sizes. There is rarely a day in the year when we lack a hatch of fly. I've seen the temperature at minus 15° and still winter olives appear. How long they last Heaven knows.'

Iron blue float down in April and the autumn; hawthorn at the end of April; mayfly are almost entirely absent.

'Do you have many shrimp and crayfish in the river?'

'We have both. Shrimp form about 75% of the diet of my trout and make the flesh pink.'

'Sometimes one sees a trout pushing at the river bed with his nose, whilst his tail is waving in the air. Can you catch him?'

'No. It is almost impossible. But sometimes they do that and then drop back a yard to see what has been churned up. You might catch such a trout on a nymph.'

'Have you found anything remarkable inside a trout?'

'A mouse. I have also seen a trout take a young rat. A rat, mind you, not a water vole. The trout must have been a four-pounder.'

On we went to an area where the river had been narrowed the previous season. The new banks, which had been white chalk, were now grass-covered and the verges planted with sedge.

'I dig up the sedges from the area of the old banks and break up the plants. Then I plant them along the edge of the river to form a new fringe. They will form a screen for anglers and be topped when they're established. Their proper name is Bur reed.'

Ron's two spaniels, Sam Browne and Snoopy, followed us, but Sam exercised his own discretion on the route. Shortly, from a willow clump on the far bank, there arose spaniel whoops of joy. Three roe deer emerged to canter along the far bank, and two swam across the river. Snoopy stayed close, looking superior.

We then went to Ron's house where his wife, Paula, gave us delicious home-made soup, with toast, cheese and coffee.

Ron's career

'I can vividly remember the first fish I caught. It was a little roach, and came from the cemetery lake on Southampton Common in 1941.'

'How about your first trout?'

'As an 8 year-old I cycled to the river Blackwater, a tributary which runs from the New Forest into the Testwood water of the lower Test. I was poaching. I had made the rod myself of bamboo, and fitted a little aluminium reel which came from Woolworths and cost 2 shillings and 6 pence. On the reel were 30yds of level Cuttyhunk line with a swan quill float. That float was also home-made, from a feather off the river bank and a few elastic bands. On the end was an Allcock's No 16 hook to gut and a worm. Worms were found by kicking over cowpats. I poked the rod out and swung the worm into a dark hole under an overhanging tree. Suddenly there was a huge splash and a whoosh, and there was my first trout. From then on I was hooked. Of course I was. Although it is now my work, it remains my major hobby.'

There followed school, college, two years National Service and a spell in agriculture. All spare time was spent fishing.

'I was there on the opening day of Chew Valley Lake in the 1950s. My father visited Blagdon Lake with me after I had saved £1 from my pocket money for the ticket. For that sum there was an eight-fish limit. I was in paradise. They were wonderful years. Since 1970 I have been keepering here, at Martyr Worthy.'

Watercress beds and fish farms

The nearest commercial cress bed to Martyr Worthy is two miles upstream. The bulk of the beds are eight miles away at the headwaters. These beds do not create any problems for Ron's fishery, other than occasional water discolouration. There are other fisheries, closer to the beds, and without full-time keepers. They are troubled with silt deposition and decomposing water cress being washed downstream. Ron is of the opinion that there ought to be some form of trap for the silt; this could then be extracted and pumped over adjacent fields as fertilizer.

Trout farms cause great problems. There is one half-a-mile above the fishery:

'It produces between 300 and 400 tons a year. The effluent is discharged into a ditch about 150yds long. That is the only conscious effort which appears to have been made to trap their solid effluent. That ditch is full, and excess effluent flows down the river. Several years ago white sewage fungus was growing on the bed of the river for 1,000yds downstream. That is one problem. The other is their inability to keep in all their fish. I know one cannot make every stew pond escape proof. Yet, I cannot tolerate mass escapes of nearly 10,000 trout which happens at about two-yearly intervals. In between there are block escapes of smaller numbers — say, 2,000 at a time. The last escape was dealt with by electric fishing — we removed 4,000 rainbows. My tenants pay an arm and a leg to fish here for wild brown. Wild brown! I've got wild rods when all they can catch are 6in rainbows which rush at every offering on the water.'

The fishery and fishing methods

The Martyr Worthy water is 1¼ miles of double bank river, fished between 1 May and 15 October. Other than the owners, the water is fished by five season rods. The river is bordered by water meadows. The water is clear, open, and not deep. In consequence trout are easily scared. Leaders of 5X, 6X and even 7X are necessary. Small flies on No 18 and No 20 hooks are often required.

Ron's order of importance in the achievement of success in dry fly fishing: presentation is foremost, followed by correct size, shape and colour of the fly. Three artificials take most of the trout: Iron Blue, Greenwell's Glory and Lunn's Particular.

'The old admiral fishes a Beacon Beige most of the time. That is his favourite. I haven't much confidence in the fly, so I don't take many fish on it. But a Greenwell, that is another matter. A Greenwell is the tops. They should be dressed in three sizes on No 16, No 18 and No 20 hooks. You are then able to imitate all sizes of natural olives. By golly, they take fish. I have a penchant for long tails, and I like my flies to be winged.'

'Do you like a Caperer?'

'That represents a sedge. It is acceptable, but we have our own artificial — The Martyr Worthy Sedge. I tie them: small ginger hackle, dark green silk body, roof-like brown hackle tippets along the back.'

'What is the annual catch of trout?'

'Our 10-year average is 710 fish weighing 1lb 3½oz. The largest wild fish I have had weighed 9lb 4½ oz. It fell to a No 16 Sedge on a 3lb point. He had been about the place for two or three years, but now spends the seasons set up on a wall at the house.'

To achieve these excellent results Ron supports his fish with extra food in the winter.

'It is difficult to persuade wild brown trout to take floating fish pellets, but I like to feed them from the second week in January until the end of April. It was necessary to find a way to induce them to eat. Martyr Worthy bridge is on a public footpath. People go there with children to feed the ducks with squares of white bread, and the trout compete with the ducks. I cut a bag of white bread chunks and feed them each morning. Then brown chunks were mixed with the white. Then brown only, and I cut those to the shape of trout pellets. Then it was just pellets.'

At this point in our discussion I asked for an amusing incident. Paula told me: 'The admiral, who has fished here for many years, and is well into his 80s, caught a trout on the top beat. He put it on the bench and went on fishing. Looking back he thought he saw a dachshund by the bench — it was an otter eating his fish.'

Ron: 'Another time I was watching the admiral. His back cast extended over the field and the fly hooked a bullock. There he was, rod up, reel zizzing, but it broke him in the end.'

Recent river narrowing, and creating a new trout stream

After luncheon we drove to the Easton Road bridge and looked upstream. The left bank of the river had been moved forward to narrow the river width, and now presented an area of white chalk which would grass over during the summer.

'Would you like to explain this improvement?'

'The river was narrowed because it was 20ft too wide for the flow. First of all we made a new bank with logs, each of which weighs about 1 ton. They were cut from across the field, dragged here and floated into place. We pegged them in with 8ft scaffold poles, driven in to refusal with a beetle. Then we back-filled with 3,000 or 4,000 tons of chalk which came from a building site near Winchester.'

We then walked up a new stretch of trout stream being created from a carrier which had been blocked with silt. The stream runs through a Site of Special Scientific Interest. 'This Site is to protect the flora and fauna. There are almost 30 types of willow present.' There is also a great range of birds. In a survey lasting 12 months Ron, and a local farmer and ornithologist counted 127 varieties.

The carrier is three-quarters of a mile long. Mud was removed to create the new stream, and the bank built up and reinforced with poplar logs and Geolon plastic hessian. Weeds, starwort and ranunculus, are starting to root in the bed of the stream into which trout have already moved of their own accord from the main river. It is a fine brook, an enterprising addition to the fishery, and a great credit to Ron and his employer.

'Who did all the work?'

'We did it together.'

I walked back to the car along the river bank. Trout were still rising to large olives on that beautiful clear intimate water.

20 February 1991

Ian Hay — The Rod Box, Kings Worthy

Personal and business history

Ian was raised in Scotland. He caught his first trout in the Pentland hills at the age of five years.

'I saw this bright little fish in a burn and caught it in a tin can. Feeling sorry for the troutlet I released him, but he swam back into the tin. I thought "that's good enough. I'll have him out".'

His is the fifth generation of fly fishers in the Hay family. The earliest records of their involvement being at the start of the 18th century. The family came south in 1955. Ian's early training was at Milward's of Redditch. There he learned various skills including the making of split cane rods, reels, fish hooks, and the braiding of fly lines. During his lunch hours he was taught to cast a fly on grass at the golf club by Capt Terry Thomas. 'He used to sit on a deck chair and drink beer whilst I wielded my fly rod.' The training was followed by a spell in Milward's London shop in Bury Street where he managed the fishing section.

Rod letting on the river beats

In 1965, with his parents, he opened The Rod Box. The business expanded through two moves to the present comprehensively stocked shop at Kings Worthy. In the middle years Ian's father started to let fishing for various owners on the river Itchen. 'It was a privilege to fish the Itchen. My father vetted all the rods. Beginners were not allowed on the river unless accompanied by a gillie, and after taking lessons. Dry fly only was the rule. We adhere to his principles today and have four instructors available.' The instructors teach all aspects of trout and salmon fishing including double haul for the lakes, and Spey casting for salmon.

The Rod Box has available for short period letting nearly 40 miles of water on Test, Itchen, Nadder and the Whitewater near Odiham. There are five beats on the Itchen taking between two and four rods; on the Test is a single superb two-rod beat; on the Nadder a single two-rod beat which rotates amongst seven beats. There are two beats on the Whitewater which is a most attractive small stream. Their Itchen beats, in the middle river between Itchen Abbas and Brambridge, are stocked solely with brown trout. Determined efforts are made to encourage wild spawning by raking over the gravel beds. Each beat is stocked with fry as well as fish weighing between $1^{1}/_{4}$–$1^{3}/_{4}$ lb. If the water has a mayfly hatch a few larger trout up to $2^{1}/_{2}$ lb may be introduced, but the emphasis is towards natural regeneration. The rods are encouraged to return wild fish, but 'catch and release' of stocked trout is not the rule due to the possibility of damaged fish introducing disease.

Pike are controlled by electro-fishing by the Head Keeper Glyn Smith and the Under-Keeper Leslie Gates. Leslie is a pike expert who takes up his spinning rod after the hours of regular work — in the last 28 months he has killed 90 pike!

On the Nadder, at Compton Chamberlayne, the owner has his own stews and stocks the water with both brown and rainbow trout.

The Test beat at Longparish is delightful. There is a fine hatch pool, two waterfalls, a long glide and two carrier streams, all stocked with Test-bred browns. The open trout seasons are:

Itchen: 15 April-30 September
Test: 1 May-30 September
Nadder: 1 May-30 September
Whitewater: 1 May-30 September

Nymph fishing is allowed on some beats in the second half of the season, but rods are always encouraged to fish dry fly. On the Test water, and one Itchen beat, grayling fishing is let from 1 October-31 December.

Natural flies

The natural fly sequence is governed by the weather. The season starts off with large dark olives and iron blues. Being a fly which hatches in cold rough weather, the iron blue has been prolific in the bleak conditions of the spring of 1991, and continued to appear until the middle of May. The water temperature in May being 10° lower, at an average of 53°, than in 1990. On one Itchen beat mayfly and iron blue hatched at the same time.

Grannom are scarce, hawthorn plentiful, and the mayfly follows them both. Pale wateries hatch after the mayfly and then blue winged olives by day. Later, in July, the blue winged olive has a double hatch, by day and in the evening. With the arrival of the final hours of daylight the female spent (Sherry Spinner) falls, nymphs hatch and the evening duns are taking off. To crown this confusion sedge flies also put in an appearance.

'How do you deal with this varied abundance?'

'You never have the right fly on at the crucial moment.'

'So, what do you do?'

'Go into the fishing hut and attack the whisky bottle.'

Black gnats are not aquatic. They are blown off the land on hot August days. Many anglers mistake the reed smut, on which trout feed voraciously, for the black gnat. Reed smuts are found in running water and The Rod Box dress imitations down to hook size No 22.

Sedges hatch in large numbers and in a range of sizes from the great red down to small black specimens. In the hot summer of 1990 sedges appeared in great numbers until September. At that time, when dew falls on the grass, daddy long-legs feed the fish, and the artificial crane fly fills the creel.

Artificial flies and nymphs

I have always felt that presentation of a hackled fly of the right size, in pristine condition, on fine nylon, is more important than exact imitation of the natural insect on which a trout is feeding. I therefore asked Ian to put forward a small selection of six flies with which he would feel confident to fish throughout the trout season. This is his selection:

- No 14 Iron Blue
- No 16 Lunn's Particular as a spent fly
- No 14 Red or Black Sedge
- No 12 Red Wulff for mayfly, and deep fishing situations
- No 14 Greenwell's Glory — winged
- No 14 Lunn's Caperer

The Caperer is little-known beyond the chalk streams, but it is a fly which accounts for many trout on hot bright summer afternoons. Ian: 'I remember fishing after lunch on a hot day as a guest at The Houghton Club. I had five brown trout; all weighed over 3lb, and all fell to the Caperer.' He waterproofs small dry flies with Permafloat, and large ones with solid Mucilin. He then selected two nymphs:

- No 14 Partridge and Orange
- No 16 Pheasant Tail

He approves of the Pheasant Tail being tied with copper wire. 'I know that Skues nymphs are very different from those generally dressed today. A nymph with copper wire does not sink far below the surface in our fast-flowing water.'

FLY FISHING TACKLE

The following is his selection of a plain working outfit for fishing the Itchen for trout.

The rod

A 9ft AFTM No 6 carbon fibre two-piece. These are made-up by The Rod Box from British-made Hardy Fibatube blanks. They have sufficient power to cast a large fly into the wind, and yet are delicate enough to fish a fine nylon point and hook trout without the leader breaking. The rod has a rosewood insertion to the reel seat, and screw reel fittings. Spare tops are always in stock, and there is a rapid repair service for both carbon fibre and split cane rods.

The reel

Again, Ian chose one of British make, the System Two in size No 6/7 from Leeda Tackle. This reel has a smooth action, disc braking, and is of medium cost.

The fly line

A double-tapered No 6 floating fly line of a pale colour: pink, cream or buff. A light shade helps the angler to see the line when light fades at evening rise. In addition Ian is of the opinion that a light-coloured line is less visible on the surface of the water when viewed from below. He suggests the AirCel by the United States firm Scientific Anglers.

The leader

The Rod Box tie their own tapered leaders, following the principles of Charles Ritz. This leader has a 4ft butt of 25lb Maxima Chameleon which helps to turn the fly over into the wind. There is then a steep taper through six sections of reducing diameter to a long fine point. Platil knotless tapered leaders are also stocked.

The net

The Hay Net is a speciality of the house. The ring is bow-headed, being 15in deep and 13^1/$_2$ in across. The hinge is of brass, a metal which does not corrode and on which the closing ferrule does not jam. The shaft has a square section telescopic extension, and the hand grip is of cork. There is a clip for suspension on the angler's belt. All metal parts are anodised matt black, other than the brass hinge. It is a piece of sensibly priced, practical, luxury equipment.

I left The Rod Box taking with me the impression of a business founded and run by anglers to cater for the needs of chalk stream fishermen.

26 June 1991

Salmon Fishing

Dick Houghton — Head Keeper, The Lower Itchen Fishery

I arrived at Gaters Mill, headquarters of the fishery, after having luncheon nearby with Dick Houghton and Tony Allen who has a rod on the water. I thus had 'keeper and catcher' together. Dick has been at Lower Itchen for 21 years, and septuagenarian Tony has fished the chalk streams of Hampshire for six decades.

Dick was born on a farm a few miles from the lower Itchen. He was brought up in the nearby country, learned about rural pursuits and, like many boys, started his angling career by catching minnows in a jar. At first he worked on farms, and on Sir Thomas Sopwith's estate at Compton Manor on the river Test; there he helped the Head River Keeper Ted Hill (father of the present Head Keeper Cecil Hill). Later, the Head River Keeper at The Countess of Brecknock's Wherwell estate gave him a letter of introduction to Col Palmer, the estate factor, following which Dick became Under-Keeper at Wherwell.

He is now managing the 3½ miles of the Lower Itchen Fishery which terminate one mile above the tide at Gaters Mill. Three miles of the water are double bank and half a mile is single. This length is divided into five beats, each of which is fished by two rods. Fishing commences at 9.00am and closes at 8.00pm. A return of fish must be made on the day of capture at the Fish Room in the Mill: date, number of salmon and weight. Salmon may not be gaffed after 15 August, and hen fish, unless obviously fresh run, should be returned to the river. The season is from 1 March-30 September. Brown trout fishing is by fly only, with a two-fish limit per beat.

Leaving the mill we drove up the right bank of the river, starting at Beat No 5 which is at the lower end of the fishery. Man-made wooden groynes protrude from the banks to create salmon lies; I asked Dick who had made them and how long they lasted:

'The wood is Douglas Fir. I cut and trimmed the trees myself at Farley, near Salisbury, and brought them home. They last 10 or 12 years. We also use Douglas for piling, driving one end of the pole into the river bed by hand with a 36lb mallet which we call a beetle. I've a student from Sparsholt College arriving tomorrow for three weeks to learn about river keeping. I'll start him off quietly by a wander up the river in the morning; after lunch I'll hand him the beetle!'

On we went up the river whilst Dick pointed out the pools: the Clump, Upper Round the Bend, Lower Round the Bend — 'That's where I caught two fish last year, in the tail of the pool', interjected Tony.

The water was reasonably clear and at a low summer level after a long period of frost. The river is normally turbid in spring but clears by July; this clearance has become later in recent seasons.

'When I first came here it would be clear by mid-May. We now have problems of reduced flow, lower levels, and increased turbidity. There is a sewage works above us. If you go up the river in the early morning the water is clear and sparkling, it then colours by 10.00am, but clears again overnight. I think turbidity is related to activity at that works.'

We passed some sluices on the overflow channel of Gaters Mill. 'When the water built up and became too high in the old days, the channel took off the additional flow.'

Tony recalled his boyhood when, at the age of 10 years in 1928, he had stood on the bridge below the mill to see groups of salmon. 'You don't see them now. There is not sufficient water.'

Dick: 'Things have changed. In 1973, '74 and 1975, before the drought year of 1976, salmon were plentiful. The 1960s were even better. If I had the same rods fishing in the early 1970s that I've got now they would have taken 350 fish, instead of the 180 or so we catch today. I'm certain of it.'

On we went to Broomfields Pool where there is a productive run. 'Just here is a deep undercut piece of peat. Salmon love that place. A bar of gravel is in the middle of the river; cast to that and then let the bait swing in under the bank.'

We passed Lower and Upper Pike Pools, and drove by a bridge and across a public footpath. A line of piling reinforced the far bank.

'Those posts are 12ft long. There are 820 of them. We put them all in by hand, driving them down with the beetle. The job took two of us three weeks. I made my own beetle from a piece of 6in steel water pipe, and turned two wooden inserts on the lathe to go inside.'

The fish population is comprised of salmon, sea trout — 'fewer of those than in past seasons' — and stocked brown trout. Other fish present are grayling, pike, perch, dace, chub, roach, bream and eels. Escaped rainbow trout arrive from elsewhere. The rods fish for trout if salmon are dour, and as a privilege they may come after the salmon season to pursue coarse fish. Grayling are taken in summer on fly or nymph, and this may continue in the winter. Favoured flies are Orange Partridge and Red Tag. I asked 'Do they fish the Red Tag as a nymph or a dry fly?'

'Well, one of my gentlemen uses a dry pattern but puts it in his mouth to make it sink.'

On we went up the river, past The Pulpit and The Horseshoe, to the top of Beat No 4, and then went on to Beat No 3. The river was beautiful, and so was the scene at The Island. When I commented, Dick said:

'The sad thing is that the river is deteriorating like the Test, but we are five years behind them in loss of condition. We have to fight increased water abstraction to supply housing and industrial development. It appals me that there is an augmentation scheme to pump water out of the aquifer into the river to increase the flow. The aquifer is the supply source of the river — the underground sponge replenished by rain — but with recent dry summers the water is not being replaced. For the first time in living memory the top end of the Arle (an upstream tributary) actually dried up last summer. It is totally wrong to pump from the aquifer to supply the river; it is robbing Peter to pay Paul.'

Above The Island we came to a pool called Ward's, after an earlier owner of the water, and then continued to the top end of the fishing road. On driving down the river Dick pointed out the site of an old duck decoy. 'There were two arms to the decoy. When I first came here, if you poked about, you could uncover the iron hoops which were netted over to form the tunnels; duck were lured into them by the trapper's dog.'

We came to Six Hatches, so-called because two hatches used to be opened or closed to control the drowning of the water meadows, and four hatches — now removed — controlled the flow down the river.

Dick does not electric-fish his water, but he caught a $19\frac{1}{2}$ lb pike which was eaten by a friend. He likes to see a variety of fish. 'I disagree with the removal of all coarse fish. I like to see a balanced population. A few pike are a good thing and they mainly eat coarse fish. I have crayfish in the river — they clean up anything that dies. Eels are present, but in reducing numbers.' Dick does not use his eel rack to trap them until after the end of the salmon season and, recently, has found it hardly worth setting the trap. The delay in operating the rack, when eels are taken elsewhere and higher up the river in the summer, is because he does not like to alter the river flow. Changing the level may cause salmon to run upstream out of his water.

In the fields bordering the river are many molehills. 'I caught 22 moles in three weeks, but there were two I couldn't catch. These are their progeny!' Before setting his mole traps he rubs his hands in earth to disguise the human scent. I commented that this was my practice before baiting hooks for salmon with worm, shrimp or prawn.

I felt that Dick was fortunate that his section of the river was bordered by meadows which filter rain before it flows into the river. One of the problems of the Test is ploughed fields alongside the river; these do not provide any filtration and silt is washed directly into the river during rainfall. Blanket weed is a problem because it clogs his broad scythe and smothers ranunculus, carrot weed and other desirable growths.

The conversation changed to fishing methods, and those practised by his rods. Dick likes the little English prawn complete with all its legs and whiskers, rather than the soft over-sized specimens from the fishmonger's slab. Natural brown shrimps, and those which are coloured ruby red, are becoming more popular than the prawn on his fishery. Both are mounted with a shrimp or prawn pin pressed in under the tail, a treble in the whiskers, and the whole bound around with fine copper wire. A few rods fish the fly. Unlike the Test, small flies are favoured in traditional patterns on single and double hooks: sizes being No 6, No 8 and even No 10 in the autumn. Tubes and Waddingtons are rarely used.

'Devon minnows don't seem to work here. I think there is insufficient draw in the water to make them revolve at once and properly. The Mepp is the most popular bait after prawn and shrimp. We cast Mepps up and down; the upstream cast commences in the middle of May when the water temperature reaches the mid-50s.'

In the river are natural wild trout and stocked brown which come from Guy Robinson on the Leckford Estate. Very few mayfly were present in the past, but they seem to be increasing. 'When I first came here you might see 10 in a season. Now I might see 150 in a day. We have grannom, hawthorn, iron blue, pale wateries, blue winged olive, sedges and other flies.'

I asked about poaching, and whether he remembered any humorous incidents. 'Poaching is not a problem. The price of salmon has fallen to a level where it is not worthwhile. As to amusing incidents, I once saw a fisherman come out of the main fishing hut in his underpants. He was beaming all over his face, having taken a $17\frac{1}{2}$ lb salmon on a fly. The fish ran him up and down the river, but he couldn't find a landing place. Eventually he got into the water but the fish ran between his legs and broke the top of the rod. He was soaked, but as happy as a dog with two tails.'

I left this salmon fishery, taking with me the impression of a beautiful oasis: green, quiet, a tranquil scene populated by many birds, and yet on the outskirts of Southampton. In the two hours of my visit I saw the following: redwings, fieldfares, a drake golden eye, pheasant, snipe, lapwings, and a family of goldfinches. We also saw The Cliff where a kingfisher burrows into the bank each season to nest.

5 February 1991

Tony Allen — Salmon Angler, The Lower Itchen Fishery

Personal history
'My first notable angling success came at the age of eight years when I caught a $13\frac{1}{2}$ lb pike. My father and a friend taught me to fish, and had taken me to the waters

of The Southampton Piscatorial Society on the river Stour near Wimborne. To mark this achievement the Society made me a member, disregarding the minimum age of 12 years. I still have a letter from the Hon Secretary about the catch. In later years on that water I caught a brown trout of 3lb 12oz on a mayfly. It was a wild fish, there being no stocking in those days. I followed that trout with many more from the Stour.'

Two remarkable salmon have fallen to his rod. The first came when, as a boy, he was spinning with a home-made copper spoon on the Stour for pike in September. It was a cock salmon of 27lb which broke the top of his rod. 'Most of the time I was playing that fish with a broken rod. I had to have help from my father.' The second, at Broadlands on the Test, weighed 25lb, being taken on a 3in Yellow Belly Devon minnow in Cowshed Pool on the beat known as Moorcourt.

His first salmon on fly was taken in 1969 in my company from the river Dart. My fishing diary records the event which took place on a wet day:

'25 April. River rose and fell previous day. Medium/low on 25th. Water 49°. Air 56°. Cold wind in am, but warmed up by 2.00pm when Tony had a fish of 12½ lb halfway down Forest Pool above the big rock on far side. He fished slow and deep with a No 1 Thunder & Lightning. One hour later I rose a fish twice in the run of Oak Tree on same fly.'

Numerous visits to Devon then followed when we both took many salmon from the river Taw. At the same time we turned our attention to chalk stream salmon fishing. At Broadlands, on the Test, we took 28 salmon between us in the 1975 season, and six each in the drought year of 1976.

Lower Itchen salmon runs

Eight years ago Tony, and his co-rod Brian, started to fish at Lower Itchen. They normally take a fortnightly rod, but for a while fished once a week. To begin with they caught about six salmon each a season, but catches then reduced. In 1990 Brian caught four fish and Tony took three. In the early years they took salmon weighing up to 14lb, but recently the fish average in the region of 6lb.

The run starts with small numbers of heavy salmon in the spring. Small summer fish and grilse now predominate, entering the river from July until the end of the season. In the autumn a few really large fish come in; in September 1990, Tony saw a salmon which must have weighed 20lb.

The salmon are of good quality. Many carry sea lice, particularly those caught in the two lower beats, No 4 and No 5.

'Cottage Pool, and the Hatch Pool, both by Gaters Mill, are only one mile above the tide. Salmon swim straight in as the tide ebbs away. More fish are caught in Cottage Pool than in the Hatch Pool, although the Hatch looks more productive.'

Tackle

At Broadlands, in the 1970s, Tony fished the prawn with a 10ft fibreglass carp rod. I thought this was long enough, but he now uses a still longer weapon of 12ft made of carbon fibre. This is a springy rod, and the length enables him to reach out to hold a prawn beyond a groyne. There is also a better chance of remaining out of sight. His reel is a fixed spool Mitchell 300, holding 100m of 17lb Platil Soft. The trace is 1m of 15lb monofilament, joined to the reel line by a swivel. The knots at these junctions being Tucked Half Bloods. He uses a Paternoster system with 8in of 8lb nylon leading to the weight which is between ½ oz and 1oz.

'I like a Paternoster which is free to run along my reel line. This is arranged by threading on to the reel line, above the line/trace junction, a second swivel to which is attached a short paternoster nylon. When a fish takes, it is able to run off with the prawn without the disturbance of the weight bumping on the bottom. In addition, I can feel movements with great sensitivity, particularly if a fish is mouthing the bait.'

The prawn and shrimp

In summer he fishes with a small English prawn or a shrimp. 'I like to fish really small. Little natural shrimps are good, they are brown with black heads, but most of the time I use a small prawn.'

'How do you obtain your bait?'

'It is no good going to the fishmonger. His specimens are too large, overcooked, and thus soft. They don't last on the hook. I have found that you can catch prawns and shrimps at Millbrook, under the bridge, in the Test estuary. I cook them myself, just for a minute or two, until they turn pink. It is as well to keep a stock in the deep freeze; take them to the river in an ice-packed Thermos, and then return the unused ones to the freezer in the evening.'

I questioned him on his method of mounting the prawn.

'Many salmon are lost on the prawn. They come unhooked. It seemed sensible to develop a new mount and to use two trebles, one in the whiskers and the other tucked-up amongst the legs. I made such a mount myself of wire; the central treble can be moved along the body of the prawn to the required position. In the Broadlands days the water was clear; one sometimes saw a salmon bite a chunk out of the body of the prawn without being hooked on the single treble in the whiskers. My mount caught those fish on the central treble. The pin of the mount goes in at the head, not under the tail, and the whole is wrapped around with fine pink wire. A prawn mounted in this way rarely works loose, and may be fished for many hours. In addition, it is common practice to break off the tail flaps which may cause the prawn to revolve in the current. The jagged spear is also snapped from the head of the prawn because this sharp spike might deter a fish.'

Shrimps, being smaller, are more likely to be taken right into the mouth of the fish. Tony thus mounts them with a single small treble in the whiskers, and a shrimp pin pushed into the body from under the tail to keep the shrimp straight. The nylon from the treble is led back between the legs, and the whole is then bound around with fine copper wire which may be taken from an electric light cable.

The fly

When the water is clear he always fishes a fly. Tubes are preferred of 1in to 1½ in in length, attached to the leader by a Tucked Half Blood. Hairy Mary, Thunder & Lightning, and the two tubes which I invented, the Black Dart and Copper Dart. All of these have sockets at the tail into which a No 8 Partridge outpoint treble is thrust. The leader is 11ft of 15lb nylon, untapered, drawn straight off the spool which he carries in his pocket. His rod is 12ft long, of carbon fibre and easy in the action. A thin white AFTM No 6 floating line is used to cut down line shadow when fishing on the surface in warm water. 'I like white. It points to the fly. If the water is cold I use a green floating line with a dark sinking tip.' He ties a Blood Bight Loop to the end of the leader and attaches this to the fly line with a Double Sheet Bend.

'Do you move your fly fast through the water?'

'No. I fish slowly, casting the fly down and a little way out from the bank, and work the rod top all the time. My flies are hair winged. Moving the rod top makes the hair open and close, just like a jelly fish. Backing-up the fly at speed doesn't seem to work for me, particularly in a narrow river. When backing-up you have to cast out at right angles to your position — the Itchen is not wide, often the water is clear, fish will see you and be scared'.

The worm

Worms are fished on a No 2 Mustad sliced beak hook, the slices being cuts in the shank which point up to the eye and prevent the worm sliding down the shank. Other than the hook the tackle for worming is identical to the prawn outfit. Three or four lob worms are fished: the first is worked up the hook to cover the shank, the other two are in loops with heads and tails hanging. The worms are collected at night from the lawn in damp weather.

'After a hot sunny day, followed by a shower, the grass will be covered with worms when night has fallen. They may be two or three inches out of the ground. You have to be quick to grab them because I suspect they feel the heat as your hand approaches and they may disappear back into their holes like lightning. Some people stick a fork into the ground and shake it — worms pop up. They can be kept in a box with wet newspaper in the bottom and grass cuttings on top to make a mulchy bed. Some anglers, those who wish to keep their worms for a long period, feed them on fish meal and bran.'

Tony is adamant that a salmon must be given plenty of time to take a worm well back into the mouth. 'When you see them close their mouths on the bunch of worms, count 10, slowly, then strike.'

Spinning

He does not use Devon minnows on the Itchen. 'I have not had a lot of success with them. It is difficult to tell when they become clogged with weed. The Itchen is not like a rocky Devon stream where weed does not grow.'

His favourite spinning bait is the Mepp spoon. No 4 for upstream casting and No 2 when throwing down the river. If the current is slow the downstream size may be increased to No 3. Gold and silver are the preferred colours. He does not meet success with the copper shade.

'A keeper on the Itchen once advised me to cast a No 2 Mepp upstream with a swan shot on the trace 1ft above the bait. The Mepp was silver with red spots. I had a fish at once!'

Salmon lies and fishing conditions

Most of the fish are caught after being spotted in the river. Individual fish are thus attacked. Few are taken when the water is coloured, when one has to fish blind, unless throwing a No 4 Mepp upstream. Clarity of water makes all the difference to success. One ought therefore to start to fish at 9.00am when the fishery opens and the water is clear. As the morning progresses the river becomes coloured and fishing is more difficult. If the water is turbid one has to fish blind, casting around the groynes — time of day is not then of importance.

'I don't mind sunny days. The light helps me to see fish. Dazzle of the salmon must be avoided. It is true that the Itchen runs from north to south, and thus the sun shines upstream at mid-day, but the river also winds. One must fish so that dazzle does not discomfort a salmon when it approaches the bait. Never fish down on a salmon with the fly when it has the sun in its eyes.'

Salmon lie in front of concrete blocks placed on the river bed. Popular lies are just off and level with a groyne, or just alongside the end of the boards. 'You can usually see the tail waggling behind the end of the groyne.' Another resting place is in any small trough in the gravel of the river bed. Some fish may be found where the bed rises at the tail of a pool, in front of and alongside weed beds.

'Would you say that more fish are caught close to the bank than in the middle of the river?'

'Certainly. Almost all fish are taken close to the bank. I walk up the river slowly, wearing Polaroids, watching as I walk. If I spot a salmon it is usually given away by the moving tail; the rest of the body then becomes firmer in outline as I peer.'

Having spotted a fish he stops, casts his Paternoster outfit some yards above the salmon, the weight rests on the bottom and the prawn swings downstream of the weight. He may then cast again, or move the weight by lifting the rod, until the prawn is swaying 2-3in in front of the nose of the fish. Provided the fish has not been hooked before, is not running, and has not been scared, he will usually swim forward and take.

'If I am working my way downstream and see a fish I cast ahead of the salmon, but take great care not to be seen. It is best to kneel down, and the length of my 12ft rod enables me to keep out of the vision window of the fish.'

A shower of rain after a dry period activates fish. Heavy rain takes some time to colour the water because few ditches run into the river which is bordered by meadows.

'If it rained during the night and stopped at breakfast-time, you would be able to fish until noon before colour tinges the water. It is much better than the Test which colours rapidly due to ploughed fields close to the river banks.'

An east wind is not good, neither are conditions suitable if the air is colder than the water. Rapidly rising or falling air pressures unsettle salmon, but Tony cannot say that either precludes the catching of fish. I asked him to describe his most productive day at Lower Itchen in the 1990 season:

'It was 25 July. I arrived at 9.00am at the Hatch Pool which was alive with fish. They were swimming around, some in pairs and others singly. Many were 5lb or 6lb in weight, but there were a few of almost 20lb. I could not catch them. They just bumped my bait aside and wouldn't look at anything. In half an hour the pool was empty, all the fish having run upstream.

'I went up to Beat No 5 where I met Dick. He advised me to put on a No 2 Mepp with a single swan shot and cast upstream. I did as he instructed and a fish took at once. That was No 1, it weighed 6lb and carried sea lice. I continued up the river. There were fish on gravel runs, but they did not respond. Near the top of the beat is a groyne where fish could be seen. I dropped in a prawn — three salmon swam off, a fourth seized the bait and was landed. That was No 2, a five-pounder.

'Nothing more happened between that groyne and the top of the beat. I turned about and came downstream. A fish was lying close to the bank. He saw the prawn and took at once, but spat the bait out before I could strike. Three times he took and ejected the bait before swimming away. At the groyne where I had already caught a salmon, a prawn tempted another fish, No 3. He weighed $6\frac{1}{2}$lb.

'All this took place between 9.00am and noon. I left the fishery at 2.30pm after lunch. I was exhausted, and three fish ought to be enough for anyone.

'In the afternoon, after my departure, Brian took three salmon on a shrimp. It was a perfect day: the water was clear, the weather mild and the sun showed up the fish. The dogs were with me. Amber (labrador) is keen to help. She stares over the bank at salmon, eyeball to eyeball. She frightens them to death, but I cannot leave her behind.'
5 February 1991

The River Meon

Trout Fishing

Capt Brian Manhire RN (Retd) — Water Manager, Portsmouth Services Fly Fishing Association (PSFFA)

Description of the river

I met Brian Manhire at The Buck's Head, which overlooks the river between Corhampton and Meonstoke. I could not have been more fortunate in my guide on a river tour for the Association controls much of the trout fishing on the Meon. Their water is open to personnel who are serving, or have served, in the Armed Forces. There is a waiting list for retired personnel; preference in the allocation of beats on the rivers Meon and Itchen being given to seagoing members.

Before we started our journey down the river Brian gave me this description of the Meon. It rises at South Farm to the south-east of East Meon to flow north, north-west, and then west to West Meon, and in these areas the bed is sometimes dry. At Warnford are springs, watercress beds and trout lakes. This top section of the river circumnavigates Old Winchester Hill. The river then flows directly south from a height of about 300ft to 50ft at Wickham. This fall of 250ft in 7 miles produces a fast flow which flushes silt from the river bed and thus, between Warnford and Wickham we have a river which has the true characteristics of a small chalk stream. Below Wickham the river, falling only 50ft over the final five miles to the sea, becomes slow-flowing and silted.

Sea trout are present in the lower river at Crofton but, due to sluggish water, are more likely to be taken on bait than on fly. The PSFFA shares some sea trout water at Titchfield with the Park Gate Fishing Club. The Association hopes to obtain sea trout fishing in the Little Posbrook/Crofton House area.

Below Meonstoke the river passes the village of Droxford where Izaak Walton must have fished. Walton's daughter Anne married the curate of St Mary and All Saints and is buried there. At East Meon there is an inn — the Izaak Walton. Just below Warnford Park the water meadows above the road bridge leading to Exton were regularly flooded until 1986, and the hatches are still in working order at the converted mill. This flooding not only provided snipe shooting in winter, and early grazing for cattle in spring, but allowed silt to settle before rainwater passed into the river.

The creation of a wild brown trout fishery

Evidence of hatches for flooding the water meadows was apparent in the first stretch to which I was taken. Below Meonstoke the river divides into two: the original looped river, and a man-made straight cut through which the water could be diverted by hatches to flood the meadows. The original brickwork of the hatch system may be seen, and is probably about 200 years old. The straight cut rejoins the river after about 300yds.

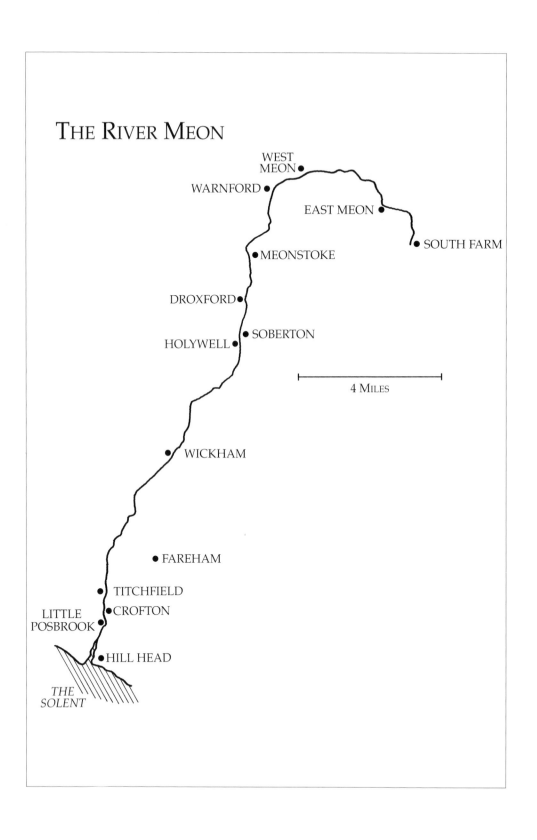

THE RIVER MEON

WEST MEON

WARNFORD

EAST MEON

SOUTH FARM

MEONSTOKE

DROXFORD

SOBERTON

HOLYWELL

4 MILES

WICKHAM

FAREHAM

TITCHFIELD

CROFTON

LITTLE POSBROOK

HILL HEAD

THE SOLENT

The Association is well on the way to transforming this cut and the original course into a wild brown trout fishery. To that end, two seasons ago, yearling brown trout were introduced in April in addition to takeable trout of about 1lb. A further two or three stockings of takeable trout will be made during the season, but it is hoped these introductions of 1lb fish may be reduced if wild brown spawn in the area. Ranunculus has been planted and flourishes, the roots being held down by stones; dams have been created to increase depth; gaps have been cut in the tree canopy to allow light to reach the stream. Brian stated: 'Three weeks ago I saw a sight which gladdened my heart — some 3in trout. They must be the product of natural spawning.' The dams in the straight cut were built of heavy gauge plastic bags filled with solids from the river bed. The bags were placed across the stream in three layers: the layer on the river bed is three bags wide; the second two bags; the top layer is of one bag. The whole could easily be removed if this proved necessary to protect the banks from erosion in time of flood.

The bed of the river is raked by hand to assist trout to cut redds. This may lead to the fulfilment of one of Brian's ambitions: 'I would like, in four or five years, if not before, to find sea trout spawning here.' This is quite possible for there are fish passes on the lower river. The one at Funtley has been in place for several years; another has been installed at Wickham where sea trout arrive after the end of the season.

Raking the bed is essential because, in times of heavy rain, the Meon rises like a spate river and much silt arrives. If this silt is not broken up by raking it solidifies and stifles spawning areas.

We reached the place where the straight cut rejoins the original river, and this we followed upstream to our starting point. There was superb growth of flowering ranunculus which had been planted three years before. The flow of water was good, but will fall by early July. Brian: 'At the junction, above the little bridge, there was a large trout. I don't know where he came from, but doubtless he was a cannibal. I thought of my wild fingerlings. He must be caught. I was determined. I got him by stealthily drifting down a weighted Corixa whilst using a 10ft rod to keep myself out of sight. I had him out, all 3lbs of him, but he turned out to be she!'

These river works, maintenance, and keepering of the other Meon and Itchen beats, is under the control of Brian and the Assistant Water Manager, John Robertson. To help them, 18 voluntary keepers, who are mainly members, are appointed at the rate of one or two per beat. Their duties range over a long trout season from 3 April to the end of October in addition to winter work. The sea trout season opens on 1 May and ends also on 31 October. Membership, subscriptions, fishing leases, cash receipts and the office work of the Association is in the hands of the Hon Sec Maj Dick Stacey.

Our journey down the river

We drove south to the road bridge over the river above the village of Droxford. Immediately below the bridge was further evidence of old hatches to divide the river: the main stream at a low level going along the eastern side; the western mill stream running into the old Droxford Mill, in the vicinity of which the streams rejoin. Hatches are also present in this area to flood water meadows. This water is not leased by the PSFFA, and permission to fish might be obtained from the landowner.

On our way down by car to Soberton we passed a winding section of the river below us to the east — the St Clair beats. Here the Water Manager has arranged the planting of clumps of trees to give cover in an otherwise windswept valley, not only to the angler, but to encourage fly life and the return of spinners to the water to lay their eggs.

We parked opposite the Soberton pumping station of The Portsmouth & Gosport Water Co. Abstraction reduces the flow down the river, particularly in July when a good flow is most needed to counteract the ill-effects of peak water temperatures and low oxygen levels. Grayling are particularly susceptible to high water temperatures — there are none in the Meon, and pike are also absent. There is thus no need to electric fish unless one wishes to carry out a fish population survey. A few perch and many dace are in the water, and there is a run of eels.

From the pumping station we walked across meadows to the Holywell beat. The banks are trimmed twice a year by four mechanical brush cutters. The first cut being towards the end of June and the second close to the end of the season. Care is taken not to make a drastic clearance and thus destroy fly life, whilst reasonable access must be provided for the members. Yellow flags and marsh marigolds grow by the river.

On the Holywell water is Brian's second type of temporary weir. This is made of 3ft wide chicken wire stretched across the river below the surface, and secured by posts on both banks. The mesh is vertical and the first 12in are turned upstream and anchored on the river bed with stones. An efficient weir is thus produced as the wire becomes blocked by drifting weed and other debris. In winter the anchoring posts may be knocked out to allow flushing of the watercourse.

Although lack of water is a major problem, too much water in winter, producing floods at intervals of several years, may cause damage to weed growth. In common with the Test, and other chalk streams, ranunculus on the bed of the river is sometimes severely reduced. If ranunculus is not cut, the long trailing growths, in time of heavy flood, are dragged upon by the current to the extent that the roots may be pulled out. There are not set weed cutting dates on the Meon because weed banks are quite small.

We then continued south, taking the turning to Curdridge to view the Mislingford beat. At this place the river runs off the chalk to become wide, slow and shallow, but with some good pools in the woods from which it emerges into scrubland.

Driving on we entered the Rookesbury Estate below Mislingford to view the stocked Chiphall Lake Fishery, alongside which the river flows. We looked over the bridge close to the lake. PSFFA has water upstream and downstream of this bridge, and these sections are stocked with trout. Although heavily canopied with trees the water is most attractive to fish, particularly in the evening. As the tidal river is only six miles to the south there is the hope that this section may become a sea trout beat.

At lunch we were joined by Capt Donald McEwen to whom I am indebted for my introduction to Brian Manhire. We discussed the fly life of the river. All the normal naturals are present: iron blue at the beginning and end of the season, blue winged olive, hawthorn, mayfly, sedges and so on. I asked Donald to tell us of his preferences in artificial flies:

'The Tups Indispensable is a winner every time. My only alternative as a dry fly is the Pheasant Tail. I also use the Pheasant Tail Nymph and a Sawyer Bug. We are allowed to fish a nymph throughout the season.'

'Have you had anything remarkable happen to you on the river — fallen in, or something?'

'Me? I'm always falling in. I get used to it. In fact I wear short waders and fill them up almost at once — my feet then stay warm in the trapped water.'

The Meon is an attractive small chalk stream. The waters of the PSFFA are maintained with knowledge and care, but the river, being of a short length, offers little trout water to the public.

8 May 1991

Sea Trout Fishing

Donald Hanley — Bailiff, Fly Fishing Section, Park Gate and District Royal British Legion

Donald had not caught a sea trout until he fished the Meon. Then, 30 years ago, on the lower river, one took his Butcher. It was a large fly, probably a No 4, attached to strong nylon by a Blood Bight loop. He still uses large Butchers and still threads a 2in long loop through the eye, passes it over the body and encircles the neck of the fly. One needed to be sure of the hook and the knot in those days for large sea trout were common — fish up to 17lb have been authenticated, and five-pounders were not rare.

In that first season he took three herling (small sea trout of up to 1$\frac{1}{2}$ lb) on a 7ft Accles & Pollock steel brook rod. Herling, on the Meon, are the equivalent of West Country school peal, but are several ounces heavier in weight. These extra ounces may be due to the young fish having been raised in an alkaline river rather than the acid waters of the south-west.

In the second season he took three in one evening but, mystery of mysteries, did not have a touch under apparently identical conditions the following night, an experience with which many sea trout anglers are familiar. Three years passed before he breached the 2lb mark with a fish of 2lb 1$\frac{1}{2}$ oz in the pool above the Anjou Bridge behind The Fisherman's Rest Inn, which is a mile to the north of Titchfield. Subsequently he has taken in the region of 20 fish of over 3lb in weight and perhaps half a dozen exceeding 5lb.

Breaking the flow of information, and bringing the reader to the present day, Donald telephoned me during the evening of the day following our meeting:

'After you left, when it was dark, I fished for an hour or two above the Anjou Bridge. There was a splash in the large pool. The Butcher searched the water, the fly I showed you in the car, and hooked the fish, a sea trout, but I lost him at the net at 11.30pm. He must have weighed 3lb.'

He has to live a little in the past whilst working for the future, for the runs are not what they used to be. One day the regular adventure of the midnight splash and tug may return, for he is working, with others, to ensure free passage up the river to spawning fish. Passes have been installed, obstructions removed and redding areas raked.

There is another problem. The old Meon Marshes Estate at Hill Head on the estuary, where many used to fish, passed from private hands into those of the Hampshire County Council. Fishing is now prohibited in the tidal waters from Titchfield Haven up to Little Posbrook and, instead of silent night-time anglers, bird watchers abound. Higher, at Crofton House, there is hope of fishing in the future, and at Hill Head, for the anglers do not accept that the fishing is lost forever.

Records of sea trout catches are reliable over the last 50 seasons. That the lower river catches have deteriorated is a fact. This is not only due to the denial of access to good angling areas, but has arisen following the reduction of water flows and the consequential silting of the slower moving river.

The fish population

The sea trout season opens on 1 May and closes on 31 October; trout 3 April-31 October.

A few large sea trout run in during the spring. Herling enter from July onwards if there is sufficient water. The main run of spawning fish arrive in the river in the fuller autumn water flows.

Grayling are also present, having been stocked by Donald to extend the season. They may be fished by upstream dry fly and upstream nymph with a maximum No 12 hook size. Trout may be fished for upstream dry and downstream wet. The reason for the upstream-only grayling rule is to prevent sea trout, after the end of their season, being taken on flies cast down and across.

Brown and Rainbow trout are introduced at weights of about 1lb. The first stocking of 50 brown and 50 rainbow takes place in April when a few large rainbow of about 2lb are also slipped into the stream. Further stockings are made in May, June and July.

Sea trout flies and tackle

'My yardstick: dark night — dark fly, Butcher or Bloody Butcher. Bright night — silver fly, Teal & Silver Blue or Peter Ross. Always a single fly, and always a single hook.'Meon sea trout anglers use large flies, rarely going as small as No 8 unless the water is very low. No 4, No 2 and even larger sizes are required, even for little herling. Donald does not like hooks with long fine shanks due to the risk that leverage may snap the hook at the bend.

His Abu rods are between 9ft and 9ft 6in in length, of fibreglass and designed for still water trout fishing. He also fishes with an old Hardy 'Blagdon', one of the first split cane rods designed for still water trout fishing. He always uses a floating fly line but has no preference in colour:

'At night one ought to learn to fish by feel and not by sight. I have to because my sight is not good. When playing a fish you can tell where he is by senses other than vision: the direction of the pull on your hands and the sound of a splash. In addition, you catch the swoosh of each cast as it travels through the air — the swish is slightly different if the leader is tangled.'

His leader is usually of 8lb nylon, untapered, straight off the spool. The length will be 18in less than the length of the rod because he joins line and leader with a Blood Bight loop and Sheet Bend.

The weather

Donald likes a mild overcast night, no moon, the darker the better. A stable water temperature is desirable in a settled spell of weather. Having described the ideal night he told me of one which was far from perfect:

'It was the night of the Titchfield Carnival when they burn an effigy of the Earl of Southampton. The sky was alight with fireworks and rockets, and the spent cases hissed as they fell into the river. It was bitterly cold. I caught five sea trout.'

I asked about thunderstorms. He does not like them because they take place in changeable weather. Settled conditions of wind, temperature and water flow are best. In tidal fishing he prefers the tide to be on the turn, ie: just starting to ebb, with fresh river water beginning to take over.

A remarkable incident

'I was in the water listening for the splashes of sea trout. Enveloped by the dim and misty glow of night I waited, the bank at my back. Nothing stirred. Then footsteps in the field to the rear caused the hair to rise on my neck. Silence followed. I fished. Then more footsteps, and as I peered the tall grass moved and parted with each step. There was no body, only feet. My eyes were wide and my hands were wet with sweat. There was a final thump and a brown hare landed on the bank. I was very glad I saw him or I would never have fished that pool again.'

Sea trout angling on the lower Meon is clearly no longer of the quality which prevailed in former years. Few of Donald's members now fish at night. He feels that, disregarding middle age, if he applied himself to night fishing he could take about 20 herling in the season by fishing once a week. On the plus side, and looking to the future, it must be noted that the best areas may again become open to anglers. The installation of fish passes, and other steps being taken to sustain the fish, may result in increased spawning runs and a high percentage of ova hatching in redds which have been cleared of silt.

23 July 1991

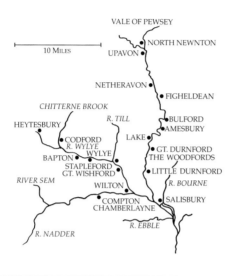

THE AVON ABOVE SALISBURY
RIVERS WYLYE AND NADDER

VALE OF PEWSEY

10 MILES

● NORTH NEWNTON

UPAVON ●

NETHERAVON ●

● FIGHELDEAN

CHITTERNE BROOK

R. TILL

HEYTESBURY

● BULFORD
● AMESBURY

● CODFORD
R. WYLYE

LAKE ●

WYLYE

● GT. DURNFORD
THE WOODFORDS

BAPTON ●

STAPLEFORD
GT. WISHFORD

● LITTLE DURNFORD

RIVER SEM

WILTON ●

R. BOURNE

● SALISBURY

COMPTON
CHAMBERLAYNE

R. EBBLE

R. NADDER

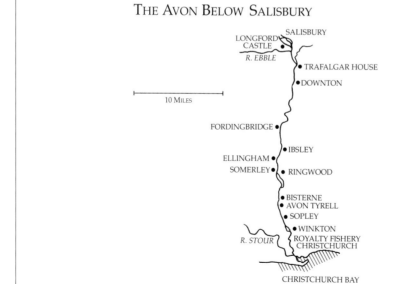

THE AVON BELOW SALISBURY

SALISBURY

LONGFORD
CASTLE ●

R. EBBLE

● TRAFALGAR HOUSE

● DOWNTON

10 MILES

FORDINGBRIDGE ●

● IBSLEY

ELLINGHAM ●

SOMERLEY ●

● RINGWOOD

● BISTERNE
● AVON TYRELL

● SOPLEY

● WINKTON

R. STOUR

ROYALTY FISHERY
CHRISTCHURCH

CHRISTCHURCH BAY

The Hampshire Avon

The river is formed in the Vale of Pewsey from two streams: the East Avon and West Avon which join at Scales Bridge at Rushall. The river then runs by or through Upavon, East Chisenbury, Fittleton, Netheravon, Figheldean, Durrington and Bulford to Amesbury. This section of the river provides good trout and grayling fishing, and as good, or better, is that section of the river from Amesbury to Salisbury which passes through the Woodford valley. Above Salisbury the Avon is joined by the Nadder which has, itself, been added to by the Wylye at Quidhampton.

The Avon is augmented just below Salisbury by the Bourne, and the Ebble comes in $2^{1}/_{2}$ miles downstream of the town centre at Bodenham. Between Salisbury and Christchurch the river, now much enlarged, changes in character. It is no longer a trout stream, fishing being predominantly for salmon and coarse fish. The best of the salmon fishing is between Fordingbridge and Christchurch where the river runs into the sea. It is a big fish river. Salmon of over 40lb have been taken and the spring fish of today, for which it is noted, still average in the region of 20lb. Pike and barbel are also large. My grandfather, who was born in 1870, regularly fished for pike at Fordingbridge at the end of the 19th century. Catching a pike of substantial weight he wagered with his companion that it would exceed 20lb. The sum between the two of them was one guinea, equivalent today to not far short of £100. My grandfather took the fish aside to find that it pulled the scales down to $19^{1}/_{2}$lb. Filling the fish with one or two stones he won the bet but, conscience stricken, returned the golden coin.

Trout Fishing

Allan Cook — Head Keeper, The Services Dry Fly Fishing Association, Netheravon

Allan's family have lived in Wiltshire, and been connected with the river Avon, since the beginning of this century, their early years being spent at Bulford. His uncle, Harold Sturgess, went to school with Frank Sawyer (Allan's predecessor and a famous river keeper), and in their early years both assisted the keeper on the Avon at Bulford.

In 1928 Frank succeeded William Pratt as River Keeper at Netheravon. In 1970, after 20 years of part-time assistance on the river, Allan took full employment under Frank Sawyer who retired in 1973. Since that year Allan has had charge of the SDFFA waters from Coombe to Bulford. Frank Sawyer died in 1980.

The Association
There are in the region of 100 rods: 70 are serving officers, 20 are retired officers, there are six civilians, and some associate members. Each member is given two

complimentary guest tickets each season, and may purchase further guest tickets. One of the oldest civilian members is Arthur J. Rycroft who also fishes at Hungerford, on the river Kennet, where I have seen him deceive trout with a skilfully presented fly.

The Association has five and a half miles of double-bank fishing downstream from Coombe Mill at Fifield, and one mile (left) bank terminating 150yds below Bulford Bridge. There are two short gaps at Figheldean and Durrington; through these the Association is allowed passage by the courtesy of the owners.

The water is divided into 14 sections which are known as 'reaches', a better name for a river section than 'beat'. There are also the Corfe End ponds at Netheravon which are known as Reach No 3. These still waters are stocked in April with 500 brown trout, with more added in July. Three sites of the Services water are available for local children to fish until they reach school leaving age. Netheravon Mill, Figheldean Mill and Milston Mill. Dry fly is encouraged, but worm, maggot and bread paste are allowed.

The trout season is from 1 May-14 October. After this grayling fishing continues until 31 December in the lower reaches. Members may fish when and where they wish, but retired and civilian members are requested to fish mid-week. This unwritten rule allows serving members greater freedom of movement at weekends.

Below the Services water are stretches owned by Dr Charles Goodson-Wicks MP and John Angus. Between these stretches and The Piscatorial Society water below Amesbury, the river is fished by The Salisbury and District Angling Club. Above the Services are a number of short stretches and the Chisenbury water of Baroness Vickers which is run by Brig Bruce Jones.

Stocking and breeding

For the last 10 years Allan has stocked the river in April with 1,000 brown trout of a minimum length of 11in. In the middle of July, after the weed cut, a further stocking is made of trout which are between 11-13in in length. The trout of this second stocking are out of the same year batch in Allan's stews as the earlier fish, but have had an additional three months feeding and growth. Eighty per cent of stocked brown are the indigenous trout of the river. Frank Sawyer made the first hatchery on the fishery in 1934-35, and a second, improved, hatchery was constructed after the war; the hatchery walls being constructed of Lignacite blocks by Frank Sawyer and Harold and Ira Sturgess.

Trout were stripped, the ova was fertilized, hatched, and after absorbtion of their yolk sac the alevins were fed on and stocked as fry, being poured through the spout of a watering can into the river at various sites. The hatchery had been abandoned four or five years before Allan started to work fulltime at Netheravon.

In 1966-67 stock ponds were dug at Haxton. Rainbow trout were in these for two seasons, but it was decided to revert to the brown trout policy. Allan repaired the hatchery and started again with pure water from the Cress Bed lake which is spring fed. In 1970, with Frank, he caught-up wild trout from the Avon and its side streams. Breeding has continued since then from these fish, with a small addition from Hungerford and Beaminster trout farms in the early years. Allan now has a very pure strain of Avon brown trout.

In the present programme fish are stripped in November, the ova hatch in approximately 70 days and Allan stocks about 25,000 fry in February and March. Other fry are fed on and some are introduced as fingerlings between April and July, and these have a better chance of survival. Six or seven thousand fingerlings are retained to run a three-year stocking cycle from three stews: the East, Middle and West ponds. The East holds one year plus; the Middle two year plus (for stocking the river); the West has the largest fish which are brood stock and trout of over 1lb for stocking. It thus takes three years under near natural conditions to raise a trout of 13in in length, for Allan relies on natural food in the ponds as well as pellets. Pigmented food is not fed, yet the trout have flesh of a full orange colour. Wild spawning also takes place but is in decline, probably due to pollution which may flow into the river from salted roads in winter. The heaviest trout taken from the upper Avon is believed to be the one which fell to Frank Sawyer in 1932. The fish weighed 10lb and was caught at Bulford in the Services water.

Grayling and other fish

That grayling are in decline is confirmed by members monthly catch return cards which must be submitted by the seventh day of the following month. These cards give the following information: date of fishing, Reach No, length of the trout, the weight of the fish and whether killed or returned, and any rainbow trout which have found their way into the water. Between 1,500-1,800 trout weighing in the region of ³/₄–1lb are taken each season. 'Catch and release' using barbless hooks is now recommended.

In the 1970s 2,000 grayling might be taken by rods. In 1990 only 5-600 were caught and returned. The scarcity was noted by Frank Sawyer's son, Tim, who fishes occasionally and was on the water a month before my visit. He remarked upon the severely reduced population.

Dace are on the increase; roach numbers are static; there are one or two perch and a few pike. The minnow population is reducing, a matter of concern since they are a source of trout food. There is one carp! Allan has a small run of eels and takes a few on his grid. Crayfish have been wiped out by disease. Pike are controlled by electric fishing in October, and also by netting and spearing. Allan showed me a photograph taken on 24 October 1984 of himself, with helpers, and 63 pike taken by electric fishing of the river below the Services water and above Amesbury.

Weed cutting

As with other fisheries on the upper Avon there are four weed cutting periods. The dates are agreed between the National Rivers Authority and The Wiltshire Fisheries Association. The cuts take place in late April or early May, June (usually after the mayfly), the end of July and the end of August. These latter cuts may not take place if weed is needed to hold up water levels in periods of low flow.

The hatchery and stew ponds

Allan showed me the concrete stew which he built in the early 1970s with the help of Frank Sawyer and his father Frank Cook. Fingerlings are put into the two sections of this stew in April, 2,000 in one portion and 3,000 in the other, and are fed three times a day. From there they are transferred to the East pond after it has been cleared of predators by electric fishing. Trout from the East pond are moved to the Middle pond, and from there to the West pond by netting at yearly intervals. Large brood fish are finally stocked into the Corfe End lakes at Netheravon after completing their breeding duties.

A feature of the rearing scene is the water wheel which Allan designed. This lifts water to two 400 gallon circular tanks from a carrier of the main river. The tanks hold 4,000 fingerlings between them. The carrier is part of the old water meadow system of the valley. These trout are of the same age as the fingerlings in the concrete two-section stew. The division into four groups removes the risk of total catastrophe through accident or disease. The fingerlings in the circular tanks were due to be transferred to the East pond during the week following my visit.

Before leaving, Allan took me to the river, a wide clear beautiful water in a meadowed valley. Looking over a bridge we saw the single carp, and a dipper flew up the valley.

25 July 1991

Alex C. Amos — Chairman;
Ron Hillier — Hon Gen Sec, The Salisbury and District Angling Club

The Club was formed in 1941 and has about 1,500 members. Of these, in the region of 750 live beyond the radius of 14 miles from Salisbury and are known as Associate members. Associates are widely spread geographically, not only in the British Isles, but are domiciled in Tasmania, New York, Germany, France, Holland and Hong Kong.

Membership subscriptions are very reasonable, even when Rods pay the Game Fishing Premium which allows them access to the stocked brown trout stretches. Membership is taken up annually, and ceases on 31 March each year.

The Club's river fisheries are too extensive to describe in detail, but are listed in the particulars sent to members. Briefly, trout and grayling fishing is in the Club's Premium Game Fisheries as follows:

River Avon — Durnford
One and a half miles of double bank divided into single-bank beats. Each beat is numbered and may be fished, if vacant, by taking the numbered tag for that beat from the tag board at Deans Farm, by Avon Bridge, Stratford sub Castle. The tag must be returned to the board on leaving the beat. Above this water is the fishery of Maj David Rasch. The angling method is upstream dry fly until 1 July, after which date a nymph may also be fished.

River Avon — West Amesbury
Two miles of double and single-bank fishing between the top of The Piscatorial Society water and Amesbury.

River Avon — Upper Avon
One mile of double, and $^3/_4$ mile single-bank, to the north of Amesbury.

River Wylye — Stapleford
Three-quarters of a mile of dry fly water. There are no beats, but there is a board of 10 tags. Members take a tag on arrival, if one is free, and return it to the board on leaving the water.

River Bourne — Hurdcott

A short stretch of brook fishing for trout and grayling.

The Club has extensive river waters in addition on the lower Avon, the Nadder and the Dorset Stour for coarse fish, salmon and trout. It also has control of lakes where rainbow trout are stocked.

The trout season is from 15 April-15 October. Thereafter fishing ceases on the Durnford water. Members may continue to fish for grayling on the Upper Avon and Wylye until 31 December by upstream dry fly and nymph.

Stocking and spawning

During the season 5,000 brown trout are purchased at the takeable size of about 1lb. These are delivered by tanker. Some go directly into the river on arrival; some are placed in the oxygenated tank on the Club's Land Rover and are distributed at once where required; some go into the new stews at Eight Hatches on the Durnford stretch. Those placed in the stews are fed and taken by the Land Rover to various sites until the next main tanker delivery takes place. All stocked trout are brown.

About 4,000 takeable trout are caught by the Rods and kept each season. A member is allowed a brace and a brace of grayling. It is not the policy to kill grayling as vermin. 'Catch and release' is not practised, other than in the Burgate Mill Stream on the Hampshire Avon. Members are encouraged to leave a beat when they have caught their brace of trout. In addition to the main stockings, 500 yearling brown of about 6in were introduced in the autumn of 1991 for the second consecutive season. For identification, these small trout have had their adipose fins clipped. Many small wild brown are present from natural spawning which peaks in November.

Ron Hillier told me that he took his largest trout from the river two years ago. A superb fish, it weighed 3lb 15oz. In 1989 the record brown trout for the Club was landed from Beat No 9 at Durnford — it weighed 8lb.

Natural and artificial flies

All the usual naturals are present and hatch in their season. Mayfly appear in the middle of that month, and the main hatch, which often takes place in the evening, continues until early June, but a few late arrivals are seen throughout the summer.

Natural fly regeneration is encouraged by the use of fly boards which were present on my visit. These, tethered downstream of bridges, protect the eggs of Ephemerids from the predations of feeding caddis larvae. The two boards I inspected had heavy depositions of eggs.

I asked Laurie Stokes, the Club's River Keeper, the most popular artificial flies and nymphs on his water. Dry flies: Tups Indispensable, Grey Wulff, Gold Ribbed Hare's Ear and, late in the season, there is little to beat a Daddy Long-Legs. In his opinion the Pheasant Tail Nymph is the greatest persuader of reluctant trout, and there is nothing to match Sawyer's Killer Bug for grayling.

Electric fishing

Ron Hillier had invited me to witness the annual electric fishing of the Durnford section of their Avon water. This took place on 16 October, immediately following the final day of the season. On my arrival at Avon Bridge, upstream of Stratford sub Castle, a red punt was already in the water. The Club has its own electric equipment, but the punt belongs to The Piscatorial Society whose Avon keeper, Tom Ellis, was on board. With him were the Chairman of the Club, Alex Amos, Laurie Stokes and one helper.

Several members, on each bank, took turns on ropes to draw the boat upstream whilst the generator on board chugged industriously. The four occupants faced upstream. Two held electric probes — these are metal hoops 18in in diameter on the end of long wooden shafts. The hoops are held beneath the water surface and swept from side to side in advance of the boat. Probes have a switch in the handle which cuts off current if finger pressure is released. The cathode, a bunch of long tentacles, trails behind in the water. Beside each probe operator is a netsman who scoops out stunned fish and eels.

The boat is pulled against the flow of the river, and momentarily unconscious fish float to the surface. Trout and grayling are left, quickly recover and dart away downstream out of the electric field. Netsmen have to be alert, deft and quick. Once a fish is in the net it is tipped into a dustbin in the punt — one bin for eels and another for pike. When the process is complete the pike are killed, and the eels put into the oxygenated tank on the Land Rover to be sold to augment Club funds. By noon, 13 pike had been taken of which the largest weighed 5lb 4oz, and about one dozen eels.

As I walked up the river, watching this operation, I talked with Roy Mellish who lives at Stratford sub Castle. 'My father worked as a gardener for Mr C.D. Woodrow at Deans Farm. In 1952 there was no electric fishing; he helped to drag a net downstream from Little Durnford Manor to Avon Bridge. I was 10 years of age. They caught 29 pike that year, and half of them weighed over 15lb. One went 34lb and was larger than me.'

It rained hard during the morning of my visit. This did not dampen the spirits of the members and those who had come to lend a helping hand. I left with the impression of a club, and hard working committee, dedicated to providing excellent chalk stream fishing in return for an exceptionally low subscription.

16 October 1991

Robin Mulholland — Water Warden, The Piscatorial Society water, near Great Durnford, Wiltshire

His angling career
Robin describes himself as a fishing fanatic since the age of seven years! He was raised in Teesdale. His grandfather and great-uncle were keen trout fishers with access to many miles of the river Tees. Robin went with them at his own request, and possibly to their distraction. His education continued through teenage years. Later he developed his salmon, trout and sea trout techniques on the rivers Lune and Hodder as a member of Lancashire Fly Fishers. In 1978 he came down to the chalk-streams where he has since fished with his wife Nicky. Robin's rods for the chalk-streams are an 8ft 3in Pezon & Michel Ritz Parabolic, and an 8ft Hardy CC de France. His $3^{1}/_{4}$ in reel is a limited edition from Orvis in celebration of the Society's 150th anniversary. The line on this reel is an AFTM No 6 Air Cel Ultra, attached to which is a 10ft home made leader tapered through six sections to a point of 6lb to balance the mayfly he was using on the day of my visit.

Twenty years ago the Society created the post of Water Warden, which position was filled by Bob Lawson for 10 years. During his period of management the Society acquired their Avon and Wylye waters. Bob handed over to Hal Thirlaway who, over a period of 10 years, slowly passed his knowledge and responsibilities to Robin who is now in his third year as Water Warden.

The work is time consuming: two evenings a week are spent in correspondence; meetings take place with water lords and neighbours during most weekends, and he meets the Head River Keeper every weekend.

The Society

We met in the Rod Room which is beside the river near Great Durnford. Twenty-two years had passed since I was last in that room as a rod in a syndicate which had the water. Much had changed. Nostalgically furnished with pictures of past generations, there are also all the facilities required by the members of today: fly dressing equipment, a library, a desk, a room to eat and entertain. Originally the members of the Society fished for species such as barbel, trout, perch and pike, this latter fish becoming the Society's emblem. Many baits were used, and a large trout was taken in the Kennet, probably from a hatch pool on a worm. The record reads:

'TROUT, taken by E.M. Mayes, from the Kennet, at Newbury, June 24th 1894. Weight 11³/₄ lb.'

The Society was formed in London in 1836 to fish the rivers of Hertfordshire. As population pressures increased, those rivers became unfishable. The Society then moved west, taking a house in Newbury and waters on the rivers Kennet and Lambourne. In 1982 a review of the Society's increased river commitments became necessary. Their waters were scattered on Kennet, Lambourne, Avon, Wylye and Itchen. Some stretches had to go to reduce management responsibilities. The Society relinquished the Kennet and Lambourne waters and, again progressing west, made its headquarters on the Avon. These successful alterations moved the Society over the years into rural situations where there is reduced intrusion on the river banks and no problems with fish farms. One of the aims of the Society is to provide members with the opportunity to fish as frequently as they wish with very few restraints and regulations, and to bring guests as desired. There are 140 members in various categories, and a few from overseas. There is a waiting list for new members who must be sponsored by two existing members.

Waters and keepers

There are three full-time keepers: George Maich — Head Keeper; 6 miles double-bank river Wylye. Ex-Royal Navy. Trout season 15 April-30 September.

Tom Ellis — 3¹/₂ miles double-bank river Avon. Ex-Royal Navy, and trained at Sparsholt. Trout season 1 May-30 September. There are no beat allocations on the Lake water, members may fish where they like, but guests are excluded from the middle sections of the river from 1 May-1 July.

The Earl of Strafford (known within the Society as Tom Strafford) — owner and keeper of the Itchen water of 1¹/₂ miles of main river and two carriers. This water is restricted to six rods fishing at any time. If a member arrives to find six rods fishing he has to wait for one to finish, but such a happening is rare. The season is 1 May-30 September.

Fish populations

In addition to brown trout the Lake water has a mixed presence of dace, grayling and pike. These fish have enjoyed prolific spawning in the warm water of recent seasons. Pike are controlled by electric fishing with the Society's own boat and generator, which also attends on the adjacent waters of Maj David Rasch at Heale House, and those of the Salisbury and District Angling Club.

Following closure of the trout season many members fish for grayling until 31 December. Thereafter the river is closed until the new trout season to enable the keepers to carry out major works. There are no regulations on whether grayling caught are kept or returned, and in trout fishing there are no bag limits, but 'Catch and release' is widely practised. Trout dominate the river, and it has been established by Richard Mann of the National Rivers Authority and others that there is no real competition from grayling, both fish holding separate niches in the ecology of the river.

The Lake water does not benefit from carriers in which brown trout may spawn. Some redds are cut in the main river but successful hatching is limited, probably due to silting of the river bed. The Wylye spawning is prolific, particularly in the Chitterne Brook which joins the river at Codford St Peter. It is known that 2,500 spawning trout are active in that small tributary.

Some wild spawning takes place on the Itchen water, but the Society's stretch is bounded above and below with waters where large trout are stocked.

It is the Society's aim to provide as near classic chalk stream fishing as is possible. To this end, at Lake, a stocking of 1,500 yearlings takes place in the autumn. These used to be of about 8in in length in November, having hatched in February, but recently, due to improved fish farming methods, they are 10in in length. The trout stock is topped-up during the season by about 250 brown trout of between 13-15in, weighing in the region of $1\frac{1}{2}$lb. The result of these two introductions is that trout average $1\frac{1}{4}$lb in weight, with the occasional fish of $2\frac{1}{2}$-3lb which has survived over a second winter. No rainbows are introduced.

Insect life and artificial flies

There are no March brown. Grannom appear before the season opens, and a few large dark olives hatch at that time together with many iron blue which continue throughout the year and are prolific in September. Medium olives form a major part of trout diet, and Skues' July Dun is important in the autumn. The mayfly hatch is early and can be relied upon by the second weekend of the month. On that Saturday the Society has an informal gathering in the Rod Room, the Mayfly Supper, to celebrate the hatch. Mayfly continue in small numbers throughout the summer. In imitation Robin favours a small Grey Wulff dressed on a No 14 Kamasan hook, and Geoffrey Rivas' hatching pattern as an alternative. Patterson's Deer Slayer represents the spent.

Artificial presentation is limited to the upstream dry fly and unweighted nymph. The classic Skues-type nymph is the approved method: No 16 Iron Blue dressed with one turn of jackdaw hackle, moles fur body, red head, red butt and tiny white whisks; Tups Nymph and emerging Olives. Such patterns fish in the surface film if floatant is applied, or 2-3in down if dosed with a bit of spit. A Pheasant Tail Nymph tied with silk is acceptable, but not with fine copper wire. Members do not use mayfly nymphs because the large hook is equivalent to added weight. Heavy nymphs are allowed in the grayling season: Sawyer's Grayling Bug, shrimps and large flies bring results from the hatch pools.

Robin was raised on the Yorkshire rivers. When he came down to the chalk streams he brought with him many No 14 hooked patterns. Over the years he has steadily reduced his fly sizes to No 16, No 18 and even to No 22. Reed smuts, Sawyer midge and many other tinies are important. A fly which is popular in the Society is the Janus, named after the Roman God of the Four Seasons and of gates, who had two faces looking different ways. The fly is a fore-and-aft pattern with the tail set high between the two hackles, so that it twitches when tickled by the wind. The Janus is a good imitation of hatching Ephemeroptera, taking trout when olives and iron blues are on the water. It is also effective during midge hatches. Some members hold that if one has the Janus from size No 16 to No 22 no other fly need be carried. The Janus dressing was published in *The Flyfisher* by Hal Thirlaway, Robin's predecessor as Water Warden. Robin told me the dressing: speckled Cree hackle at the back and for the tail, red game for the front hackle, with a body of black or yellow silk.

In addition Robin fishes Black Gnats, Tups Indispensable, Baby Sun Fly, Rolt's Witch for grayling, Beacon Beige, and Skues Little Red Sedge. His basic spinner patterns are Lunn's Particular and Lunn's Yellow Boy, with the Caperer held in reserve by his wife, Nicky.

In the last two summers the hot weather has dried off duns so quickly that they have not spent much time on the water. In contrast, spinners have returned easily to the river in the settled conditions, and their patterns have been to the fore. Robin commented:

'One thing that I have learned on the chalk stream is that the emerger is incredibly important. Patterns like Terry's Terror with a buzzy peacock herl body are effective — it is the same as the Yorkshire Treacle Parkin. That fly will take when olives are hatching, and on summer evenings when the blue winged olive is in the air. It is the peacock herl body which is important.'

Water flows, silting and rainfall

The Society's Avon water is bordered by water meadows which are no longer flooded and are grazed as permanent pasture. Silting of the river bed is primarily due to low flows resulting from reduced rainfall, rather than run-off from ploughed fields. Over the $2^{1}/_{2}$ years to the time of my visit a total of 18in of rain had not fallen when compared with average precipitation. In the result, springs have not run well or for long periods and water levels are low. Because of poor flows there has been little ranunculus. The absence of this growth, the cutting or non-cutting of which reduces or increases the hold-up of water, has meant that the keepers have been unable to manage water levels. There are normally four weed cuts: a minor cut in April, a major cut in June after the mayfly, and two trimmings in August and September. Deep areas are controlled by the Society's weed cutting boat, and the shallows are cut by hand. The dates are governed jointly by the National Rivers Authority and the Wiltshire Fisheries Association. The NRA sets up booms across the river at Salisbury to catch the cut weed before it drifts down to the salmon fishing areas. Water quality is of a good standard. Algae growths have been apparent recently due to sunshine, warm water, and lack of shade from ranunculus. These growths have detracted from the appearance of the river but have not reduced the quality of the fishing.

Summing up, Robin confirmed his view that lack of rain is the major factor which has caused reduction in flows, and this has resulted in a reduced growth of ranunculus.

He is not troubled by fish farms, having none above him on the Avon other than the stews on the Officer's water, and only one on the Wylye. Sewage treatment has been improved at Amesbury, and there are no major watercress beds upstream.

An unexpected benefit of recent mild winters has been that trout have continued to grow throughout the year. In 1990 a wild $3^1/_2$ year-old trout was caught at a weight of 3lb 9oz, the scales of this fish, when read by The Institute of Freshwater Ecology, showed even growth throughout its life. Native crayfish are no longer present, having been wiped out by crayfish plague following the introduction of Signal crayfish at one point upstream five years ago. Salmon spawn at Lake but do not arrive until late in the trout season, and they are not fished for by the members.

Recovery of the river banks

Much work is being done to improve banks where they have been trodden in by cattle, and been generally neglected. Narrowing the width of the river by moving forward and facing the banks with logs, back-filled with chalk, increases the rate of water flow and encourages ranunculus. One bank is developed as a fishing bank, and the other is planted with shrubs pruned to lean out over the water to act as cover for fish and wildlife. In some places willows have been laid into the river to form a groyne, with their trunks only partially severed as in hedge laying. The tree continues to grow, the area silts below and may be hardened by the addition of chalk. In some places the banks are preserved by a nylon net through which plants and grasses grow to form a firm edge to the river.

The right bank is generally the fishing bank, but there are a few left-handed members who appreciate short sections where the left bank has been cleared and is kind to their casting.

Walk up the river

We visited two sections: one above the Rod Room — the Chalk Pit length, and the other below which is named the Broadwater. A hobby flew up the river. Robin commented: 'They take mayfly and crane flies in addition to young swallows and house martins. There are only about 150 pairs in the country, and I have seen five since I have been here. We have grasshopper warblers, and sometimes an osprey passes on migration.'

Much of the river bank at the Broadwater has been firmed-up and narrowed by the cut trunks of willow trees blown over in gales. Islands formed in mid-river below Aylmer Tryon's house, Kingfisher Mill, after the floods of February 1990. Robin and his keepers turned these into permanent features, protecting their banks with logs. In the reduced space the water flow increased on either side of the islands and ranunculus started to grow. Aylmer commented that from his bedroom window the lower island resembled *The African Queen*, even though Humphrey Bogart and Katherine Hepburn were not camped thereon. The name has stuck!

8 June 1991

The river Meon – Holywell beat.

Top: A brown trout from the river Avon at Durnford.
Bottom: The river Avon at Ibsley.

Top: The river Avon – Netheravon. Home designed wheel to lift water to the trout stews.
Bottom: The trout stews at Netheravon.

Top: The river Avon – Netheravon. Feeding trout in the stock ponds.
Bottom: Pike taken by electro-fishing boat at Durnford on the Avon.

Salmon and Trout Fishing

Mike Trowbridge — Head Keeper, Trafalgar and Longford Estates

Mike looks after five miles of double-bank fishing on the Wiltshire Avon, and several miles of carriers. Avon Turn at Britford is the top boundary. The river Ebble joins the Avon on the estate close to Longford Castle, and the fishery, sometimes in three streams, continues to Downton where the town bridge is the lower boundary. Below Downton the river passes into Hampshire but is no longer Mike's fishery, although the estate owns $1\frac{1}{2}$ miles of single bank which is let to a fishing club. He describes his water as a mixed fishery: salmon, trout and other fish. No sea trout have been caught during his term of office. He has 100 rods who may fish for any species which is in season over the 12 months of the year. The water is not divided into beats, and rods may fish when and where they wish. Many come from London, two from St Helens, and others are local. The wide geographical origins of the fishermen suits the extensive river and types of available fishing. The locals only go out when there is a chance; those who come from a distance may not hit the best times, but these are usually businessmen to whom the environment brings pleasure as well as the fishing.

Salmon runs are unreliable. The smallest catch during his time on the estate was two fish during the drought year of 1990; the greatest was 65 salmon in 1980. Until 1977 a salmon syndicate fished the water, but as the runs of fish reduced the water could no longer be let as a salmon fishery. Mike offers good trout fishing. Part of the Ebble, two carriers and some shallows on the main river are stocked. The two stocked carriers are, themselves, as wide as some trout fisheries on the Itchen.

The stocking is of brown trout: 800 two-year-olds; 4,000 yearlings of about 8in, and up to 10,000 fry.

It is estate policy to kill all pike. About 300 are removed annually by electric fishing the carriers, but the volume of water in the main river precludes a similar cull.

'I appreciate that some anglers like to go after pike. If someone catches a large one and slides it back I tend to turn a blind eye. Likewise, when electric fishing, if we turn up a big one, and he gets away, we don't pursue him. I think you must not break the balance in a river. Large pike serve a purpose.'

Mike likes to see barbel, chub and shoals of roach of which he breeds up to 11,000 a year. They are spawned at the side of Standlynch Mill, the eggs are lifted to a pond and stay there for 14 months. During this period they exist solely on natural food for, at a pH of about 7.00 the water is a prolific provider of sustenance. The roach are then put into the river, having attained a length of 5in.

Weed cutting is kept to the minimum to protect stocks of coarse fish. The river is usually fairly free of weed in the salmon areas until the middle of June, thereafter it becomes a nuisance.

'Growing weed is not a problem. It is the floating weed, cut higher up the river, which causes us trouble, it comes down from the Woodford Valley. The NRA undertakes to extract drifting weed, but because cuts take place early, when the weed is short, it is not trapped by the booms.'

Mike's river is mainly bordered by old water meadows and, at the top of the fishery, there is a farm where the drains are kept running. There was a risk of silt being washed into the river from ploughed areas close to the banks, but the Government 'set-aside' subsidy has encouraged the grassing-down of these areas, and the water flow remains reasonably clear.

Mike's career

'As a lad I was a poacher. Tom Williams was our keeper on the Itchen. He got so fed-up with me poaching that he offered me a job at Kingfisher Lodge at Brambridge. He then knew where I was.'

The Itchen was where he caught his first trout. The river went by the garden of his parents' house and he fished there with a hand line. In those days trout and eels were the quarry. His first salmon was taken when he came to Longford to take charge of the estate rod fishings.

'It was in May 1980, early on a Sunday morning. We had a fisherman staying in the house, but he liked to sleep late. I left him in bed and went to the mill to feed my fish. While I was there I had a couple of casts with a $2^1/2$ in wooden Blue & Silver Devon in front of the hatches. There was a bit of weight on the line. Lo and behold, I got into an 11-pounder. It was quite an experience.'

Tom Williams developed the estate fish farm in the early 1970s. This left him little time for the river, for the farm was a great enterprise. A river keeper was needed and Mike joined the staff in 1980 after 22 years in the Royal Marines. Tom continued as Fishery Manager until his retirement. Mike has been responsible for the river since he came to the estate, and this is his 11th season.

'I don't do much gillieing because I am occupied with other work. If I see a rod into a salmon I would help him if he wished me to do so. It is not a good idea to hook a salmon for a rod — he ought to do it himself. I carry a gaff in the back of my truck in case it is needed, but the gaff is not allowed after the end of July. You need a gaff in the early season unless you are proficient with a tailer. At that time the pressure of water is too great to hold a net out against the flow.'

The runs of salmon

Tom Williams came to the river in 1960 and started a salmon syndicate. Since then there have been records of salmon caught. Prior to that there is evidence from 1935 of 'fish — various', including one of $25^1/2$ lb, but whether of salmon or pike is not known.

Salmon have difficulty in passing up the river due to fish farms and other obstructions, but passes are being created. Not only have mature salmon to overcome obstacles in their upstream passage, but smolts are lost on their downstream migration in the complications of fish farms. Considerable attention has been paid to allow open downstream passage to smolts at Trafalgar Fisheries by the alteration of weed screen positions.

Spawning sites on the estate have altered over the years. At one time many redds were cut on the shallows above Mike's cottage, but this area is no longer favoured, probably due to lack of water depth. Many salmon spawn in the river Nadder which joins the Avon above Salisbury, and a few venture into the Wylye. Because the river provides rich feeding many parr smoltify after one year. Salmon start to arrive at Trafalgar in May, and some grilse appear at the same time. In 1989, of the first three fish caught in that month, two were large grilse of $7^1/2$ lb and 8lb in weight. In 1990, due to floods in February, salmon arrived in March, but none were caught. Sometimes a salmon may be taken in the Nadder at Wilton before a fish is grassed at Longford — 'Lord Pembroke beats us occasionally by landing the first salmon'.

'Where do your salmon lie?'

'Mainly above obstructions such as hatches. Further down the river they are taken in the hatch pools. With us they swim up and lie in front of the buttresses which divide the hatches. We have one wooden groyne, and I have only known two salmon come from that place. Later in the season they tuck in under the banks in deep water.'

Monthly salmon catches

In the last 20 years only one salmon has been recorded for February, and that was taken in 1973.

YEAR	Mar	Apr	May	Jun	Jul	Aug	Sep	TOTAL	Av Wt (lb)
1970	0	1	20	6	5	2	0	34	
1971	3	4	25	21	12	8	12	75	
1972	5	11	27	22	5	0	6	76	
1973	0	6	6	2	0	0	0	14	
1974	0	3	0	0	0	0	0	3	
1975	1	9	4	0	0	0	0	14	
1976	0	0	0	0	0	0	0	0	
1977	1	1	17	7	1	0	0	27	
1978	2	3	2	0	0	0	0	7	
1979	0	0	3	3	0	7	7	20	
1980	0	3	30	24	5	2	1	65	12
1981	2	9	36	15	6	2	1	71	14$\frac{1}{2}$
1982	0	7	1	2	1	2	0	13	14$\frac{3}{4}$
1983	0	1	10	5	1	0	0	17	15
1984	0	0	0	3	1	0	0	4	12$\frac{1}{2}$
1985	0	6	3	5	3	0	0	17	14$\frac{1}{2}$
1986	1	2	6	5	8	6	5	33	9$\frac{1}{4}$
1987	0	0	9	10	5	4	0	28	9$\frac{3}{4}$
1988	0	0	10	3	0	0	1	14	10$\frac{3}{4}$
1989	0	1	12	2	0	0	1	16	10$\frac{1}{2}$
1990	0	0	1	1	0	0	0	2	11$\frac{1}{2}$

Spinning

This is the common method of angling until 15 May when bait fishing is allowed. In the early season a wooden Devon minnow is the normal lure, fished on the Paternoster system with a 1oz or 2oz weight. Wye leads used to be common, but have fallen out of favour with the banning of lead weights of less than 1oz (28g), because anglers dislike the lighter lead substitutes. For summer spinning the upstream No 3 or No 4 Mepp is frequently used, normally in the colour gold.

Bait fishing

After 15 May bait fishing is allowed: prawn, shrimp and worm. These natural baits, primarily the English prawn, account for 75% of the Trafalgar salmon catch. Local prawns from the south coast are not readily obtainable. Two years ago Mike purchased 7 stone and froze them as a stock for his rods. The English specimen is tough and lasts well on the mount. One or two of his rods use rubber artificials and dip them in prawn juice before starting to fish, but they are not as effective as the natural. Fly fishing for salmon is little practised on his water, but a prawn imitation such as the General Practitioner is sometimes given a swim.

Trout fishing

The season starts at Trafalgar Fisheries on 15 April, two weeks after the opening day above and below them on the river. A grannom hatch is usually in progress at that time but the fly is not popular with trout, although it deceives a number of chub.

Trout stocking takes place in the first week of May, by which time the water flow is reducing. There is then a good hatch of hawthorn, followed by mayfly in the middle of June. Spasmodic mayfly hatches continue until October. Stocking continues at fortnightly intervals in those areas suited to fly fishing. Large flies bring results on Mike's water:

'Mayfly imitations such as the Grey Wulff and Grey Duster; also mayfly nymphs. We don't allow the nymph on the Ebble. The Pheasant Tail Nymph is popular in the early season. It is not sensible to fish finer than 3X leaders. There is a lot of weed in which trout can take refuge and, later in the season, my stockies are two-pounders.'

About one-third of the trout stocked are caught. Some remain in the river to spawn, and trout kelts are caught and released by coarse fishermen. In general, those trout taken on fly weigh between $1^1/_2$lb and 2lb. 'Occasionally a very large trout is caught. One of $14^1/_2$ lb took a prawn — the angler thought he had hooked his first salmon.'

Grayling were scarce when Mike arrived, but seem to be returning. They are mostly caught by coarse fishermen, but a few fall to the fly on the Ebble where they can be seen in the shallow water.

Wildlife

About 15 mink are trapped over a 12-month period; this is a reduction on 10 years ago when 30 might have been taken in the traps which are constantly set. Otters are no longer present.

Bird life is prolific and varied: migratory duck, snipe, plovers, bitterns in hard weather and, as we spoke, two female goosanders were on the river. Kingfishers are common and nest in the river banks and the boles of upturned trees. There is a large heronry of 50 nests on the estate. Herons cause more problems for the fish farm than the river, although they take trout from the shallow carriers. Cormorants — 30 or 40 at a time — are predators which Mike could do without, and there are far too many swans.

'The swans are alright at this time of year because they are in small herds of 15 or 20 dispersed in the fields. Once the crops start growing the farmers drive them off, they come to the river and tear up the ranunculus until there is none left.'

I was taken on a riverside tour: Longford Bridge, Longford Castle, the Ebble, and his eel stage where wrens and wagtails nest at Standlynch Mill.

Mike has charge of a beautiful river which gives pleasure to many and receives his constant care.

5 March 1991

Salmon Fishing

Alan Jones — Head Salmon Keeper, The Somerley Fishery of the Earl of Normanton

Alan welcomed me to his house which is near Ellingham Bridge on the Somerley Estate. Over coffee in the warm kitchen we discussed his angling career, and the estate river. I was glad to be inside; it was a bitterly cold morning.

His angling career
Alan caught his first salmon before the 1939-45 war at the age of seven years on the upper reaches of the river Severn. 'It was only a small fish of about 9lb. My bait was a worm, which was the common method of fishing in Wales.' After he had been in the Services he started to fish on the north-west coast of Scotland, and then went on to fish the Aberdeenshire Dee and the Spey. 'The worm is not a method much used in Scotland. In fact it is very much frowned upon. You fish by the method which is acceptable to the region. In Scotland salmon readily take the fly, and so fly predominates.'

In the late 1940s and early 1950s he stalked, fished and shot in Scotland. Gradually, in the late 1950s, fishing became his main interest. He later found a part-time position under the head gillie of an estate on the Dee, and this led to private employment by individual rods. His experience widened on the major Scottish salmon rivers, and he took charge of groups of rods sent north as a means of corporate entertainment. Ultimately there was hardly a free day during the fishing season which was spent on the rivers Don, Dee, Spey, Conon, Deveron and other waters. In addition he worked on river alterations and improvements, and coarse fished on the match circuits in the North of England.

Salmon, river work and coarse fishing provided an ideal background of experience for the Hampshire Avon where, with coarse and salmon fishing, the river is open throughout the year. Alan has now been at Somerley for five seasons.*

The salmon and coarse fishing seasons
The official salmon season is from 1 February-30 September. Historically the Avon was regarded as a spring salmon river. Fishing by the rods commenced in February and tailed off at the end of May and in early June when it was replaced by limited coarse fishing. The records show that very little salmon angling took place in the summer, though, no doubt, a grilse run came in to the river.

Alan produced some records of fish caught by those staying at The White Hart in Ringwood in the late 19th and early 20th centuries. The majority of these fish were taken below Ringwood at Bisterne and Avon Tyrrell, with one or two noted for Somerley. The average weights were high, and the fish were taken in the months of February, March, April and May. Entries for June are few and far between.

---

*Alan Jones, a salmon angler and head keeper of long experience, died in the spring of 1992.

YEAR	Catch	Av Wt
1885	25	23lb
1886	31	21$\frac{1}{2}$lb
1887	23	23lb
1888	(record is missing)	
1889	17	23$\frac{1}{2}$lb
1890	17	23$\frac{1}{4}$lb
1891	20	22lb
1892	28	23lb
1893	16	25lb
1894	17	24lb
1895	15	22lb
1896	18	23lb
1897	30	25lb
1898	8	21$\frac{3}{4}$lb
1899	16	23lb
1900	10	23lb

The catches then increased: 30 being taken in 1904, 41 in 1908 and 38 in 1914; the weights being well maintained.

In recent years Somerley spring fish weigh in the region of 20lb. In a full season the estate catch is expected to be about 100 fish, but this was not achieved in 1989 and 1990 due to these being summers of drought and low water which held back the grilse and small summer fish.

Two years ago it was decided to change the salmon and coarse seasons on the estate. The salmon season was altered to open one month later on 1 March, and close on 31 August to take advantage of the grilse run. The new grilse arrangement has not yet had a fair trial due to the droughts already mentioned. The salmon rods thus have six months of fishing. The other six months are let to Christchurch Angling Club, whose members fish from 1 September–28 February. During the six months of salmon fishing no coarse fishing takes place, and thus there is no conflict of interest. During the Christchurch Anglers months they may fish for salmon in February and September.

Alan has 5$\frac{1}{2}$ miles of river under his control on one side of the river, and 4$\frac{3}{4}$ miles on the other. Most of the fishery is thus double-bank. There are six beats: five are double-bank, and one is double-bank for half of its length. Each beat is fished by one rod who may bring a guest, and the beats are rotated weekly.

The condition of the river — the wildlife

I asked: 'Are you suffering from water abstraction and decreased flows?'

'Indeed we are. It is a serious situation. Unless strenuous efforts are made to contain the amount of silt and nitrates being washed down from altered farming methods upstream, in addition to increased outfall from sewage works and trout farms, I do not see the river improving.'

'When does the river clear after the winter?' Alan paused to gather his thoughts.

'Last year there were tremendous floods in the winter. When the level peaked the river was coloured from the washed banks, the roads and the brooks. As the river dropped slightly to just below the top of the banks it ran absolutely clear. It really was beautiful. This was because our water meadows and flood plains had worked in the old way, filtering out the silt. In addition, the washing velocity of the high water swept away the silt and mud from the river bed. I imagine that what we saw then was the river as it used to be.'

We left Alan's house to drive to the river, and crossed over Ellingham Bridge. Sixteen years had passed since my last visit to the Avon, but at once the scene was recognized as a place of triumph in 1975. My fishing diary records the capture of a fish with Bill, my father-in-law:

> '1975. March 6. Somerley Beat 3. Joined Bill for riverside lunch and had six casts with his rod. 2½ in Yellow Belly. Hooked a fish at 1.00pm. Bill played it and I gaffed. 15lb. A nice clean fish about 100yds above Ellingham Bridge.'

That salmon was unlucky. The minnow was mounted on an old wire flight which had been used for mahseer in India. The wire broke, but became twisted around one of the hooks of the treble, being prevented from slipping by the barb!

We continued in the car to a bridge which had been built across the main river at the head of Mackenzie's Pool, named after Gregor Mackenzie who was a keeper on the estate. Beats No 4 and No 5 were single-sided, but the new ability to cross the river will make them double-sided and improve the fishing. The bridge is a monument to the versatility of skilled workers on the estate. Alan described the construction:

'There are two main trunks of Douglas Fir, 84ft in length when trimmed down, and weighing 5 tons each. They were cut in the top woods and loaded on to a 40ft trailer which was pulled here by two tractors. With the aid of the tractors and ropes we dropped them in position, with the butt of one and the point of the other on each bank. Cross slats were then nailed down and hand rails constructed.'

On the way to the bridge we passed a small group of black and white geese. Alan prompted my memory — barnacles. It was 40 years since I had seen them on the Solway Firth. 'Lord Normanton keeps them. Birds are one of his main interests. He is keen on wildlife conservation and the preservation of the old water meadow systems.' That this is so was clear. It was the first time I had seen properly operated water meadows, although I had often read of the work of the 'drowners', in charge of their operation, in the writings of Arthur Street. Controlled by hatches the water level of the carriers is adjusted to flood surface channels, sometimes called drains, in the meadows. Benefits acrue: grass is protected from frost; silt is deposited on the meadow instead of being washed into the river: intricate water channels over a large area provide cover and feeding grounds for birds. To an amateur ornithologist the scene was fascinating: green plover, snipe in abundance, duck, great crested grebe, Canada geese and mute swans were present. Visiting swans arrive from Siberia: the little straight-necked Bewick — named after Thomas Bewick the wildlife engraver — and the large Hooper which appears from time to time.

The water meadows are flooded in mid-November and the drains remain filled and running until the end of February. At that time the level is dropped slowly to ensure fish are not stranded.

'These carriers are a great nursery for coarse fish. They spawn here and find their way into the river, keeping it stocked. A few pike are present. I don't mind large pike. The small ones have to be controlled. A small pike of up to 6lb is like a schoolboy — he never stops eating and he never stops running.'

Spinning baits

On a subsequent visit to Alan's house he produced a box of wooden Devon minnows: black & gold, black & yellow, blue & orange, yellow bellies, and a plastic Spey yellow belly. They were in sizes between 2in and 2½in in length.

'What is this frightening device?'

'It is a Blair Spoon. The original Blair was made by Willie Blair of Kincardine O'Neil. He is now dead. This is a copy. If he knew you well enough he'd knock you one out, but he never let you have more than one. It is a killer in streamy water.'

That copper spoon was about 3½in in length, silver on one side and natural copper on the other. A No 2 treble was attached at the tail. The body was punch-marked to imitate fish scales.

In Scotland slim minnows are fished, weighted inside with lead wire wrapped around the flight; it is unusual to add a weight at the line/trace junction.

On the Avon buoyant wooden Devons are fished with weight at the top of the trace, or they are swum off a Paternoster. Alan's fat Devons are lined with Biro tube to protect the nylon of the trace, and the hook is held into the tail of the minnow by a tulip bead. These Devons are hand-made by a friend who lives in Downton. They are fatter at the head than towards the tail and, being made from various types of wood, are of different densities. They fish beautifully off a Paternoster, lifting and swaying in the current.

Flies

Alan prefers to fish the fly and is used to Scottish patterns: Stoat's Tail, Willie Gunn, Garry Dog, Hairy Mary and Michael's Fancy — a yellow fly which is effective on the Avon.

'The fly must fish. It is no good putting a leaded tube fly on a Wet Cel 2 line; the fly will drag across the bottom. That is lifeless. The fly must be balanced and buoyant, just like the wooden minnow.'

He likes the fly to fish about 1ft above the river bed; to this end his tubes are very light in weight.

Hooking salmon on the fly

'Would you describe in your own words the cardinal points to be practised to hook a fish on the fly off a floating line?'

'There are three essentials: the first is to hold the rod so that the tip is low and points straight down the line to the fly. The rod must not be held at an angle to the line. The second is to set the reel correctly and lightly, so that fine nylon is not broken, and not to hold a loop of line in the hand. The third is to fish straight off the reel so that fish will pull line off the drum. As the drum starts to revolve the angler should sweep up the rod without touching the line and the fish will be hooked. The rod should then be held high to prevent the line being drowned.'

6 February 1991

Salmon Fishing

Bruce Penny — Salmon Rod, Somerley Fishery

We met at the keeper's cottage at Ellingham, and at once drove to the top of Beat No 3. Rain being forecast Bruce wasted no time in tackling-up whilst we talked.

Fly tackle
First out of the back of the car came a 15ft Bruce & Walker carbon fibre salmon fly rod. Rated at AFTM No 10-12 the rod is the Walker model which is stiffer than the Bruce of the same length. On went a Bruce & Walker 4in fly reel loaded with a double-tapered No 11 Hardy Wet Fly 2 dark green sinking fly line. A 2ft collar of 25lb monofilament is permanently attached to the end of the fly line by a Nail Knot, the joint being smoothed-over with Bostick. The collar is Blood Knotted to a leader of 6ft of 18.6lb Bayer Perlon.

A box of tube flies now surfaced. These were 2in and $2^{1}/_{2}$ in in the length of the tube, but overall, including the dressing, some attained a length of 4in. A 6in black Collie Dog was curled up in a corner. Bruce selected a 2in tube he had dressed of yellow and black bucktail. The aluminium polythene lined tube was only very slightly weighted, and had a short length of bicycle valve rubber at the end to hold the No 6 treble hook in line. The overall length being in the region of $2^{1}/_{2}$ in.

The majority of Bruce's tubes have black bodies with wide flat silver tinsel ribbing. The wings are of bucktail in various colours. A silver bodied tube was also present with a blue and white bucktail wing — this fly strongly resembled a Teal and Silver Blue. All tubes are socketed at the tail to retain the eye of the treble; most of the hooks being black Partridge outpoints. I removed an odd-looking tube fly which resembled a Hong Kong grasshopper:

'That is a Thunder & Lightning dressing on a $^{3}/_{4}$ in tube. This weighted treble flight fits inside the overhanging dressing to give a total length of $1^{1}/_{2}$ in. It is not a long fly, but it fishes deep when the water is close to 50°. I like to use it off a sink tip line.' With his permission I christened the fly The Grasshopper.

Spinning tackle
The second rod to be assembled was also a Bruce & Walker, a 10ft carbon fibre spinning rod which has seen 10 years service. This rod is versatile and will handle lines from 8lb to 20lb breaking strain with little risk of smashing the finer monofilament. A shorter and lighter spinning rod is used in lower and warmer summer water.

Other than rods and landing tackle Bruce's equipment is contained in two large suitcase-style boxes. These open into display trays and compartments. One suitcase is for fly fishing and the other for natural and artificial baits and spinning equipment.

There were three multiplying reels: a fast retrieve Ambassador 6500C which is close to 11 years in age; a 5000C which is about 25 years old, and a new carbon fibre Ambassador 823.

He mounted the 6500C loaded with 18lb Maxima nylon on the rod, threaded the line through the rings and tied on a 1oz Wye weight with a Tucked Half Blood knot. The security of Bruce's Half Bloods is ensured by taking two turns through the wire loop of a minnow flight or Wye weight.

It is rare for him to use a Wye weight in March; he would normally employ the Paternoster system which enables the bait to be fished more slowly in a full fast river. On this day the water was low, at summer level, the water temperature was 43°F and Bruce felt that a fish might move in the clear flow to a slightly faster moving bait. The trace was 2ft 6in of 15lb nylon. This slight reduction in strength ensures that the trace breaks instead of the reel line of 18lb if the bait snags on the bottom. We then looked through a selection of Devon minnows, and picked out one which was 3in in length and of unweighted wood. He does not favour metal minnows or those of wood with a weighted tube down the centre. Plain wood is best: it sways and swims with enticing freedom in the current. This particular Devon had a green back, a fluorescent pink band down each flank and a dark yellow belly. It had been found in the river. Looking at it with a critical eye Bruce commented that the yellow was rather darker than he preferred; a lighter yellow would present a less dense image which might prompt investigation by a salmon.

Of the other Devons in the box some were blue and silver, red and black and gold, yellow bellies, and a spotted creation. 'That was made by my nephew. He gave me a box of them for Christmas. They look as though they have caught measles.' This was so. The minnow was orange with white stripes, and red, black and white spots. 'I'm sure it will catch a fish.'

The hook flight was of unweighted wire passed through a red tulip bead, the eye of a No 4 treble and bound most securely around the shank of the hook. He considers that the treble must be sufficiently open in gape to protrude well beyond the width of a plump Devon body. To use too small a hook is a great — but common — mistake.

Trebles were present in three colours: black, brown and silver. All three are used for spinning baits, but only black and brown for shrimp fishing.

I examined a selection of Toby spoons in the box. In all cases the treble had been moved away from the spoon tail. This had been accomplished by the addition of a second split ring between the original ring and the eye of the hook. This extra gap does not affect the action of the bait, and Bruce loses fewer salmon through the hooks being levered out by the length of the body. The particular Toby which I examined was 3½in in length and armed with a No 2 treble. It seemed to me that the extra split ring was a simple and effective improvement. The other alteration sometimes used is to attach the treble to the swivel at the head via a wire or nylon trace. The trace length places the hook at the tail of the Toby where it is held by a twist of fuse wire — the fuse breaks loose when a salmon takes. Whilst this ensures that the Toby body cannot lever out the hook, the method is more complicated.

Also in the box was an old brass Hardy spring balance reading up to 40lb. The largest salmon Bruce has taken at Somerley weighed 33lb. The heaviest fish he has landed weighed 43lb and came from the Wye. This was hooked by a friend, a trout fisherman by inclination, who had only fished for salmon for two days. Having hooked the fish, and being at a loss to know how to proceed, it was eventually landed by Bruce.

Landing equipment

A 20 year-old Hardy three-section brass gaff with a 3in gape, and a Hardy tailer are carried. The Avon in spring is not an easy river from which to extract a heavy salmon due to the high banks. The tailer is used on kelts and the gaff on fresh fish. In early spring the waterflow is too strong for a Gye net to be held out against the current. Sometimes the water meadows bordering the river are flooded; it is then possible to swim a salmon over the bank and onto the grass. Even in such conditions the river remains reasonably clear for such a tactic.

'Many years ago, in February, I had been invited to fish this water but I did not know the river. My friend left me on my own without any landing equipment. To my astonishment a salmon took hold. There I was; there was the salmon charging about; there were the flooded water meadows. I swam the salmon over the bank and jumped on him. That was the first fish I caught on this river.'

The river and fishing methods

Leaving the car we walked across the meadows to the river. Lapwings made territorial display flights, and Canada geese could be heard in the distance. Last summer Bruce found plover and redshank nests, he often sees wild swans, shelduck and snipe.

'There are many different fish in the river. On several occasions I have hooked barbel whilst spinning for salmon. They are not foul hooked. They actually manage to take the Devon despite their small mouths. Last year I had the spring balance in my pocket and weighed one — it went 11½ lb. I have landed and returned five or six over the years.'

The water was running clear, but at summer level, and as the morning progressed both minnow and fly were tried, the latter by Spey casting. Normally, in March and April, the river would be higher by 1-2ft. Until the end of April Bruce does not expect to take fish in deep water, instead he concentrates on the streamy runs of between 3-6ft in depth. This might be because the deeper pools hold slightly colder water close to the river bed.

The fly

When Bruce first started to fish at Somerley he tried persistently in summer with a floating line and small flies, and experimented with large patterns. Many fish were moved but refused to take. One fish is clearly remembered: it circled the fly three times, failed to take, but fell first or second cast to a No 3 upstream Mepp. In recent seasons he rarely fishes the fly from June onwards, instead a single worm is cast upstream. Before June, in the full cold waters of the early season, he enjoys the fly, and meets success with large tubes on a sinking line.

The worm

'Years ago, in the Highlands, a keeper taught me to fish the upstream worm on a fly rod. That is now my summer method at Somerley. A 13ft light carbon fibre rod is ideal, fixed spool reel, a swivel, one light shot, a 3 hooked Pennel tackle and a single lob worm. If the water is coloured I might add another worm.'

He starts at the bottom of the beat and works up the river, spotting fish through polaroid spectacles. All the little streamy runs are visited, and places which others fail to fish. It may take 30 or 40 casts, throwing the worm above a salmon and allowing it to trundle down, before the fish takes.

'After a while his mouth opens and closes; his fins quiver; then he takes. You must not touch the fish with the line or he will scoot off. Casting must be to either side and as close as possible to the fish without lining him.'

Bruce does not fish the worm after the middle of August. This is because fish are usually hooked far back in the mouth, and a gravid hen, or red cock fish, cannot be released. Worms are purchased. He used to collect them on wet nights with a friend in a park.

'One night I arrived in the dark. He was using his torch and dropping the worms into a bucket. I crept up behind, silently, gave him a push and sent him sprawling. The only trouble was it wasn't my friend!'

On another occasion Bruce and a friend were collecting worms in the dark on Reading University cricket pitch. The police arrived, having been tipped-off by the warden who assumed they were vandalizing the pitch. The police were so interested that they joined the collecting team. It was a case of coppers and collectors.

Prawn and shrimp

At one time he fished the prawn. Pricked salmon resulted, spoiling the fishing for himself and others. The method was discarded. He fishes the shrimp, starting at the bottom of the beat and casting upstream as with the worm.

'If the water is clear I start by fishing upstream for salmon which are visible. In my pocket is a roll of loo paper. If they fail to take the place is marked with a piece of the paper, and I continue to the top of the beat. On the way back I stop 20yds above the loo paper, where the salmon cannot see me, and cast downstream with a 'sink and draw' action. Sometimes they take.'

Upstream spinning

A No 3 Mepp cast upstream is effective in summer when the water has warmed. Sometimes a No 4 is used. An additional tactic is to cast a large Toby upstream and reel back fast. Salmon rarely take the Toby but they give chase, reveal themselves and may then be sought with an upstream worm or shrimp.

Remarkable incidents

On one occasion Bruce was fishing below Ibsley Bridge. He cast a worm up under the bridge, and a fish took. After a while the salmon swam up through the nearside bridge arch and went down through the far arch. A friend then cast a large Toby over the line from the far bank, caught and cut Bruce's line and tied the fish to his line. The fish then returned the way it had come through both arches. It was now the turn of Bruce to tie on a Toby, cast across his friend's line, catch, cut and re-tie. The salmon of 18lb was eventually landed by Bruce who had hooked it in the first place.

On another occasion he was fishing below Ibsley Bridge on the left bank. A salmon was hooked and promptly shot down through the weir hatch on the right bank into the weir pool. Glad of the 200yds on his multiplying reel Bruce let 50yds run free, cut the line and tied a piece of wood to the end. The wood floated through the hatch after the fish and swirled about in the weir pool. Bruce then ran up the river, crossed the road bridge, came down the right bank, located the wood, hooked the line on a Toby, re-tied and landed the salmon.

At one time his partner was on Beat No 3 when an angler hooked a salmon when fishing from the far bank. This man had no landing tackle. A gaff was thrown across but fell short and was lost in the river. Six years later this angler hooked his own gaff whilst spinning. He sent it back to Hardy's at Alnwick who cleaned it and returned it in new condition.

Catch record

1991 was his 20th season at Somerley where he has a Saturday rod. In that span of years, one of which was missed due to ill health, he has landed well over 100 salmon. The largest as already disclosed, was 33lb, and in addition several have been taken between 20-30lb in weight. Recently, fish have reduced in numbers and average weight.

'I don't want to kill a lot of salmon any more. Last season, in the drought, I fished for 17 days and took four fish. The year before, also a drought, I only took one. 1988 was wet and that was a different story. On one Saturday I had four fish from Beat No 3. I couldn't come to the river the next Saturday, but the following week I had five fish from Beat No 2. The river was packed with grilse. Mind you, in some seasons I have drawn a blank.'

Bruce keeps a meticulous diary recording Beat, pool, bait and so on.

'What is this bait you've entered. BBB?'

'A blackbird's breakfast.' (Worm)

Contents of his car boot in addition to fishing tackle: Fish basses, loo roll, sun tan oil, unbreakable steel coffee flask, whisky flask, fish carrier with cork handle and cords, bag of spare clothes, cold bag in summer for fish, beer and worms, towel, midge cream, rod clips for car roof, Balaclava, caps and sun hat, Polaroid spectacles (two pairs), fish gutting knife, camera, boomerang otter (home-made, for releasing snagged baits).

5 March 1991

The River Wylye

(See map, page 86)

Trout Fishing

River description

The river, which rises above Kingston Deverill, is still extremely narrow where it passes by Monkton Deverill and Brixton Deverill. At Longbridge Deverill the river is wider, belongs to the Longleat Estate, and is fishable, as is the case at Norton Bavant and Heytesbury. Over the next six miles to Bapton, with a few short gaps, the Wylye is in the hands of The Society. This water is fished by about 30 members who may only fish the Wylye, and by full members who have access to all the waters of The Society. The Wylye stretch is not divided into beats; members fish where they choose. Below The Society's water Bapton Farms have a syndicate. Downstream of Bapton are private stretches, and waters fished by both The Wilton Fly Fishing Club and The Salisbury and District Angling Club.

George Maich — Head Keeper, The Piscatorial Society, The River Wylye

His history

Whenever George had a spell ashore during his years in Royal Navy submarines, he fished. On leaving the Navy a month of educational and vocational training is available. George chose river keeping, going in 1969 for his month to the river Arle, an Itchen tributary, under keeper Jim Collins. A year on the Test followed at Timsbury. Leaving that river in 1971 George moved to The Piscatorial Society on the river Kennet at Kintbury, and other waters which The Society fished at Thatcham, and on the river Lambourn. I asked George if he had seen or caught a notable trout:

'I caught a 7lb brown in the Kennet at Newbury. I saw a pike and set a line for him; then patrolled up the river Lambourn. When I came back he was hooked. After this I baited with a small perch. Returning the next morning I found this 7lb brown had swallowed my bait — we swallowed him at the Keepers Supper!'

The year on the river

Trout fishing starts on 15 April and closes on 30 September. Grayling continue for members until 31 December, and also for one or two non-members who have helped with river work during the year. A fly fishing club from Yorkshire visits the water annually for a grayling competition against The Society.

By 15 April the banks and margins of the river have been cut and trimmed. Weed cutting is in four periods which are arranged by The Wiltshire Fishery Association, the main cut taking place over three weeks in June. Other cuts are in April, July and September. On the Wylye those who cut weed are responsible for 'clearing down'. This entails freeing all cut weed held on bridge supports, in rafts stranded on growing weed and on the banks. The floating weed is then pulled out of the river at various points downstream by NRA-operated draglines.

George cuts his weed by hand with a Turk scythe, the river being too shallow for a weed cutting boat or the use of a chain scythe.

The banks of the Wylye are steep and much above the water level in places. This is due to the river having been dragged during the 1939-45 war to create a line of defence against tanks if invasion had taken place. George trims access points down the banks at intervals to enable members to enter the river. He does not encourage wading up the stream — just descent into the water at these places for a cast or two upstream.

Stocking is solely with brown trout. During the season takeable fish are introduced above the size limit of 11in at Heytesbury and Knook. There is no bag limit. The main aim of The Society, being to provide fishing for wild trout, was fulfilled by the introduction of yearling fish. These entered the river after the end of the season, and followed any electric fishing to remove the very few pike, and once a single 4lb carp. The yearlings grew on from a length of 6in to a good size after two or three years. The last introduction of these juveniles took place in 1985. Since then George has relied upon wild spawning and the annual stocking of about 100 trout of 11in. If larger trout are released they have been found to lose condition. The heaviest trout taken from The Society's Wylye up to the time of my visit in 1991 weighed $2\frac{1}{2}$lb. Wild redding is successful, being helped by loosening gravel beds with a garden rake. The Chitterne Brook is heavily frequented by Wylye spawning trout. It has been established that about 2,000 trout travel up the brook to cut redds. Salmon spawn in the river, but not above the village of Wylye where there is a mill with hatches.

Winter work includes the restoration of the river to its original width. This has the effect of narrowing the channel and thus speeding the water flow which has reduced due to abstraction from a pumping station at Codford St Mary, and as the result of recent dry seasons. The banks are reinforced with a fine plastic net which has the trade name of Nicospan, and is described as 'prefabricated double-weave revetment fabric'. The net is held upright along the edge of the river by stakes. These are passed through vertical sleeves, incorporated at intervals in the fabric, and driven into the bed of the river. The area behind the plastic is then filled with stones, chalk and earth. Weed grows through the net and the bank rapidly acquires a natural appearance. Nicospan was used on The Society's water at Knook and, in places, the banks have been reinforced with tree trunks.

The river work of George, and his Under-Keepers Tom Ellis and Tom Stoppard, was recorded in the year of The Society's 150th Anniversary on a video which took 12 months to complete. The vocal descriptions of the scenes are by Sir Michael Hordern, himself a member.

Summary of 1990 Wylye fishing season results
(1989 season)
(1988 season)

    TROUT (sizeable)

Kept	208	*Released*	711	*Notable*	85	1990
	(106)		(286)	(over 1lb)	(27)	1989
	(340)		(850)		(85)	1988

TROUT STOCKED

Sizeable	100	*Yearlings*	500	1990
	(100)		(–)	1989
	(200)		(500)	1988

GRAYLING

212	1990
(282)	1989
(126)	1988

Rod visits per day including guests

3.26	1990
(3.00)	1989
(3.90)	1988

GUESTS

69	1990
(58)	1989
(105)	1988

TROUT CATCH PER VISIT

1.69	1990
(1.30)	1989
(1.80)	1988

Natural fly life

The grannom hatch, usually sparse, is improving. Large spring olives and iron blue are abundant. Hawthorn are blown off the land in good numbers. Blue winged olives, sedges and pale wateries appear in their season. Mayfly hatches commence at the end of May, are not as prolific as on the Avon but are sufficient to bring up the fish. The hatch continues in small numbers into July, and a few mayfly were present on the day of my visit.

River weeds

Ranunculus, starwort and water celery are the major water plants. Water parsley and watercress are also present. George drove me to Heytesbury where he removed a sample of all five plants from the river and described them, including a few pieces of Canadian pond weed. In the sodden bundles which we laid out on the road were ample populations of freshwater shrimp, caddis, nymphs, snails and the eggs of various insects. I asked him to describe the plants:

Water Celery — not a problem provided it does not cover too large an area. It likes to grow in the shade.

Water Parsley — beneficial, but the flowers come above water level and have a magnetic attraction to angler's artificial flies as well as drifting cut weed and other debris!

Starwort — this thick weed is desirable in small quantities. If allowed to spread it gathers mud. Blue winged olive favour starwort, and the armful which George removed from the river held more invertebrate life than the other samples.

Ranunculus — (also known as water buttercup and crow's foot) is an excellent weed for the maintenance of insect life. It is attractive when in flower, and has the desirable quality of holding up water levels in dry seasons.

Watercress — grows mainly in the latter part of the season on the river edge, and is a haven for insect life. If left it will spread across the river, and thus has to be controlled by pulling out excessive growth.

Canadian Pond Weed — tends to prosper in mud and slow flowing streams. A minor plant which appears in the summer when water flows are reduced.

Of all the weeds described trout prefer to hide in ranunculus and starwort because they form a flap over the river surface beneath which trout take refuge.

Before I left, George, with characteristic care for river life, rescued many of the struggling nymphs and shrimps from the road and returned them to the water.
18 July 1991

Norman Smith — Head Keeper, The Wilton Fly Fishing Club

We met in the Club room which adjoins Norman's house at Great Wishford. On the walls are cased trout, including a most remarkable brace:

Hen. Union Stream.   Cock. Summer House Stream.
17 May 1927. 5lb 10oz   20 May 1927. 6lb 11oz.

At the window table is the fishing record book in which members record their catch, whether killed or returned, the weight and sometimes the length, the fly, and other matters. Beside the book is a selection of flies, dressed by the Club's river watcher, Taff Stephens. It is a small but comfortable room, with an intriguing library of modern fishing books and those by angling masters of bygone eras.

Formation of the Club

When Norman took up his duties 27 years ago there were 19 members. This has now increased to 45, and there is a waiting list.

The Club was founded in 1878 under the name The Hungerford Fly Fishing Club, with waters on the river Kennet. In 1891 they moved to Wilton. The Inaugural Meeting is recorded in the Club Minutes:

> *'The First Annual Meeting of The Hungerford Fly Fishing Club was held at The Three Swans Hotel, Hungerford on Monday 4th February 1878 at 1.00pm. Present were: . . .'*

(The book records that there were eight members. The originators of the Club being Mr H. Collins and the Rev. H.G. Veitch.)

The transfer to Wilton and the change of name are recorded in Minutes of Meetings held in London. The 15th and final Meeting of The Hungerford Club took place on Monday 29 February 1892 at 4.30pm, one year after the first Annual General Meeting of The Wilton Fly Fishing Club on 23 February 1891 at 4.30pm. The Meetings took place in the offices of Messrs Smith and Pitts, 14 Cornhill, London. From these records it is apparent that the Wilton Club was formed one year before the winding-up of the Hungerford Club. In the records is the following circular letter to members:

Reading, 13th September 1878

Dear Sir,

The Committee of The Hungerford Club desire me to acquaint you that the exceptional expenditure specified below compels them to appeal to members for a donation of five pounds each. The Committee cannot foresee a recurrence of this appeal which they trust will receive your favourable response. Cheques could be forwarded and made payable to   *Mr H. Collins.*
                                                        Signed on behalf of the Committee
                                                        H. J. Simonds
                                                        President of the Club

P.S. Should you wish to contribute to the keeper's fund (limited to 5/-), please add this amount to your cheque.

Items of exceptional expenditure:	£
Surveys and reports on Marsh	8
Trout nursery	15
Nets etc	30
Books and printing	10
Stock trout and grayling	40
TOTAL	103

N.B. The sums debited for the last three items are arrived at after a deduction of a future Annual Expenditure under each of such heads.

The Club waters

These are leased from The Wilton Estate. The fishery extends from Stapleford, commencing about 500yds below the river Till junction, to Wilton, a distance of approximately five miles which is almost entirely double-bank. Due to the presence of carriers: the Hudd Stream, the Union Stream below Seven Hatches, the Butcher Stream and the Summer House Stream, the length of water extends to nearly seven miles.

The fishery is divided into 24 reaches, of which two require fitness and a pioneering spirit! Members do not book a reach, being able to fish where they wish, but the reach system identifies where fish have been caught through entries in the record book.

Immediately above Norman's water, the river is fished by The Salisbury and District Angling Club, and above them are some small syndicates. Downstream is The Wilton Estate water which extends to below the junction of the rivers Wylye and Nadder.

The trout season runs from 15 April-14 October, the nymph being allowed throughout as well as dry fly. Grayling fishing continues thereafter for members through the winter. Amongst the membership are one or two pike experts. They help to control this predator by spinning in the trout close season. Electric fishing by the Club's own boat, with an ancient but effective generator, keeps grayling and pike numbers at a reasonable level, the catch being transferred to coarse fishing waters. Netting also takes place, and pike are trapped when entering side streams to spawn. There is no eel grid on the Club's section of the river, but some are taken during electric fishing.

Spawning and stocking

Wild Wylye trout spawn late, in December, mainly in side streams such as the Till and Chitterne Brook. Some trout are taken down to the Club's water from the Chitterne Brook and these, together with an annual introduction in April of fed-fry from Stockbridge, provide a good population of wild brown trout. Rainbow trout are not introduced. Salmon spawn in the river as far upstream as Wylye. Crayfish are absent following disease from the Avon.

Weeds

Norman considers ranunculus to be the most beneficial weed in a trout fishery, but its presence has been reduced through grazing by swans. Reduction in ranunculus (also known as crowsfoot) has allowed the entry of other weeds, such as potamogeton in summer. Starwort, water celery and milfoil are also present.

Natural and artificial flies

We looked at the fishing record book for confirmation of the natural fly cycle, and the artificials with which these had been imitated. The following entries of catches on artificials are representative. Not all of the trout recorded are killed, there being a column for those returned.

1991
April   20, 21 & 28   Grannom

May   2   Large Dark Olive
               8   Black Gnat
                            Hawthorn
                            Shrimp
               11 & 12   Hawthorn
               12   No 16 Gold Ribbed Hare's Ear
               19   Hawthorn
               20   Sedge
               19 & 22   Pheasant Tail
               23   *Note*: 'Just coming on the May'. 3 fish taken on Mayfly
               26   Hawthorn

June   2   Royal Wulff (for mayfly)
               5   Small Olives
               8   Mayfly
               10   Mayfly spinner
               10   Greenwell's Glory
               11   Tony Hayter — Mayfly. 3lb 7oz. 19$^{1}/_{4}$ in long.
                            Note: '5.00pm. A good hatch from 4.15pm to 6.00pm.'

Norman commented about this fish: 'I remember him telling me that during the evening there had been the best mayfly hatch he had seen this season. The trout is our largest so far in 1991.'

               12   *Note*: 'No May to speak of'.
               12   Tony Hayter — nymph. 3lb. Reach No 19. 18$^{1}/_{4}$ in in length.
               21   Blue Winged Olive. Mr Bell took and returned four trout
                            1lb 4oz
                            1lb 4oz
                            2lb 0oz
                            0lb 15oz
               24   Hamish Anderson. 2lb 1oz (contained $^{1}/_{2}$ digested mouse).
                            Author's note: artificial not mentioned!

July   2   Blue Winged Olive
               6   Blue Winged Olive
               10   Red Sedge
               13   Cinnamon Sedge
               17   Pheasant Tail Nymph
               21   Greenwell's Glory

August	1	Sherry Spinner
	4	Greenwell's Glory and Pheasant Tail Nymph
	5	Pheasant Tail Nymph and Sherry Spinner
	9	Sherry Spinner
	9	*Note*: 'Fish still taking mayfly'
	11	Greenwell's Glory
	14	Sherry Spinner
	19	Hamish Anderson took 3 pike
	28	Beacon Beige

September

Entries to the day of my visit included Greenwell's Glory, Sherry Spinner, Black Gnat and Daddy Long-Legs.

Grayling fishing

Norman then drove me to Stoford Bridge where we found Taff Stephens fishing for grayling, casting upstream with a nymph of his own design. He has christened this nymph the Silver Head.

The Silver Head

- Hook — No 16 Partridge Code E1A. Down eye with small barb
- Body — Rabbit fur
- Rib — Fine copper wire
- Head — Metal silver bead from a wash basin plug chain, secured by fine wire

(He dresses a similar nymph, but with a gold bead, for trout.)

The cast was 3lb Drennan, greased from the line/leader junction to 2ft from the nymph — the downward twitch of the greased section indicates a 'take'.

If Taff were limited to one fly for his trout fishing throughout the season he would choose Skues' Little Red Sedge. To this he sometimes adds a striped teal wing sloping back over the body. For grayling, a nymph — Frank Sawyer's Grayling Bug. Innovative in his fly dressing, he also produces a beetle in which the horny wing sheath is one half of a sunflower seed case — 'but it only does for one trout, because the case breaks'.

16 September 1991

The River Nadder

(See map, page 86)

The river rises from a series of very small streams in the Charlton, Donhead St Mary and Donhead St Andrew areas. It trickles north-east to Tisbury, being joined on the way by the river Sem. Above Tisbury it is much overgrown and barely fishable. To the north of Tisbury are the stocked lakes of the Fonthill Estate. Charles Patrick (see below) fishes these lakes which originally held wild brown trout. They are now stocked with rainbows which grow on naturally to a large size, some reaching 2-3lb in weight. The Font, a trout holding stream fished by a small syndicate, flows out of the lakes to join the Nadder east of Tisbury.

The Tisbury Angling Club holds the water downstream of the town as far as Upper Chicksgrove, fish present being trout and coarse fish. A short section is privately owned between Upper and Lower Chicksgrove and there, from the bridge, I saw children fishing for trout with bread paste.

The Teffont Flyfishing Club hold four miles of water from Lower Chicksgrove to Dinton Station. In this section the Nadder is joined by the Teffont Brook from the north. The Fovant Brook, flowing from the south, is added just below Fovant Mill.

Charley's double-bank water of nearly three miles runs from Compton Wood to the Hurdcott Estate, the water of which is fished privately. There is also a short private section above Barford St Martin below which, down to Quidhampton, the river belongs to the Wilton Estate of Lord Pembroke. The Wilton water between Barford and Wilton is fished by The Burcombe Fly Fishers Club.

On the Wilton House water is a syndicate which also fishes the Wylye which joins the Nadder to the east of Wilton Park. The joint river, fished by Salisbury and District Angling Club and still called the Nadder, joins the Avon to the south of Salisbury.

The Compton Chamberlayne water is divided into seven beats, each of which may be fished by two rods a day. John Newman, Charley's employer, keeps one beat per day and The Rod Box at Winchester and the timeshare cottage at Dinton Mill each retain a beat. This leaves four beats per day which are divided between syndicate rods. Rod Box anglers are usually day rods. Those sent down by Mr John Newman are often anglers waiting for a place on the syndicate, but it is possible for others to obtain a day's fishing.

Trout Fishing

Charles Patrick — Head Keeper, Compton Chamberlayne Estate

Charles Patrick's career
He was brought up in Yorkshire and fished the becks which ran into the Swale. Wild trout were stalked with a lob worm and weighed up to $1\frac{1}{4}$lb. The heaviest was hooked and played from the crook of a tree above a pool. It was never landed! As he hauled it up he slipped — fish and boy fell into the river.

He worked for a while as a gamekeeper, went to Sparsholt College, then Broadlands Estate under the Head Gamekeeper Harry Grass. Two years followed assisting in the running of a pheasant shoot north of Paris. After this he came to Compton Chamberlayne to look after the river and fishery, and has now been there for ten years.

Stocking and spawning

The trout season lasts for 23 weeks from the final Sunday in April. Grayling are in decline and are not pursued after the end of the trout season.

About 1,000 fingerlings are purchased in August from the spawning of the previous November. These brown are fed on in a stew prior to releasing into the river in October. There they are fed with those trout which have survived the season, and together these fish form the backbone of a semi-wild stock. Wild spawning also takes place in the shallows of the river and in several small side streams.

During the season brown and rainbow trout of between $1^1/_4$-3lb in weight are stocked every two or three weeks. This joint method provides an annual catch of approximately 2,500 trout at an average weight of 2lb.

The largest truly wild Nadder trout on the Compton water which Charley has seen taken weighed $1^3/_4$lb. Two years before my visit a grown-on brown stock fish which weighed 7lb 14oz was taken in the Dinton Mill Pool. This hen may have been the fish of 5lb which had been caught and released three years previously. The trout fell to a Grey Wulff, and the rod had it smoked. In favourable years, when there is sufficient water, salmon spawn in the area. In the winter of 1989 there were 20 redds between Dinton Mill and Hurdcott hatches. Lord Pembroke catches salmon in the Nadder just above the Wylye junction, and sometimes takes a fish there before one is taken downstream at Longford Castle on the Avon into which the Nadder discharges. A salmon will, occasionally, arrive at Dinton during the trout season, but this only happens if there is full water.

The Nadder is suffering from water abstraction. In the 10 years of Charley's stewardship the flow has decreased dramatically. Wessex Water abstracts above Fonthill and there are a considerable number of private licences. Low rainfall has also contributed to low flow, and the heavier rainfall of 1991 has not increased the volume of water running down the valley, but it has lowered the water temperature and thus reduced the incidence of Furunculosis in trout and grayling. Crayfish are present, and there is an untrapped eel run.

Electric fishing takes place in March in conjunction with the Teffont Club. This not only controls pike, but provides a fish population survey. There are roach weighing up to 2lb, and last year a carp of 15lb was caught in the Dinton hatch pool and transferred to the Compton Estate lakes which are managed for the production of coarse fish. These are netted annually in February, the fish being sold to coarse fisheries. Small coarse fish are then stocked to grow on to form the next crop.

Fishing tackle

Charley uses an 8ft Hardy Graphite rod with The Featherweight reel of $2^7/_8$in diameter. The line is an AFTM No 5 orange floater. His leader is comprised of 5ft of Orvis braided nylon, with a tippet of Drennan 'sub-surface'. The fly is waterproofed with Permafloat but the leader is not greased and thus fishes, almost invisibly, in or under the surface film. In fact, Charley is so determined that his leader shall not show that he de-greases the final 2-3ft closest to the fly.

Natural and artificial flies

Charley uses a parachute fly for most of his Nadder fishing. He calls the fly the Wee MacGregor after Col Robert Leith MacGregor who brought it to England from Portland where it is called the Float-n-Fool. The colonel had some tied by Farlows of Pall Mall, but they are now dressed by Charley. Trout, grayling, dace and chub all love the Float-n-Fool.

The dressing:
- Hook   No 10 to 16. Down eye
- Body   peacock herl
- Tail & Post   continuous white calf tail (soft hair)
- Hackle   2 ginger or red, with 1 grizzle hackle in the middle tied around the Post
- Silk   Black, pre-waxed

Sawyer's Pheasant Tail and Killer Bug nymphs are excellent for trout and grayling. As Charley says 'the Killer Bug is the fly fisherman's maggot, and just as effective'. Rods use the Grey Wulff as a mayfly pattern for several weeks for, in 1991, the hatch continued until the early days of August. Sedge patterns should be carried. Blue winged olive imitations, Sherry Spinner for the spent, are needed when the natural is present. Pale watery imitations are required. Lunn's Particular is a favourite. Of early season flies the iron blue is in decline, but the large dark olive hatches in good numbers as do alder and hawthorn. A hawthorn artificial should be small — when trout are feeding on the natural, which may be blown on the water, they frequently take a white-winged Black Gnat in preference to hawthorn patterns which may be of too large a size.

In some seasons there are tremendous hatches of grannom, but their numbers are tailing off just as the rod season opens. Even so, grannom bring up trout which become used to surface feeding by the time anglers arrive on the scene.

Poaching

Seeing poachers fishing off the road bridge on Beat No 1, Charley telephoned the police who took an hour to arrive — too late. He complained at the police station the next morning and, by chance, came across a single poacher that afternoon. A telephone call was made. At once two police Panda cars arrived, a patrol car, a helicopter and a police dog in a van. The helicopter crew flew up the river and arrested a farmer, Edward Williams, who was searching for some stock. All ended well. The poacher was caught and a stolen car was recovered.

14 August 1991

The River Kennet

In common with many of the tributaries of the river Thames the Kennet holds trout, grayling, roach, rudd, pike, chub and other fish, salmon not amongst them.
It is a long and substantial water which rises above Marlborough, where there are trout, to pass Ramsbury, Chilton Foliat, Hungerford, Kintbury and Newbury before joining the parent Thames at Reading.

Trout Fishing

Cdr Jack Langworthy RN (Retd) — Rod, Chilton Foliat Estate

Jack was born in 1906 and started to fish at the age of 17 years for ½ lb trout in a small river in Yorkshire. Other than during his years at sea, three as navigating officer on the battle cruiser HMS *Repulse* — when he was known as Pilot, or Vasco da Gama — he has since fished on every possible occasion and has had a rod at Chilton since 1972.

During 19 seasons on the river he has noticed a reduction in fly life, with fewer large dark olives in spring, and a smaller number of medium olives and pale wateries as the season progresses. He also feels there is a reduction in flow, partly due to water abstraction, and an increase in silt deposition resulting from increased arable farming. He believes that before the war the river was bordered by water meadows grazed by sheep, the meadows filtering and cleaning the water entering the river. Today, with ploughed fields adjacent in some areas, quantities of mud wash into the Kennet.

Jack fishes the river on Tuesday and Friday. The length of fishable bank is hard to calculate, but the main river is double-bank from Chilton Foliat bridge almost down to the Hungerford town water, with four carriers in addition. A total of approximately 28 rods fish the estate water on specific days. I asked Jack his choice of flies:

'In the old days when there was plenty of insect life you had to get roughly the right fly, otherwise you wasted your time. My eyesight is not what it was, I have some difficulty in tying on my offerings, but I could now go through the season with three flies: a No 16 Black Gnat, a Red or Grey Wulff and a Gold Ribbed Hare's Ear. After 1 July a nymph is allowed: Pheasant Tail Nymph, Grey Goose, and a Shrimp if you want something heavy. There is another fly I'd like to tell you about which nobody uses but me. It is called Eric's Beetle, after Eric Horsfall Turner who, I think, was a surgeon from Yorkshire. It is a simple fly: yellow wool body, of which two turns are left exposed at the tail, covered with bronze peacock herl to the head where there are two turns of a black hen hackle. It doesn't last well, and only more or less floats. It suits me because my sight is not good. I find it hard to see the tweak when a sunk nymph is taken, but I can spot a rise to Eric's Beetle.'

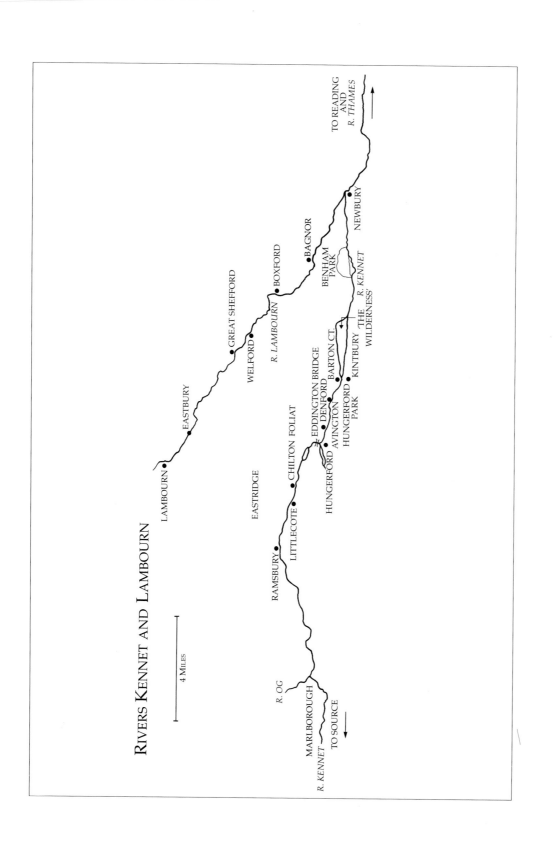

RIVERS KENNET AND LAMBOURN

4 MILES

Jack searched in an ancient fly box. 'Here's one' he said, handing it over. The fly he produced resembled a Caperer on a No 14 hook. 'We're not allowed hooks larger than No 12.'

Next out was a Shrimp on a No 12 hook. 'That's got a bit of weight under the dressing.'

'What is this nymph in the box, the one with a bit of red?'

'It will be a Buzzer. I've got a few of those.'

'How long have you had the box?'

'A very very long time. I know there is a mixture inside, but my sight is poor and the compartments become mixed. When my grandson comes to stay he sorts them out. He is 14 years-old and a damn sight better fisherman than me. It is some comfort that I taught him. There really ought to be a Hawthorn in the box for there are plenty about in May, and by June we have many sedges. Mayfly are almost entirely absent, but that doesn't mean they won't take an artificial. I remember two occasions, not at mayfly time, when I became so exasperated with a fish which wouldn't take my imitation of the small hatching natural that I put on a huge Mayfly. Had him in the net at once.'

Jack's rod is a No 6 Hardy Fibalite of 9ft in length. He has never felt the need of carbon fibre. 'I always use a 4X tapered leader. You ought not to go finer than that because we have some large fish.'

He produced his fishing diary which is a meticulously kept record:

'In 1975 we went through a bad patch. That was before Stephen, the present keeper, arrived. I nearly left. We had a lot of what I call 'downstream draggers'. The diary revealed success to an orange nymph: 'I used to tie those myself, and wish I could get them now. They were very good with a hot orange body.'

I read through the result of that year: 42 brown trout and 38 rainbow at an average weight of 1lb 9oz. I observed, 'That's a good size. You have just as much fun with a fish of 1½lb as one of double that weight.' Jack, momentarily, agreed. Then 'Well, up to a point. Those big blighters, they don't half give you a run for your money. I've been in the river twice!'

'Do you go out for grayling in the winter?'

'I used to, but not much now. They're a bit of a trial because they breed like rabbits. Another trouble is that they often take the fly far back into their throats; that wastes time when you are after trout. The Killer Bug is the thing for grayling, but I refuse to use it now because it resembles a maggot. I have one. I lifted it from a bush and it worked well, but then my conscience saved me.'

Two more flies featured in the diary: Treacle Parkin and an Alder. 'Both good flies. Last year the fish were being tiresome. I rested on a bench and an alder came and sat on my hand, so I tied on that fly and caught a trout.'

'What is this fly called a Dog's Body? I see that caught a trout.'

'It came from the coat of my wife's Pekinese. That made the body, ribbed with gold wire. The tail whisks were pheasant tail, and the hackles a mixture of red cock and grizzle.'

In 1981 Jack noted a catch of 50 brown and 44 rainbow at an average weight of 1lb 9oz. He wrote in his diary: 'The best and most interesting season for many years. The banishment of downstream draggers has enabled a dry fly to be effective most of the time, except in July and August.'

The catch of 94 trout were taken: 24 on nymph and 70 on dry fly; 12 fish came from the Pump House, 4 from the Mud Ditch, 2 from Lower Main, 21 Main, 17 Island, 21 Lower Pump and 17 from the Water Gardens.

'I see you have noted a fly called the Fore & Aft.'

'Oh my word. That is a dreadful fly. I acquired that when I fished once or twice as a guest on some lakes near Aldershot. A friend tied them on a mayfly hook. In front is a red hackle and a bit of white behind. He used electric light flex for the body. A terrible, but effective, creation which floats like a haystack.'

Jack's companions on his Tuesday fishing day are all octogenarians with one exception, Philip, 'who is a superb fisherman'. The others: a retired Governor of Hong Kong, and a retired High Court Judge.

We then left Jack's house at Eastbury in the Lambourn valley to drive to Chilton Foliat where we met the Estate Keeper, Stephen Jones.

5 October 1990

Stephen Jones — Head Keeper, Chilton Foliat Estate

Jack, Stephen and I sat around the table of his house to drink coffee, and then inspect the river which runs nearby.

The stocking on the estate is 80% brown trout, and 20% rainbow of which a higher percentage are caught than the brown trout. Stephen: 'We keep the rainbows back until July and August. The brown trout keep their heads down at that time and fishing is difficult. Up until then, if you catch a rainbow, it will be a fish of the previous season.'

'How do the rainbow go through the winter?'

'Very well. I feed them in the lean months with floating pellets which are carried down the river.'

Stephen buys in his little fish at 100 to 1lb and keeps them for 18 months. As soon as the season is over he puts between 60% and 70% of next season's brown trout stock into a large hatch pool at the top of his river. He feeds them on: 'Through the winter they learn what they can and cannot eat. They become very fit, and learn how to survive and live in fast water.' The rainbows he buys from Brian Parker of the Bossington Estate on the Test, feeds them and then stocks into the river at 18 months of age.

The rods at Chilton fish named days. Some fish infrequently, in fact one rod, from America, just comes over in May and June for three weeks and does not otherwise appear. 'May and June is the best time. We have a few mayfly. If you see 20 in a day, that's a lot. Normally, there are just enough to interest the fish.'

'Which flies appear as the season progresses?'

'I've seen large olives in January. It all depends on the weather and if it is warm. We start fishing on 15 April which is not too early in the mild springs we have been experiencing recently. We do not have any grannom. Hawthorn are prolific; we kill many fish on the artificial. There are small olives in May and the blue winged olive later on, and sedges too. Plenty of sedges.'

I asked about water quality, flow and abstraction. 'At the top of our water is a wide section of the river by an old mill. A skin settles there on top of the silt which forms on the river bed. This skin lifts off and drifts downstream when the sun warms the water and stimulates gas production. If it washes through a hatch it will break up, making the water unfishable. We try to push it all into a carrier. In this way only one stretch is affected, but the condition becomes worse year by year, and lasts for a longer period.'

Stephen continued on the subject of water flow: 'Four or five years ago we had a very wet summer. Even so, in June and July, the river level went down drastically. We were shutting down the hatches every day. I swear it is a direct effect of pumping from boreholes for Swindon. The river seems to fall each year to a certain level and then no further; I believe this is controlled by the amount they pump out of the ground. It seems to me that Thames Water has decided on a level which is just acceptable before people start screaming.' It appears that this is the position the whole way up the valley.

'What is the state at Marlborough?'

'When I first came here they would fish right through until August at Manton, which is the other side of Marlborough. This year they didn't cut the weed. If they had cut, all the remaining water would have run away. The river grows shorter every year.'

Stephen allows friends who have helped him during the season to fish in the winter for grayling. The majority prefer the fly, but a few trot a maggot down the pools. He has not electric-fished the river for two seasons. 'I have a rod who is absolute mustard at taking out pike in the winter — he had 64 last season, the largest was 21lb.'

There is trouble with poachers: 'They never come alone. They arrive from London, Bristol, anywhere. They fish a hatch pool by a public footpath. Their method is a hand line and bread paste. If I am about they drop the line, and then whose is it? I protect my stews with an alarm system.'

There are many kingfishers which nest in a high bank downstream of Stephen's water. After the young have fledged they return to his section of the river. There are mink, which he traps, but no otters. Water rails, moorhens and herons — 'too many of those!'

We then left the house to walk to the river, and the Fish House where anglers take their lunch. In the centre of the floor is a trap door with a cage underneath where trout were kept for consumption in the house. On one wall is the cast of a monster trout with a green coloured back. 'When Kennet wild brown trout exceed 3lb they have deep bellies, and their backs go dark green with large spots. There are not many left.'

On another wall is the painting of a trout caught by S.B. Horn on 5 June 1948. The fish weighed 6lb, the length was 24in and the girth $14^1/_2$in.

Outside the hut is a lily pond. 'In the old days, 25 years ago when only house guests fished, one of the first jobs of the keeper each morning was to turn all the lily leaves the right way up in case the owner came down to enjoy the scene.'

Walking along the river we came to three 7m circular tanks holding rainbows. They will stay there throughout the winter. Stephen rears trout for other fisheries. 'If you are going to rear 2,000 trout you may as well make it 4,000 and sell the surplus.'

Close to these tanks is the large hatch pool which holds next season's brown trout. They will be fed throughout the winter until 1 April. Feeding then ceases and the trout drop down river, populating a stretch of $^3/_4$ mile of their own accord. This method provides fit fish with perfect tails — educated too. No foolish fish for Stephen's rods! 'In the pool there are trout which have been there for three, four or even five years. Eventually they move into the river. They are really wild, and all specimens.' The hatch pool method applies only to the brown trout. In contrast, rainbows are placed out over the length of the water in July and August.

When we discussed fishing tackle I asked about the strength of nylon leaders he recommended: 'I have some people who come and try a 3X leader with small No 18 flies in late summer. How they manage to pass the nylon through the minute eye is a mystery. You need 3lb to match a No 18 Black Gnat — go thicker, trout will be frightened and you will fail. Having said that, this year we had many daddy long-legs on the water: for the artificial you need 4X.'

'Which flies do you favour?'

'A Tups is very good if it does not have too much crimson. A dry Pheasant Tail is excellent. The Black Gnat takes many fish and can be used when the hawthorn is about.'

Weed cutting is not limited to specific periods, as on the river Test. Stephen cuts weed when necessary and removes it from the river into weed pits. This year (1990) he did not cut any ranunculus because it failed to grow. He had one bare area when he came to Chilton, but having cleared off the mud, by staking out corrugated iron sheets mid-river to flush away the silt, the weed started to grow of its own accord. 'It's always there. All you have to do is clean the bed and it will appear in the fast-flowing places.'

As the three of us walked along this beautiful river Stephen told me of the largest wild brown trout he had seen caught on his water: 'It was 4lb 12oz and came from the Broadwater'. He looked at Jack: 'What fly did you take it on Commander?'

Jack searched his memory. 'I think it was a little Red Sedge.'

With some persuasion Jack admitted that he had taken 2nd Prize with the fish at The Fly Dressers Guild, but had been defeated by Geoffrey Bucknall who had taken an even larger one from the Test — 'but I know that mine was wild'.

5 October 1990

The Hungerford Fishery

A day on the river and a meeting at the John O'Gaunt, 4 July 1990. Present:

Col Donald Macey — Hon Manager & Secretary

Bill Waldron — a rod for 20 years

Tony Allen and the author — guests

It is not my purpose to describe the history of this ancient fishery. This has been achieved in admirable detail by E.L. Davis, a former Constable of Hungerford, and Hon Sec & Manager of the Fishery from 1972-75. In 1978 Jim Davis published a small limited edition book *The Story of an Ancient Fishery* of which I am fortunate to possess copy No 21.

It is the normal course in this book to describe the experiences and methods of anglers who have fished for many seasons — or with marked success over a shorter period — a particular beat on the river. In the case of the Hungerford Fishery I have tapped the memories and recent practices of Bill Waldron, my father-in-law, and relied upon my own fishing diary. Bill, an octogenarian, has fished the water for 20 years but, more than that, he has a photograph of his grandfather Henry Trengrouse, with other rods, standing in front of Eddington Mill in the final years of the reign of Queen Victoria!

The following is a description of 4 July 1990 taken from my fishing diary:

> 'River Kennet, Hungerford. Rainbow trout 3. Total 4lb 9oz. No 14 Pheasant Tail Nymph dressed by Tony on Partridge long shank sedge hooks. Wet morning. Tony and I met Bill at Eddington Bridge at 9am. Sat in car for coffee. We then caught 3 trout and 1 grayling above the bridge. All had lunch with Donald Macey in John O'Gaunt. After lunch we parked cars at Denford Mill. Lost 3 trout, came unstuck, in The Meadows. Returned 3 brown. Found kingfishers nest above Duffer's Pool in butt of blown-over tree.'

There is nothing like a drop of warm rain to bring fish on the rise. Oliver Kite, twice a guest at Hungerford in 1967, wrote: 'If I go fishing to catch trout, give me a wet day'. So it proved on 4 July. With windscreen wipers in action we sat in the car and watched the river. As the rain eased trout and grayling started to feed and we ventured out to tackle-up. Bill and I use 9ft carbon fibre rods of AFTM No 6/7 by Bruce & Walker; Tony a rod of the same make but 8ft 6in in length. We attached 4X Platil knotless tapered leaders and knotted on No 14 Pheasant Tail Nymphs.

The river above Eddington Bridge is wide. There are open gravel spaces between bars of weed; swallows skim, ducks paddle and dabchicks dive. It is idyllic. However interesting the scene the angler, if he is worthy of inclusion in the brotherhood, remains alert for the black nose of a trout stretching the water skin. Tony crept up the left bank to set about a trout bulging steadily mid-stream. There was no noticeable hatch of fly and he judged the trout to be nymphing. So it proved. The Pheasant Tail deceived that fish and the rod bent into a lively arc before the net enclosed a rainbow of 1lb 8oz. It was now my turn with a beautiful wild brown, barely 11in in length, which was released by tweaking free the nymph without removing the fish from the water.

There have always been trout of aldermanic size above that bridge — I call them the 'tail-wavers'. Others may catch them — not me. They spend their days, nose down, grubbing in the gravel for shrimps and caddis larvae, and in so doing their tails come up to wave in the air. They are tantalizing. Waste no time on their pursuit. Perhaps one falls from time to time when the mayfly is up in June.

Mayfly

Mayfly — there's a word to raise the pulse rate. They still hatch at Hungerford. Bill tells me they start in The Meadows below Denford Mill and tend to keep to the lower part of the fishery. I recall taking trout on mayfly from the Bracket Stream 15 years ago with Bill's brother Maurice. He favoured a soft artificial with hackles from the breast of a partridge rather than those with stiff wings. He may have been right. He certainly caught trout, and so did John Waller Hills who fished at Hungerford in 1901. Hills:

> 'But, when all is said, however good your tackle, whatever you do, however accomplished you are, and however long your experience, trout on the mayfly are extraordinarily hard to hook. This remains the eternal difficulty of the mayfly. I

think the reason is partly because of the still whole-feathers with which most patterns are winged. If you change to a soft hackled variety you often hook more. A stiff fly is hard to suck in. Partly too, no doubt, the difficulty is due to the fact that so large an insect takes time to eat; partly to the trout's fear that it is something dangerous: and partly, perhaps, to his anxiety to secure it.'

Hills may have been right, particularly in the slowness with which the fly is devoured. He advises: 'Strike slowly, you can hardly be too slow, and, if a floating fly is refused, try a hackle one, waterlogged.'

But a soggy dry fly, including the mayfly, somehow seems to me to be not quite right. I prefer a dun which retains its shape to ride high on the needle points of stiff hackled feet. When the spent is on the water you may use up the waterlogged specimens from your box. Tony has his own dressing of a mayfly which I recommend for deception and a long casting life:

- Hook: No 8 Partridge Long Mayfly
- Body: Seal's fur dyed yellow ribbed fine gold wire
- Front hackle: Blue dun
- Palmered hackle: Blue dun
- Tail: Three ginger cock whisks
- Wing: Brown bucktail. Split shaving brush tying

One cannot leave mayfly without mentioning ducks and ducklings. Ducks abound at Hungerford. Family planning means nothing to a duck — ducklings are in dozens at mayfly time. They scuttle across the water to take the natural, and would readily take the artificial if given the chance. I have always managed to lift off just in time. Swifts are different. They scream, and scythe down the valley on scimitar wings and no fly is safe, neither is the fly on the end of a leader. I once caught one in mid-air by the Black Hut, dried him and threw him into the air — up and away he went.

The nymph
The trout season at Hungerford opens on May Day and closes on 30 September, with grayling fishing allowed until 31 December. From 1 July one is permitted to fish the nymph on hooks no larger than No 14. The Pheasant Tail is my favourite and is simple to dress.

The Pheasant Tail Nymph
Clamp tight on a No 14 single hook with your fly-tying vice. From head to tail wind on fine copper wire, with extra turns near the head to form the thorax of the nymph. Cut out eight long fibres from the tail of a cock pheasant. Tie these in at the tail, slightly on the hook bend, with the copper wire, leaving the fibre points free and pointing to the rear by ¼in. Wind the wire up to the head, wind the fibres over the wire and up the body to the eye of the hook where they are secured by two turns of the wire. Double back the fibres over the thorax to form a hood and tie down, lay them forward once more, tie in, trim off and secure the wire with four whipped turns. Time: three minutes. Product: a nymph which will take trout from 8oz to 8lb. Well, I have not proved the 8lb mark but have come within 8oz. My diary records:

Top: The river Nadder at Compton Chamberlayne.
Bottom: Brown trout from the river Nadder.

Top: The river Kennet. Hungerford Fishery, Meadows water.
Bottom: Eddington Mill pool, Hungerford Fishery.

Top: The river Kennet, the Hungerford Fishery, feeding trout in a natural stew pond.

Bottom: The author (with trout), the keeper and The Hon. Manager and Secretary of the Hungerford Fishery at Eddington Bridge. (Tony Allen)

Top: The river Kennet, the Fish House, Chilton Foliat estate.
Below: Above Bracket Hatch, on the Kennet, the Hungerford Fishery.

'16 July 1976. Hungerford. An outstanding trout. 7¹/₂ lb rainbow. 3X leader. Pheasant Tail Nymph. Had probably escaped from a pond which had not been used for 2 or 3 years on Peart's trout farm   Had to jump in and follow the trout downstream.'

If you go up the Bracket Stream that runs past the house in which Lancelot Peart lived, leaving the Duffer's Pool on your left, you will come to the scene. The trout's downfall came about in this manner. A trout had risen over the far side of the stream. I then watched the place for 10 minutes, trying to make out his exact location for an accurate throw. I peered through the rushes on my side, eyes focused on the water as it swirled under the far bank. Failing to find the trout my gaze relaxed and there, unsought, almost under my feet was the grey back of the largest trout I'd seen in my life. Bill came by, walking lightly, as far as possible from the river. He wanted his lunch as much as I wanted that trout. He is senior to me; the trout must wait.

Over sausages, eggs and chips in one of the inns of the town we plotted his downfall. A deception was devised. Returning to the river, the 4X was replaced by a 3X leader, the Pheasant Tail Nymph tied on, and the rod pushed forward. He was still there, just below the surface, and not at all excited or disturbed. In went the nymph 3yds upstream, out of sight behind the rushes. The grey back eased forward, the tail waved, the trout moved out of sight. I raised the rod after three or four seconds and he was on. Down the river we went, down and down, in the water over the tops of my boots I waded around the bankside trees. We almost reached the Duffer's. It was only when I tried to slide him into the net that I realised his master size. He was vast. But he was slain and remains my largest trout.

Further evidence of the effectiveness of this nymph is contained in my diary:

'1979. July 13. Hungerford. Bill and I had a good day. 8 rainbows, 6 on PTN, 1 on a Daddy Long-Legs and 1 on a Mayfly. Total weight 16lb 8oz. Two best were 3lb 12oz and 3lb 6oz. 4X leader.'

To fish the nymph is fascinating, but war must be waged on individual fish; half the fun is lost if one fishes the water, just casting into likely turbulent places. The first requirement is a good pair of polarized spectacles. Choose those in which the lenses let through as much light as possible — dark glasses, even if polarized, are not the requirement. The nymph needs a bit of weight if trout are deep, and this is provided by the copper wire in the dressing I have given. If the nymph is dressed with silk instead of wire, and is of a small size, a bit of old fashioned spit will help it to cut through the water skin. Wander slowly, very slowly, up the river — and up is better than down — looking all the time for a nymphing trout. The habit of looking into, and not at, the water is a knack which must be cultivated. You will probably spot a trout, firm in outline against the chalk river bed, about 12in below the surface. He may be swinging in the current, lifting and falling and moving from side to side to take the nymphs as they drift downstream. Go down on your knees, take a look behind for trees reaching out their branches to catch you on the back cast, then chuck the nymph 6ft above the trout. The nymph will drift down towards the quarry, sinking as it goes. If you have done it right the trout will stroll over, open his white rimmed mouth and — you lift the rod. As soon as you see those white lips open — react.

Sometimes he will just back down with your offering, and then give chase when the nymph has passed. Such fish are hard to hook, their mouths being open and towards you — you need a little luck.

Then there is 'the black hole'. Have you seen nylon slide forward and down into 'the black hole'? It happens with cruising trout. Why do large trout cruise so that one is hard put to know where to pitch the nymph? Perhaps it is to keep those of lesser status out of their feeding area. Anyway, portmanteaux rainbows tend to patrol a territory. Up under one bank and down the other, or along the side of a weed bed they go. Up, around and down. Slowly. Again and again at regular intervals. Pitch the nymph to his next port of call, even if you cannot see him as he glides out of sight. If you've done it right the nylon will slide forward with a twitch into 'the black hole'.

The dry fly

I once had the privilege of talking to Mick Lunn in the club room of The Houghton Club at the Grosvenor Hotel in Stockbridge. Mick: 'If I had six fishers who went out and they came back with six fish each at the end of the day, it would be found that they would have been taken on different flies: Caperer, Tups, Iron Blue. What you would then notice is that the majority would have fallen to flies of the same size. Size is more important than pattern or colour. This, coupled to presentation are the crucial factors — more than a purist's correct insect identification.'

I agree. The following selection of flies for Hungerford accommodates the need for a range of sizes. The smallest might be a No 18 Black Gnat for use in the summer, or a No 18 Iron Blue in rough weather in the spring or any other galesome time.

The Black Gnat
- Body: Black silk
- Hackle: Black cock or starling's neck feather
- Wings: Pale starling tied flat on the back.
               The wings may be omitted if a hackled fly is preferred.

The Iron Blue
- Body: Stripped peacock quill dyed claret
- Wings: Cock blackbird or starling dyed inky blue
- Hackle: Dark blue dun cock hackle
- Tail whisks: Fibres of pale blue dun cock.
               The wings may be omitted if a hackled fly is preferred.

Then a No 14 Olive. Who could better Oliver Kite's Imperial? He fished as a guest of Mr Gerry Golding in 1967 and recorded one of the days in an article in *Shooting Times* of which the following is an extract:

'As I put my rod up, I noticed a fish rising only a few yards away. It must have seen us, but if it had, it was in no way disturbed. Presently, when I was ready, I pointed the trout's position out to my host, who invited me to try for it. The rule being dry fly only, at that time, I had on an Imperial, which was taken as soon as it dropped accurately in the teasing wind. The trout promptly tore across the wide river and fought it out under the far bank. A strong fish, this, and one I was delighted to net in due course, having made such an encouraging start.'

Kite's Imperial

- Working silk: Purple
- Tail: Honey dun
- Body: Three natural heron herls from a primary wing feather, ribbed with fine gold wire
- Thorax hump: Ends of heron herl doubled and redoubled
- Hackle: Honey dun cock

Of course one must carry a sedge. My favourite is a No 12 Red Sedge. Many fish have fallen to that fly, including:

'1978. June 14. Hungerford. 1 brown 1lb 10oz. 2 rainbows, 1lb 12oz and 3lb. All on a very fat Red Sedge.'

The Red Sedge

- Body: Red fur ribbed with fine gold wire
- Body hackle: Red cock
- Wings: Brown hen
- Shoulder hackle: Red cock

The wings of a sedge in the natural state, particularly of that large member the great red sedge, are large and prominent. This is one of the few flies which I prefer to fish winged rather than hackled.

Sedges are substantial. One must fish a good mouthful. Such a fly is the Grey Wulff which will do as well as any sedge in June, and then on through the season. Donald Macey is sure the Wulff is the fly for Hungerford and Bill agrees. In summer it may be fished from 9am (when fishing starts) to one hour after sunset and whether there is, or is not, a rise! I have watched and followed Bill up the river. He drops the Wulff tight below the edge of his bank. Trout live beneath the overhang. He tempts them out. The Wulff is versatile — a large one on a No 10 hook does very well as a mayfly.

The Grey Wulff

- Body: Blue/grey fur
- Wings: Brown bucktail, divided and sloping forward
- Hackle: Blue dun cock
- Tail: Brown bucktail

The large Wulff and the mayfly already described have a further use. If a trout is 'on the fin' you may catch him on what he is eating. The trout which is deep, half asleep and clearly uninterested in food may be woken by the thump of a fat fly dropped just behind his head. He may react and take.

I add one more fly for luck, a tested local fly. Terry's Terror is described by Peter Deane in John Veniard's *Further Guide to Fly Dressing*.

'This wonderful fly was devised by that first-class fisherman Dr Cecil Terry of Bath, the doyen of Hungerford, and the late Ernest Lock of Andover.

Terry's Terror
- Hook: No 12
- Body: Bronze peacock herl — one strand only
- Rib: Fine flat copper tinsel
- Tail: Equal parts of orange and yellow goat hair, cut short to make a stiff tag
- Hackle: Medium red game.'

The lunch and the afternoon

Enthusiastic description of the fishing has caused me to digress from 4 July. Bill, Tony and I met Donald Macey at the John O'Gaunt for lunch. Donald told us of trout purchased from Dave Walford, the Laverstoke Head Keeper on the Test, which are being fed-on in the pool below Bracket's hatch; of the floods and gales of the 1989-90 winter, and showed us photographs of the Kennet and Dunn joined by flood water. We heard of early solid-tyred fire engines, and his family's long service to the town as Constable, and taking their turn as Tutti men as the decades passed.

After lunch Tony and I fished the meadows below Denford Mill. We lost three brown trout which came off barbless hooks and released three more. It was a good day.

The River Lambourn

(See map, page 122)

The river rises, or used to rise before it became reduced, between the villages of Upper Lambourn and Lambourn. It flows for approximately 12 miles in a south-easterly direction, passing through a number of picturesque villages, including Bagnor, the home of Sir Michael Hordern. Within a few yards of his house it is joined from the north by a much depleted brook, the Winterbourne. At Newbury it flows into the river Kennet.

Trout Fishing

Sir Michael Hordern CBE — Rod at Bagnor Manor

'I can remember my first fish absolutely clearly. I was five years-old. I was with my elder brother with whom I still fish. He is now 85 and was fishing the Wylye yesterday, but didn't catch anything worth keeping. We lived in Hertfordshire, at Berkhamsted, where he took me down to the canal. There was a bunch of rushes upstream, or rather, above me, for there was no current. I saw my float go down and slide away. My brother shouted at me. Up came a little roach, $4^1/_2$in in length. I was so proud that I burst into tears. I often shed tears when I caught something. My brother had been fishing on a trout stream with his godfather, and had seen undersized trout put back. He made me return my fish, when all I wanted to do was to take it home to show my mother, and put it in the greenhouse tank.'

'Do you remember your first trout?'

'Yes, I do, by God. It came from a little pond on a wealthy property in Sussex, I believe just after the Great War. There have been so many wars, it is hard to remember which one. The pond was in the woods. They had put in some fish, including a dozen trout. I was fishing with bread paste, or a worm, expecting to catch a little carp or something else. I caught this unfamiliar fish and took it back to the house. There was a terrible row. It was one of the 12. I tried to revive it in the bath, but it expired.'

In 1921 his family moved to Dartmoor. There, Michael fished in the Webburn for trout with a worm before progressing to the fly. At the age of 21 years he caught Polio and became paralysed down one side.

'I asked Dr Ironside, a lady, if I might go out to fish for salmon. It was the last day of the season. She was reluctant, but agreed that I might go if accompanied by my mother who knew nothing about salmon. We went to Dartmeet to struggle up the West Dart. I limped past Queenie Pool to Coombe Weir and there, by God, I hooked a salmon. It played me. After a while it came in to my feet and my mother gave me the gaff. It decided to have another run and swam out slowly to the middle of the pool. It never came back!'

Forty years ago Sir Michael became a member of The Piscatorial Society which had fishing on the Lambourn, which it subsequently relinquished. He purchased a house close to the river in the 1950s, and thus began a close association with this small tributary of the Kennet. Over the years he has seen a marked deterioration in the river, and considers this is due to reduced flows caused by abstraction, trout farms which allow rainbow trout to escape, and the replacement of the larder by the deep freeze.

'Anglers fill their freezers. I am ashamed to say I have a trout in my freezer from last season. By now it will not be worth eating. Before the age of the freezer you took what you could eat, and returned the rest.'

Abstraction has reduced the river to a shadow of its former self. The bed is usually dry at the head of the valley. Little weed grows in the depleted depth. Many rainbow trout escape from a trout farm, 'but I fish on private water which is beautifully looked after. Last winter Bruce, the keeper, electric fished to clear out rainbows and reduce the grayling. He does not stock. We have wild brown trout. Last year I caught my first on the Upper Water at the end of April on a dry Pheasant Tail. I returned him as an offering to the river.'

We discussed the fly life of the valley. Sir Michael: 'I am not an entomologist. I might be if the flies called out their names as they landed on the water.'

There is a heavy hatch of mayfly, followed by sedges and blue winged olive. Early season appearances are made by iron blue and large spring olive. There are no grannom. Michael relies substantially on the Pheasant Tail, both as a dry fly and a nymph, dressing them himself.

'I once had a nymph named after me: The Hordern Pheasant Tail. I tied them. There was nothing very special about that nymph, but perhaps it had a few extra whiskers. I gave one to a fellow member of The Piscatorial Society who passed it on to one of the Hardy brothers who wrote to me from Alnwick. He had experienced a wonderful day with my nymph on the Aln. Could he put my nymph in the Hardy catalogue? I replied that I would rather have such an honour than a knighthood. There it was, in the booklet, in colour, The Hordern Pheasant Tail Nymph. Subsequently The Queen knighted me, and Hardy took the nymph out of the catalogue.'

Sir Michael dresses most of his own flies which are usually hackled. We looked through three Wheatley boxes which he takes to the river. The contents covered all possible occasions, and every practical size from No 18 Iron Blue to No 10 Grey Wulff for the mayfly. There was a huge Spent Gnat. Kite's Imperial, Red Sedge, Lunn's Particular, Alder, Tup's Indispensable — all found a corner in a compartment, or a lifeless place, flat on the foam of the lid.

We then looked at his fishing diary:

> '1973. September 2. 3 trout. Mist. Afternoon. Many trout rising. Silver Witch, intended for grayling.
> '1973, September 3. 1 trout. 3 grayling. Warm and dull. Grayling caught on a large deep grayling bug, dressed by Kim Debenham, Head Keeper at Leckford on the Test at that time.'

In 1982 there was an entry:

> '4 trout. All returned. Blustery showers. 3pm to 6pm. Goodish mayfly hatch started at 5pm. Trout on to them at once. Could have kept my fish, but larder full as I had done well on the Avon the day before.'

'1964. May 31. Very hot. Thundery showers. Reported — there was a huge hatch of mayfly at 4pm in the thunderstorm. I arrived at 6pm in misty rain. Not a fly hatched or a fish rose.'

'I like to fish during a thunderstorm. Once, on the Kennet, during the mayfly, I cast as the thunder rolled — the trout went mad.'

'1989. May 29. Upper Water. Water full of good fish and all beautifully kept. On the river 5pm to 7.30pm. Heavy hatch of mayfly. Fish unwilling to take floating fly, either natural or artificial, but Straddle Bug Mayfly fished damp, or preferably very damp, fairly took them. I returned four, all between 1lb and 2lbs.'

At the end of the season he fishes for grayling until Christmas, using Red Tag, Silver Witch and Grayling Bug. I asked Sir Michael to comment on the deterioration in water flows down the Lambourn:

'The reduction in water volume over the 35 or more years I have been here has been tremendous. There is no comparison with its past state. One tries to think that the cause is lack of rainfall, but it obviously is not. It is abstraction of water. The Winterbourne, a small brook, joins the Lambourn just outside my house. It used to be full of trout. Now, two miles up the valley, it has ceased to flow. It is dry. There are no fish. It is the same at the top of the Lambourn — the river has gone. I doubt that my grandson, Nicholas Curzon, who is aged seven years, will ever see the Lambourn in good heart as has been my good fortune.'

29 April 1991

The River Allen

The Allen rises north of Wimborne St Giles in Dorset, flows south for about 13 convoluted miles to join the river Stour below Wimborne Minster. On the way it passes mainly through large estates where it is well preserved, the first of these being the Wimborne St Giles estate. The Allen is joined on the right bank by the Gussage Brook one mile above the Horton Inn at Stanbridge. I lived in Gussage All Saints for 15 years, the Brook flowed at the bottom of my garden, and I had the privilege of fishing the Upper Allen and the water belonging to the next estate — Crichel. The river then continues south past Witchampton, where there is an inoperative mill — one of eight mills on the Allen — and through the Gaunts estate. Below this is the High Hall water, followed by the National Trust and the town water of Wimborne. After passing through the grounds of Deans Court it joins the river Stour one mile below the town.

The Allen is a beautiful small chalk stream noted for clear water, although there is less of this vital commodity than in former years. It is well populated by wild and stocked brown trout. Salmon and sea trout enter the lower reaches, and used to spawn below Stanbridge before the over-abstraction of water reduced the flow, making their journey almost impossible. Other fish are also present, particularly in the lower reaches. In the last 20 years the river has been the victim of serious water abstraction. This depletion of the chalk aquifer and reduction of flow down the river gave rise to the formation of The River Allen Association, of which John Ashley-Cooper and Bill Humphreys were founder members. I served on the Committee for a few years at the invitation of Bill, who is the Hon Secretary, and attended the inaugural Meeting on 28 October 1972. The Association concerns itself with all matters bearing on the well-being of the river, and has spearheaded the fight against excessive pumping of water from the aquifer, and the export of the water to Bournemouth and its surrounding areas.

In an attempt to mitigate the depletion of the river, and return the flow to an acceptable level, augmentation boreholes were sunk above Wimborne St Giles at Wyke Down, and between Gussage All Saints and Gussage St Michael. These pump water from the aquifer and channel it into the Allen and Gussage Brook. A further stream support discharge was established above Crichel Lake, with doubtful benefit. These river augmentation arrangements were the work of Wessex Water. The pumpings have not prevented river flows reducing in times of drought to an unacceptable level. Bill commented in an article published in *The Field* (September 1990), that the flow had reduced on 31 October and 1 November 1989 to 1.5 million gallons a day (mgd): 'The sort of flow best described as coming out of a 9in drainpipe when full'. This is far below the minimum prescribed flow of 6mgd. At the same time 10mgd were being, or were licensed to be, abstracted!

For 20 years Bill has laboured to save the Allen, confronting water companies with unpalatable truths. He has drawn attention to lack of ranunculus, the stifling presence of blanket weed and silt, and the fact that fishing, at times, may take place in galoshes instead of thigh boots as in earlier seasons. His efforts are likely to bear fruit. With the assistance of Dr Terry Newman and Dr Richard Symons of the NRA, and Peter

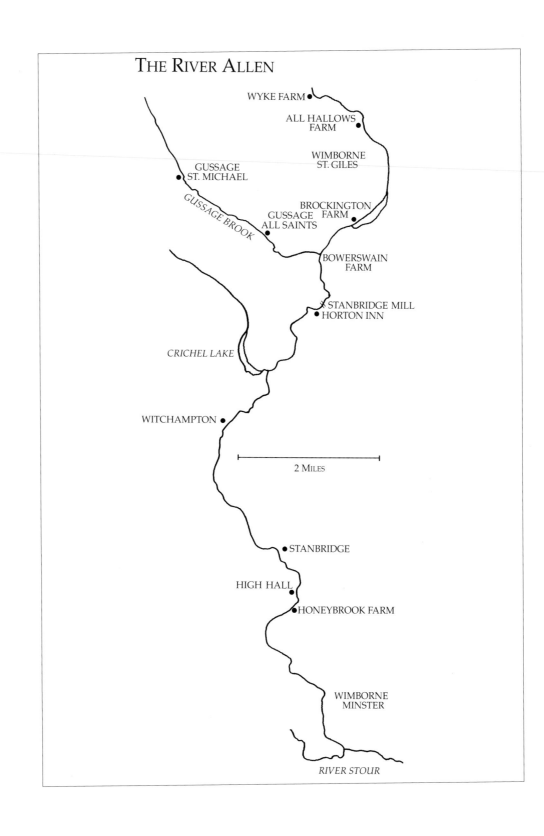

THE RIVER ALLEN

WYKE FARM ●

ALL HALLOWS
FARM ●

WIMBORNE
ST. GILES

GUSSAGE
ST. MICHAEL ●

GUSSAGE BROOK

BROCKINGTON
FARM ●

GUSSAGE
ALL SAINTS ●

BOWERSWAIN
FARM

✕ STANBRIDGE MILL
● HORTON INN

CRICHEL LAKE

WITCHAMPTON ●

2 MILES

● STANBRIDGE

HIGH HALL ●
● HONEYBROOK FARM

WIMBORNE
MINSTER

RIVER STOUR

Rippon and Robin Wardlaw of Groundwater Developments of Cambridge, the NRA is to spend £3.5 million in investigating, identifying and solving the river Allen reduced flow situation. The outlook is brighter!

Trout Fishing

Harry Teasdale — Fishery Manager, Upper Allen Fishery, and a Committee member of The River Allen Association

The beats and catches

Harry is head forester on the estate; he also looks after the physical well-being of the river and those who fish the beats. Necessary work is carried out by himself and the staff of the forestry department who help him with weed cutting and other tasks.

Progressing downstream from Wimborne St Giles there are three beats: Brockington, Bowerswaine (previously known as Stanbridge) and Crichel. Above these is the village water which provides additional fishing if any of the permanent beats are out of order.

Harry took over the management of the water from a syndicate in 1970. In that final year 84 trout were taken at an average weight of 14oz. The average catch for the three beats since that season has steadily increased to a total in the region of 500 fish averaging close to 2lb in weight. There was a slight reduction in the catch in 1989 and 1990 due to drought and the temporary closure of the Crichel beat. At the same time, rods staying in the area were allowed to fish the water running through the village of Wimborne St Giles. One rod fishes each beat on two or three-day lets, is issued with a map of the water and a return card. These cards eventually come to Harry who notes the catches in the estate record book.

The statutory season on the river is from 1 April-15 October. Upper Allen Fishery, and Gaunts Fishery lower down the river, delay their start until the final week of April, in common with the Crichel Estate. Gaunts closes early on 30 September, and after that date few people fish the Upper Allen water. I asked whether any rod had made a remarkable catch:

'One rod was named John Marshall. He started on a Saturday morning, only to find cattle had broken into his beat and were churning up the mud. The river was unfishable. He left and came back after taking lunch in the pub, only to find a couple of strangers with dogs walking down the river. They disturbed everything, splashing and chasing up and down despite being asked politely to leave. Again he was unable to fish. For the third time he went to his beat. It was evening. He went to the big pool at Stanbridge where he could see fish moving. Unable to see what they were taking he knotted on a little nymph, the smallest he could find. First cast, he was into a heavy fish which he landed. It weighed 4lb 1oz. He looked down its throat to see that it had been taking tiny nymphs which, by luck, he had imitated. The next large fish cruised by and, again, he took that first cast. He only made two chucks on all those expeditions. He wrote in the record book that night "Just a brace of four-pounders today".'

The Upper Allen records

YEAR	No of fish	Weight of largest	Average fish
1970	84	2lb 0oz	0lb 14oz
1971	186	3lb 4$\frac{1}{2}$oz	1lb 3$\frac{1}{2}$oz
1972	187	6lb 0oz	1lb 3$\frac{1}{4}$oz
1973	237	not noted	1lb 3$\frac{1}{5}$oz
1974	310	4lb 4oz	1lb 5oz
1975	326	4lb 10oz	1lb 4oz
1976	147	4lb 5oz	1lb 6oz
1977	178	2lb 14oz	1lb 5$\frac{1}{2}$oz
1978	231	2lb 14oz	1lb 5oz
1979	277	2lb 8oz	1lb 4$\frac{1}{3}$oz
1980	290	3lb 8oz	1lb 5$\frac{1}{8}$oz
1981	310	3lb 8oz	1lb 6$\frac{2}{3}$oz
1982	315	5lb 3oz	1lb 7$\frac{3}{4}$oz
1983	335	5lb 8oz	1lb 8$\frac{1}{2}$oz
1984	557	6lb 4oz	1lb 9$\frac{1}{5}$oz
1985	650	8lb 3oz	1lb 10$\frac{3}{5}$oz
1986	515	8lb 13oz	2lb 2$\frac{3}{4}$oz
1987	590	7lb 8oz	1lb 15$\frac{3}{4}$oz
1988	584	4lb 12oz	1lb 12oz
1989	384	5lb 8oz	2lb 4$\frac{3}{5}$oz
1990	468	5lb 4oz	2lb 3$\frac{3}{4}$oz

Fly life and artificials

All the normal natural flies are on the river, and they are imitated in the various stages of their life cycles by artificial dry flies and nymphs. Harry produced a list of the nymphs and artificials which had accounted for 1,226 fish, the total for the 1984 and 1985 seasons of which 19 were not noted on the return cards.

NYMPHS

Pheasant Tail	181
Olive	63
Various	54
Mayfly	12

DRY FLIES

Iron Blue dun	72
March Brown	9
Hawthorn	54
Black Gnat (early — large)	80
Black Gnat (midsummer — small)	87
Alder	54

Direct imitation Olives	— Large Dark — Small Dark — Medium — Pale Watery	} 152 (total)
Kite's Imperial		33
Tups Indispensable		32
Beacon Beige		7
Gold Ribbed Hare's Ear		35
Ginger Quill		23
Greenwell's Glory		24
Wickham's Fancy		7
Blue Upright		6
Sherry Spinner		9
Olive Spinner		10
Lunn's Particular		9
Houghton Ruby		5
Red Spinner		14
Pheasant Tail Spinner		7
Red Quill		2
Sedges — various		38
Mayfly		16
Blue Winged Olive		52
Blue Winged Olive Quill		9
Coch-y-Bondhu		13
Coachman		8
Rough Brown		5
Grey Wulff		10
White Wulff		3
Silver Wulff		3
Corixa		6
Chironomid larvae		5
Daddy Long-Legs		10
Grey Duster		7

A maximum hook size is not stipulated. 'The fishermen who come here don't have to be regulated in that way. They normally know pretty well what they are about. Some may lack experience, but I don't intrude to help unless I am asked.'

The river has never had a mayfly hatch of any consequence, but on the Brockington beat there are flutters from time to time. 'The strange thing is that on the Kennet or the Itchen you can have mayfly up for a fortnight in May or June. On the Allen the hatch may start and stop and start again until July or August. This long hatch may have a historical background. There is evidence that some anglers tried to plant mayfly on the Brockington beat, bringing them from different rivers. If the mayfly hatches on those rivers took place in varied weeks, this might account for the long hatching period now experienced on the Allen.'

I commented that trout on the Kennet and Test often take three or four days to start feeding on mayfly after the hatch commences, possibly due to fear of so large an insect.

'If you are on the Kennet, and blue winged olive hatch at the same time as mayfly, the trout will take the Blue Winged Olive in preference to the larger fly. On the Allen there is no such hesitation — they are on the mayfly at once. I have known people catch a limit bag by 11am on Mayfly in July.'

Harry told me that William Lunn, appointed Head Keeper to the Houghton Club at Stockbridge in 1887, held that rows of poplars should be planted at right angles, and not parallel, to the river. This gave wind protection to mating mayfly which were able to perform their mating dance and return to the river to deposit the fertilized ova without being blown away. On the Upper Allen water a stand of poplars, planted in this manner at the turn of the century, may be seen at the bottom of the Brockington beat.

'What do you fish in stormy weather?'

'I go along with Courtney Williams. The Iron Blue is the fly. We used to have two hatches: the first in May, and the second of rather smaller flies at the end of September. I dress the first on No 15 hooks, and go down to No 16 for the autumn hatch. I don't fish our water very much, but I try to have a day or two at the end of the season. One morning at about 11 o'clock a hatch started. They were coming down in groups, continuously, one after the other, and all the fish were on the feed. It was the end of the season, and yet trout were everywhere. Now, I tie my own artificials using dyed mole's hair of an inky colour for the male fly, dubbing in a bit of orange seal's fur with the mole for the female. The flies coming down were males, so I knotted on a male fly. Not a fish offered. Nothing. Yet all the flies passing before my eyes were males. Then it dawned on me — the trout had eaten all the females. That was the most astute example of selective feeding I have seen.'

As another example of selectivity I mentioned that a friend of mine was watching a mayfly hatch one morning. Resting his rod he sat beside the river. Mayfly were coming down thick, in bunches, and the trout were feeding. He then noticed that those sucked from sight all had three tails. Damaged flies with two tails passed unmolested.

I enquired whether his trout were pink-fleshed due to eating shrimp.

'Yes. There is a heavy population of freshwater shrimp. At the top of the valley there is a compensation borehole to augment the water flowing down the river. Last year, due to mechanical faults, the pump failed nine times. As the borehole has stolen the water from the upper springs the river flow ceases at once if the pump stops. One weekend in late October it broke down and it took them 12 hours to repair the fault. The top end of the valley was full of spawning fish and there was no water. The trout were gasping, and we were considering netting them out. But the point I want to make is that every little remaining currentless pool was full of moving shrimp. They were panicking. They knew something was wrong. There were thousands, in fact millions of shrimp on the move.'

Artificials for the evening light

Harry considers that the evening light has a marked effect on fly fishing on rivers which flow east. On these the angler would be casting upstream and the fly would drift down towards the trout with the light behind the hackles from the sun sinking below the westerly horizon.

'When you have an east-flowing river the setting sun gives an orange tinge when shining through the wings of an artificial. An orange/brown wing enhances this light and the feathers acquire an extra glow. Red Sedge, Cinnamon Sedge and Orange Quill are great flies in the evening. I often think the sunset is the secret of the success of the Orange Quill. People say that it represents the blue winged olive, but if you look at the two flies against a white table cloth they are not alike. I think it is the sunset on the Orange Quill which does the trick. It doesn't work all the time, but more times than enough. It is a great little fly in the evening.'

Wildlife

A few unwanted mink come up the valley from the river Stour. On the way they have to pass through three well-keepered estates, and not many survive. In the mid-1960s otters were present. Harry saw the last otter whilst delivering Christmas trees on the estate:

'I had my four year-old daughter with me in the truck. We went over the bridge between the two watercress beds by All Hallowes Farm. Looking down the river we saw an otter surface, it looked at us, then popped off and went away. I can be certain of the date — it was Christmas 1968.'

Water voles are present. There used to be many at the Crichel end of the water until the banks were altered.

'I was on the Gaunts water one day with David. We crept up through the woods to a large pool where there was a mass of floating weed. A water vole sat there, on the raft, eating, his plump back towards us, the food clutched in his hands. David reached forward with his rod and tapped him on the shoulder. The vole looked around, but continued eating — he looked just like an absent-minded professor. It was not until David said "Excuse me, are we right for Witchampton?" that he dived.'

I asked whether a bat had ever taken his fly at dusk.

'No, but I have caught a number of swallows. Fortunately they can be released. In the old days, when rods had a spear in the butt, a friend stuck his into the ground and left the fly free in the wind at lunch time. A swallow took the fly. He released the bird, but let the fly go, and whilst showing us the swallow a second bird took. He unhooked them both and they flew away quite happily.'

He told me about kingfishers:

'I arrived at the overflow of the lake at the top of the Allen. A kingfisher had just dived in, but the turbulent water had tumbled him over. He swam downstream with the flow until he came to a small stick protruding from the bank just above the water. He managed to flap onto this, and sat there in a state of shock, trying to dry himself. He had obviously seen me but I waded down to him, thinking I might be able to put my finger under his chest, give a little push, and he might sit on the finger like a budgerigar. I reached him and he put one foot on my little finger before losing courage and flying off.'

Fly fishing tackle

For years he used a two-piece 8ft split cane rod named The Kestrel, which is one of The Falcon series made by two brothers in the Midlands. Two years ago he made up a kit rod of carbon fibre and caught a fish on it with the first cast. Close to his heart is an Allcock's rod, The Dalesman which he uses in high summer when fine nylon is necessary due to the clear water. 'Being a Dalesman myself it appeals to me. The action is so soft that I can use a 1lb point. No matter how hard I hit a fish on the strike that rod saves a break. It is of split cane, very old fashioned, and no good against the wind.'

His reels are small ancient Hardy Perfects.

'Those reels are beautiful. They take a No 3 or No 4 line, green in colour. I don't like white. If I had a white line I would dye it green with Dylon. On the Allen there are a lot of dark bushes; if you have a white line going to and fro against the background it scares the fish. White lines are alright on a reservoir where the background is the sky.'

The leader is 3yds in length and tapered to 4X or 5X for normal use. In high summer 6X is necessary. The strength may be increased slightly when fishing a sedge in the evening.

The weather

Little notice is taken of the barometer; whether it is rising or falling. Harry feels it is tempting, if the fishing is on your doorstep, and it is an unpleasant day, to wait for better weather. On the whole the finest days are not the best for fishing, even though it may be idyllic to be beside the river: warm, no breeze, sun in the sky and perfect for casting. 'I prefer a broken sky, dark cloud, a bit of blue here and there, and a breeze to ruffle the water. A mixed up sort of day. A mildly unpleasant day for the fisherman is usually a good one for taking trout. I'm slowly reaching the stage where the actual catching of fish is secondary to being there to stand and stare. People give up shooting because the killing shot is final. Fishing is different. Even at the peak of your success you can still play God and let the fish go.'

A late October day

I asked whether people fish for grayling on the lower sections of the river. Harry responded:

'Three years ago a few of us who fish the Gaunt's water had a little meeting at which we decided to give it a go. I went down to the Honeybrook end, where there is a little wood and a big deep bend with lily pads. I had seen grayling in that place. I caught three or four. Good fish they were, all just below 2lb. That was before I reached the lily pool where the river comes down in a right-hand curve. As I looked into the pool a fish or two rose to iron blue. Several fish then started feeding, and I thought "That's got to be a shoal of grayling". On the point was a barbless fly. I often fish barbless. Well I threw for the last fish in the shoal. First cast Bingo! Bang! Off he went like a shot. Eventually he was unhooked — a 3lb brown. I thought "That's odd, perhaps he was lying at the tail of the shoal". So I tried for the next fish. Another brown of almost the same size. I thought "Well, that's very odd, but I'll try one more". That was a trout as well, so I packed up, waded across the river and there, ahead, were 300yds of gravel covered over ankle deep with water. That is where they had come from. The whole population of that shallow stretch — trout in a line — had sought sanctuary in the lily pool.'

19 February 1991

Bill Humphreys — Tenant 1966-90, The Crichel Estate

History

In 1966 John Ashley-Cooper invited Bill to join him on the Crichel water. Since then he has looked after and fished that stretch for 25 years, for four or five of which I joined him as one of a few rods. Downhearted by the desperate conditions resulting from diminished flows, he gave up his tenancy in 1990.

The fish population and coarse fish control

The Crichel water is just over one mile in length, and is well stocked with wild free-spawning trout and those which are introduced. The Allen trout is a bold deep fish of a yellow green colour with large red spots. Stocked brown trout acquire these natural shades after being in the river for two or three years, which period is quite possible due to a light fishing demand on this water. The system of trout stocking was finely calculated and based upon factual evidence. In early March the water is electric fished to remove pike and grayling; at the same time the turned-up trout are counted. This survey may be subject to an error of about 10%. In 1984 the trout count was 252 fish. In the years 1984 to 1986 inclusive, 320 trout were stocked at a length of 12in. In those three years the rod catch amounted to a total of 295 trout. In 1987 the trout count was 264, almost exactly equalling the 1984 population. All was thus stable, the fish in the water being capable of support by the food-producing capacity of the river. This was confirmed by the weight of trout caught by the rods which averaged just under $1^{1}/_{2}$lb a fish. This substantial weight reflected well on both the fishing policy and the fertility of the water, particularly as the river is mainly comprised of shallow runs without many deep hidey-holes for heavy fish. This picture of stability has not been maintained. As flows and conditions declined so did the electric-fish count. In March 1990 there were 163 trout observed, and when the Crichel estate electric-fished the water in 1991 the numbers were halved to 81.

Of passing interest, Bill mentioned that whilst electric fishing, an eel of 7lb had surfaced; it was removed to a gravel pit near Basingstoke where it lived for many years and eventually died. In addition, pike of up to 20lb have been taken from the water at Witchampton Mill. Really large trout are absent. A fish of $3^{1}/_{2}$lb would be remarkable, but those of $2^{1}/_{2}$lb are not uncommon.

The electric fishing having been completed, the river was stocked at the end of March, the fish being introduced along the whole beat. In this way the trout had a month to settle down and acclimatize themselves before the start of the fishing season.

Abstraction, having reduced depth and water flows, has made it difficult for migratory fish to enter the river. At one time, before excessive water pumping to Bournemouth and Poole, there was a good run of sea trout into the Crichel water in October, after the end of the season. In the early 1980s a high percentage of salmon redds in the Stour catchment were found in the lower reaches of the Allen, up to 40 redds being counted. Salmon are no longer able to run the river, and are spawning higher up the Stour. I asked Bill whether grayling are present:

'We never had grayling until about 1986 when, I believe, Wessex Water stocked the Stour below Wimborne and grayling came right up the Allen. At the bottom of the river is a coarse fishery owned by the National Trust and let to Wimborne Anglers. A grayling which held the British record for some time, weight 3lb 10oz,

Top: The river Lambourn – The Mill House at Boxford.
Bottom: The river Lambourn – Sir Michael Hordern at Bagnor Manor water.

The river Allen at Stanbridge.

Top: The Peacock Bridge over the Frome at Frampton Court. The bridge was designed by Sir Christopher Wren.
Bottom: The river Frome, Lulworth Castle estate water above the Bunny Bridge at Bindon Abbey.

Top and bottom: The river Piddle near Tolpuddle.

was caught on 28 August 1983 by Ian White on the Allen. It is set up in a tackle shop in the town.'

When Bill took over the Crichel water there were considerable numbers of coarse fish, including some large-sized chub. When electric fishing, these fish were saved, put in tanks and taken down the river with the approval of the Water Authority. The River Allen Association now has its own electric fishing boat which may be used if required. In the early years 30 pike might be removed each season. Today only about half-a-dozen are found and, other than grayling, trout have the upper waters to themselves.

'Do crayfish still inhabit the water?'

'Yes. Twenty-five years ago you couldn't move a bit of weed without finding crayfish. They have reduced and take a bit of finding, but they are still there.'

I was glad to have his assurance on this matter because many chalk streams are now denuded of crayfish. In addition there was a personal interest. When I was one of Bill's rods we operated three pike traps which were inspected every other day on a rota basis between the rods. For some reason the timetable went astray, the traps were not visited for 10 days and in one a pike died. Being first on the scene after this interval I found three dozen crayfish feeding off the pike. These were released with the exception of five or six which I put in a bucket of water. After a short talk on crayfish, and a demonstration of the contents of the bucket to the pupils at Witchampton village school, these also were returned to the river. The crayfish is beneficial. If a bird, fish or animal dies in the river the crayfish acts as dustman!

The fishing

The trout fisheries on the Allen open in the final week of April. At this time a prolific hatch of hawthorn is in full swing. The usual insect sequence follows: olives, blue winged olives, sedges, and the iron blue on rough days in spring and autumn. I asked Bill to name his preferred artificials:

'For rough water and fast runs I go for a Gold Ribbed Hare's Ear. It is an excellent fly. Also Beacon Beige, an olive dun imitation.'

I asked about nymphs:

'We have no rule about nymphs, neither do we use them. It is just our custom. Of course, if you're taking out a guest on a difficult day, one might feel obliged to fall from grace and put on a nymph.'

'Do you have any mayfly?'

'When I first started they were entirely absent. Then, about 1982, they began to appear. Perhaps this was due to lower water levels resulting from abstraction, and the increased deposition of silt which mayfly favour in their life cycle. In recent seasons one might see three or four dozen in a day.'

We continued to talk about flies:

'Spinners don't seem to work for us, but sedges do, throughout the day. Then there is the Caperer, a great fly, particularly at dusk.'

I asked whether he is careful about stalking trout, creeping along the bank, or took to the river to work upstream:

'I think the most enjoyable fishing I had, when the river was in good condition, was in shorts and gym shoes. Working up in that manner, keeping close to the bank, one only needed to cover 200yds to experience a very good morning's fishing.'

Weed cutting and dams

After 25 years on the river Bill considers that correct weed cutting is the key to successful management on the Allen. If cut too early fly life is damaged; if too late the ranunculus does not flourish. Ideally, weed must be cut lightly on several occasions, both to channel the flow from bank to bank, and provide shallow runs between pools. Scoured areas must be kept scoured. A central weed-free channel is always to be avoided.

In addition, hollow concrete blocks were formed into small dams held in place by hazel sticks. Experience showed that one dam, about one-third across the river and placed at 30° is best, but in shallow runs a pair from each bank leaving a 2ft gap between is effective. If one dam of the pair is slightly below the other, a pool will be scoured below the gap. Dams are generally moved in the autumn when flows rise, to avoid damage to the banks and comply with Water Authority requests.

Fishing tackle

Bill has always fished the Allen with a Hardy Sussex brook rod, made in 1934 and then costing £4 10s 6d.

'Because just a few of us fish, and we know the river very well, we try to make it difficult for ourselves, and even more difficult for our guests! To this end we leave more overhanging branches than would be welcome in most places.'

This little rod is matched to a DT5F line and a tapered leader with a 2lb point.

'I am particular about my leader. It must be fine because the water is so clear. It is true that I lose a fish or two in the weeds, but no doubt they would be lost even on a 4lb point. Hauling trout out of weeds rarely works.'

Wildlife and birds

'One of the seasonal appearances which gives me the greatest pleasure is the June hatching of the Scarlet Tiger Dominula. That is a wonderful sight as it goes up and down the river.'

'What is a Scarlet Tiger Dominula?'

'A moth.'

'Good Lord. That is a relief!'

There are all the usual birds on the Crichel water, and of recent years the valley is visited by osprey and hen harrier. Sedge and reed warblers are not as common as they used to be. Mute swans have increased and are a nuisance, tearing up and scattering weed.

The tale of two trout

As we sat in Bill's drawing room I recalled the time when I had fallen from grace, at least by Crichel standards, by the use of the nymph. The incident is recorded in my fishing diary of 1971.

> *'River Allen. In June I caught a brown of 1lb 11oz on a Caperer at dusk above the lake outflow. In August, on a Pheasant Tail nymph, a trout of 2lb 6oz by the blackberry bush above the paper mill at 8.30pm.'*

Both of these trout were wild, tough and educated. This was particularly so of the blackberry bush fish whose retreat was below the brambles which overhung the bank.

I spotted him one evening, but he saw me and glided into the blackberry hole. A week passed; it was again my turn to fish. The approach was made from downstream. Dim in outline, there he rested, 2ft down. A dry fly would be no use, being mostly wings and legs. He would decline to stir his fins to lift his bulk to the surface for such an unsustaining mouthful. It would be beneath his dignity. On my knees I tied on the Pheasant Tail nymph, the one with the twist of copper wire beneath the pheasant fibres. Swish, swoosh went the almost horizontal rod but, just before the nymph plopped in, he moved. Yard by yard he strolled upstream. I scrabbled forward on my knees. Around the corner the alderman departed. In desperation, to his position blind, I pitched the nymph. All now stilled. Out of sight, beyond the bend, my offering sank. I waited, then twitched the line towards the rod tip, and lo, the line twitched back! I stumbled along the bank. He splashed and splurged and was, no doubt, most cross, but failed to reach the blackberry bush. That, as they say, was that.

The presence of the lake outflow trout was not suspected. The day had been full; now it was almost dark. Sedge hour had arrived. Bats jiggered above the water beneath a canopy of trees and the dark silent river snaked into the distance. The fall of night is the hour of the mysterious wallop and the widening wave. Seated beneath a tree with my back to the trunk I watched the water whilst knotting a Caperer to the cast. Then there was a rise, a small one the size of a raindrop, in a black passage between the fronds of weed which swayed in the current. How disappointing — it would be that large and lazy chub which occupied the place, looked at my fly from time to time, but never disturbed me or himself by taking. Time to teach him a lesson as his caution fled with the approach of night. By the mercy of St Peter the fly alighted just right, drifted down and was recovered. He was at it again. Next time there was a little bulge, the fly was sucked into a dark vortex, and a bubble the size of a walnut shell drifted on the surface. The rod arched over and I knew I had him solid, and so I did, the trout, but the chub may just have smiled and gone away.

19 February 1991

The River Frome & River Cerne

Description of the rivers

The Frome starts off as a series of tributaries up in the Cattistock and Hooke areas; the river Hooke joining the Frome at Maiden Newton. The river Cerne runs down through Cerne Abbas and joins the Frome just above Dorchester. The areas upstream of Dorchester are good for trout, and much of the water is fished by the Dorchester Fishing Club. Christopher Pope has water at Stratton, and above him there are various private owners. In these upper reaches the river is narrow and clear, with a stock of brown trout — a typical small chalk stream.

At Dorchester there is a large sewage works at Loud's Mill which discharges into the river. From that point on there is some evidence of man's effect on the river. Trout continue as the main quarry for several miles until the river reaches the Moreton Estate.

Below Moreton, salmon fishing predominates down to the sea at Wareham where the first of the proper salmon beats above the tide starts at the railway bridge and runs up past East Holme Priory. Above Wareham there is a salmon counter, but there is no major obstruction on the river until the hatches are reached at Bindon Abbey just downstream of Wool.

The runs of salmon

The salmon season on the Frome opens on 1 March and closes on 30 September; sea trout commence on 15 April and continue to 31 October; trout 1 April-15 October. Salmon spawn over almost all of the river below Dorchester, and even as far downstream as Holmebridge which is only a few miles above the sea.

One has to be careful about kelts of which there are a great number in the river when the season opens. There is a pool known as Kelt Alley which, if fished in bright weather on opening day, may yield four or five well mended kelts. Sadly, every season, a number of these are killed by anglers who are just starting their fishing careers and do not have the experience to make a correct identification.

Bright days seem to suit the river which runs almost due east in the salmon areas downstream of Dorchester. Although the river has many twists and turns, there is the advantage that it is rare for fish to be facing the sun.

The river had a reputation for large spring salmon. In the 1920s, when these multi-sea-winter fish were dominant in the salmon population, fishing took place largely in the spring. Then, 40 or 50 fish of 20-30lb would be caught in March and April. Few anglers visited the river in summer. Today, there are still a few large spring salmon, perhaps four or five being caught in March, but the emphasis has shifted to summer runs of grilse. Salmon runs have settled in recent seasons into the following pattern:

- Up to the end of April a small run of fish weighing between 20-30lb;
- May — 12-18lb in slightly greater numbers;
- June — 10-12lb;
- July onwards — grilse arrive at weights of 4-7lb.
- In September some of the long term residents, heavy cock springers and black hens, become active.

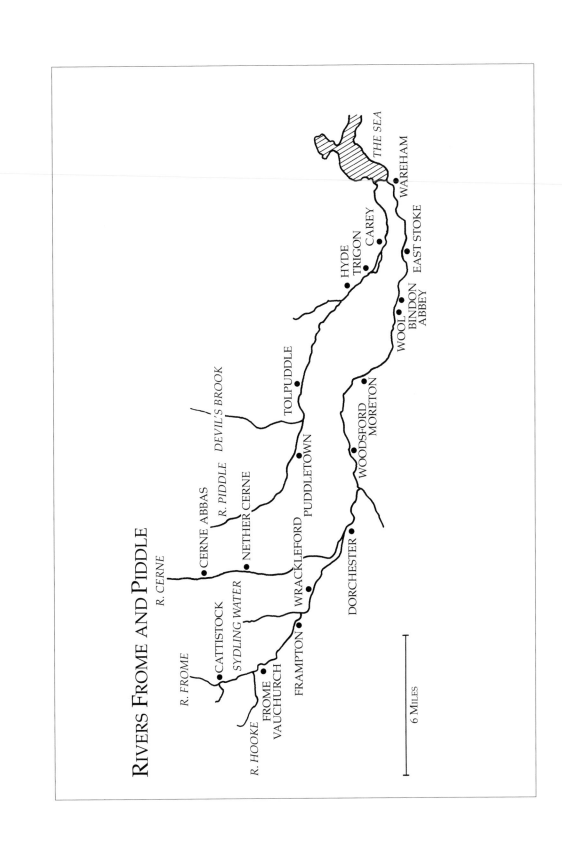

RIVERS FROME AND PIDDLE

R. CERNE

R. FROME

CATTISTOCK

SYDLING WATER

CERNE ABBAS

R. PIDDLE

DEVIL'S BROOK

NETHER CERNE

R. HOOKE

FROME
VAUCHURCH

FRAMPTON

WRACKLEFORD

PUDDLETOWN

TOLPUDDLE

DORCHESTER

WOODSFORD

MORETON

HYDE

TRIGON

CAREY

WOOL

BINDON
ABBEY

EAST STOKE

WAREHAM

THE SEA

6 MILES

There is a fish counter on the lower reaches. This has shown that the salmon entry averages between 2-3,000 fish, of which 4-600 may be caught. This is a healthy ratio, but the authorities would like to see an increased number of three-sea-winter salmon arrive in spring. To encourage this it might be wise to start angling at a later date in March, and introduce as parr or smolts progeny of this category of salmon.

The river is alkaline, there is good feeding, and many parr smoltify after one year instead of the two years common in many other rivers. This may be the reason why they spend a longer time at sea than is the case with the fish of acid rivers, and thus return at heavier weights. Whilst the run of salmon is, at present, satisfactory in numbers, constant attention must be given to the possibility of silt clogging the spawning beds which may, in future, have to be raked between Moreton and Wool. There is an army tank testing ground at Bovington, a large area devoid of vegetation from which, despite precautions, fine silt finds its way into the river when it rains. Abstraction of water reduces the flow which used to wash away silt, and increased deposition arises from the run-off of rain from ploughed-up water meadows. The level on the river during my visit in mid-April was the height which would have been expected at the end of May 20 years ago. Grayling are sensitive to pollution and their populations are decreasing on the Frome.

Trout Fishing

Godfrey Gallia — Riparian Owner and Rod, the upper river Frome and the river Cerne

Godfrey lives at Nether Cerne Manor which is partly Georgian and partly 17th century. The house stands three or four miles below the source of the Cerne above Up Cerne and Cerne Abbas. The river runs through the garden and the land, of which he farms 1,300 acres. Godfrey keepers the river himself, the water being fished for brown trout by guests. It is a superb small chalk stream whose springs above Cerne Abbas continue to flow throughout the summer, although the rate reduces as the season progresses. He cuts his own weed, but has not done so after the mayfly in the last two dry seasons because lack of cover in low water would increase the heron kill of trout. There are no pike.

Godfrey rarely fishes the Cerne himself until the end of July, and then continues through August in that most enjoyable pursuit — stalking individual fish. Sometimes he mops up a few trout after his guests at the end of the mayfly.

He also takes a rod on the river Frome at Frampton, above which the fish population is solely wild trout. Below Frampton there are still wild trout, but the river is also stocked. There are no grayling in the upper river which is maintained by riparian owners, tenants and part-time keepers. Godfrey believes there to be no full-time keeper on the river, many parts of the upper waters being tragically derelict.

Grannom are the first flies to appear on the Frome, but are not seen on the Cerne. Hawthorn are present in the valleys of both rivers, as are mayfly for three weeks up to about 20 June, and all the usual olives put in an appearance. There are prolific hatches of blue winged olive, and many caddis cases are visible on the river bed in summer. If a trout is caught in June the cases may be felt crumbling if the stomach of the fish is squeezed after it is dispatched. I asked Godfrey his favourite evening flies when the blue winged olive is on the water:

'I like a small Grey Wulff on a No 14 hook. The Red Sedge also works. Their performances are improved if given an illicit twitch!'

Very traditional in his approach, he prefers split cane for trout fishing and considers that the finest fly line is the silk Kingfisher now, sadly, unobtainable. He has many ancient fly reels, and other tackle, in a rather jumbled state in a huge canvas Bos bag: Marquis salmon reels, a St George, wading socks, two $3^1/_8$in Perfects, a 4in Silex Major and a tiny St George Junior.

Godfrey's wife, Sylvia, who also fishes, produced the fishing diary of her father, Edward Walker. In 1943, on the Frome at Frome Vauchurch, he caught a total of 196 trout with a weight of 106lb 2oz, showing that wild trout in those days averaged just over $^1/_2$lb. This size is confirmed by the 1944 entry. The season total for 59 days was 181 with a weight of 102lb 5oz, with the following fish over one pound in weight:

MONTH	WEIGHT	MONTH	WEIGHT
24 April	1lb 0oz	8 June	1lb 5oz
5 May	1lb 2oz	14 August	1lb 7oz
13 May	1lb 2oz	18 August	1lb 6oz
23 May	1lb 2oz	6 September	1lb 1oz
24 May	1lb 0oz	21 September	1lb 0oz
1 June	1lb 1oz	23 September	1lb 0oz
6 June	1lb 0oz		

Godfrey: 'If I went to Vauchurch today for an evening with the Blue Winged Olive I would expect to come back with three or four trout averaging an Irish pound in weight.'

It is clear that the size of wild trout has increased over the years. In 1988 on 10 June, on the lower Frampton beat, Godfrey caught three fish, each weighing over 1lb.

'To what do you attribute this increase in the weight of wild trout?'

'I don't know. It may be due to the extra by-products of a growing human population finding their way into the river. This might increase the nutrients available to plants and fish.'

Again, in 1988, on 27 June when there was not a fly on the water he took four trout weighing 3lb 3oz, the largest being 14oz. There is also the diary entry:

'*15th August 1988. Frampton. Blue winged olive on the water. Best $1^1/_4$lb out of 3 trout weighing a total of 3lb 3oz. I was fishing in the morning but couldn't make out what they were on. Tried a Black Gnat — failed. Got them on a Ginger Sedge and a BWO. However, they were full of black flies. Found several more beauties and proposed to return for them in the evening, but the Council Meeting went on too long.*'

This was followed by:

'22 August 1988. 2 trout, 1lb each in the morning. In the evening, went for the whopper and ended up hooking him beautifully at last light. I got the line around the butt of the rod, and our ways parted. Kept waking up all night — losing him.'

On the Cerne, by the house, the 1991 catch to the time of my visit included 16 fish of over 1lb, out of a total of 25 trout, all of them being caught on Mayfly. The rods are guests of the house, but Godfrey gives away several days to The Salmon & Trout Association for their annual auction, the proceeds going to game fishing improvements.

Historically, the Walkers and Gallias had a family fly, often dressed by Sylvia, the hackled Red Quill Bumble. On a No 16 hook, this has a peacock herl body, a red tag and a single turn of olive hackle.

Wildlife

I asked about the wildlife of the Cerne valley. Godfrey sees a number of hobbies and has witnessed them taking mayflies: 'They catch them in their talons and eat them in the air, holding the insect just as one would a banana'. The osprey visits, and twice a Cetti's Warbler in past years, a Black Tern and a Little Bittern have also been seen. Salmon spawn in the Cerne in the Charminster area, but only one has been seen higher up at Godmaston, and that fish was a grilse found dead on the bank, probably killed by a mink.

Later in the day we went over to visit Hugo Wood Homer who kindly showed me three specimen fish in his house. The first was a carved salmon mounted on a board. The inscription read:

'Salmon. Caught river Piddle 1st July 1931 by G.C. Wood Homer. Weight 40lbs. Length 46³/₄ins.'

G.C. Wood Homer being Hugo's father.

There was also a vast cased trout caught by his grandfather. Behind the glass is a newspaper cutting:

1907. FISHING RECORD

'12³/₄lbs trout caught with a dry fly, landed in a clothes basket. The Reverend S.E.V. Filleul of All Saints Rectory, Dorchester has just achieved a record in dry fly fishing, catching in the river Frome a trout weighing 12³/₄lbs. Mr Filleul was using a small Hare's Ear on a No 0 hook (about ³/₈in in size) and the finest tackle. It took an hour and a quarter to play the fish which was landed in a clothes basket. The fish, which was in splendid condition, was 29¹/₄ins long and 18¹/₂ins in girth.'

The largest salmon in the house was truly enormous. It was taken from the Frome by Hugo's father. The inscription reads:

'Taken at Rushton Pool by G.C. Wood Homer. April 12th 1925. Weight 47¹/₂lbs, length 49ins, girth 27¹/₂ins.'

I asked Godfrey to compare these with the first fish he had caught in his life:

'I was aged 11 years and went fishing in the Windrush with my sister. We caught a minnow which was, I suppose, the first fish. We still come to blows over whether it was mine or hers. But, with the minnow as bait, I caught my first trout which weighed 2³/₄lb.'

10 June 1991

Salmon Fishing

Chris Rothwell — Land Agent, The Lulworth Castle Estate
For 20 years Secretary of the Frome, Piddle and West Dorset Fishery Association. Presently, Chairman of the Wessex Regional Fishery Advisory Committee of the National Rivers Authority and a member of the Regional Advisory Board.

His personal fishing history
He started as a boy aged 12 years, in Cumbria, fishing the tarns for trout, and the river Crake, which is a tributary of the Leven. At the age of 14 years his father gave him a steel-centred 12ft split cane salmon rod by Hardy — the A.H.E. Wood No 2, and a St John reel. He still has them! Various expeditions to the Dee at Ballater and other rivers followed. The first salmon came from the river Exe, not far below The Fisherman's Cot water at Bickleigh:

'I was spinning with a Brown & Gold minnow. A chap walked by and I stopped to talk to him, but left the minnow hanging downstream in the river. After a while he walked on and I started to reel in. The bait wouldn't move. I yanked from upstream with no result. I tried from downstream. At first the bait did not shift, but then moved off across the river. I called to my acquaintance who returned to watch me land a salmon of 13¹/₂lb.'

Chris's largest sea trout from the Frome weighed 15¹/₂lb and his best salmon 28lb.

Fly and spinning tackle
We met at 10am on the river at Bindon Abbey. Chris was tackling-up whilst wearing a pair of unusual spectacles. These had polarized main lenses, below which were small lenses of clear glass of 2X magnification for tying knots.

First out of the car was an old brass ferruled 9ft tubular fibreglass spinning rod — an ideal length for the Frome. Known as the Dorchester, the rod was equipped with a Daiwa AB 1650 fixed spool reel accommodating 120yds of 18lb Maxima monofilament. This main line led to a lead substitute Wye weight of approximately ¹/₂oz. Beyond this, the 3ft trace was of the same 18lb nylon. He chose a 2¹/₄in blue and silver metal Devon minnow, adorned on the flanks with pink spots — a bilious bait! He chooses metal in early spring, when there is plenty of water and the temperature is low, for the weight of the bait assists deep fishing. Towards the end of May a plastic or wooden minnow is preferred. Mepps spoons are also used. In summer a No 2 Mepps Aglia is cast upstream and reeled back quickly. In April a No 4 may be fished downstream, followed by the medium sized No 3 in May. So large a Mepps for downstream spinning is justified by coloured water. On our day the river was a cloudy green shade but not muddy, and there was a prolific hatch of grannom.

He then assembled a three-piece 15ft fly rod of carbon fibre and the $3^7/8$in Hardy St John reel which held a brown slow sinking fly line. This was the reel given to him in 1947 by his father, at which time it probably cost £2 10s. I, myself, purchased the same reel from the Hardy shop in Pall Mall in 1958 at a cost of £5 plus Purchase tax, and the reel is still in use. Today, the St John remains in production and sells for £69.50.

The chosen fly was a 2in brass black and yellow polythene-lined tube at the end of a 7ft leader of 16lb monofilament. A rod of 15ft may seem excessive for the Frome which is a narrow river, but that length is well matched to a heavy brass tube fly. A short rod of 12ft is adequate when fishing small flies off a floating fly line in summer. In the mid-season months Chris favours a No 8 Shrimp Fly and, occasionally, a No 6 or No 8 General Practitioner. His shrimp has a black and yellow body, jungle cock wings and a tail of Red Ibis. In hot weather he sometimes uses a No 10 fly with a 10ft leader of 10lb breaking strain.

You ought to carry two rods when fishing the Frome: some of the water is suitable for the fly; other sections yield more to a spun artificial bait. Chris carries a haversack of tackle inside which is a small telescopic gaff which may not be used after the end of August when its place is taken by a net.

We left the cars and walked across a narrow bridge known as the Bunny which is on the Bindon Beat. My guide recalled an incident of fishing determination:

'You can see that there are two arches to the bridge, and a set of hatches 50yds below. Salmon lie just above the bridge. If you hook a fish, the best move is to try to walk it up to just below the willow trees 70yds upstream. Several years ago Lord Pembroke was prawning and hooked a fish which went down through one arch of the bridge and came back up through the other. He got through the first arch and managed to draw the fish down through the other, only to find that it shot past him and rushed through the hatches. He launched himself after the salmon and was washed through the hatches behind the fish. His troubles were not yet over. Having regained terra firma the line became entangled in brambles. He gaffed the line, cut out the tangled section, rejoined the line and landed the fish. The salmon weighed 11lb and the battle took 50 minutes.'

In summer fish may be discerned lying like grey torpedoes on their chosen places on the river bed. When fishing the fly off a floating line they can be seen moving off the lie to follow the fly and take: 'It needs a brave and steady man to watch and wait for the fish to complete his take before raising the rod'.

Fishing fly and spinning baits

Chris now moved 75yds up the river to fish down to the Bunny Bridge with his fly rod. I noticed that he held a loop of line below the handle of the rod. When a fish takes his fly fished deep off a sinking line he releases the loop on feeling the draw of the fish. When the loop has gone he traps the line under the forefinger of the hand up the rod which is then raised. Salmon have usually turned away by this time and are hooked in the scissors. He does not strike — all movements are slow and well timed.

Having fished down to the bridge with the fly he covered the water a second time with the Devon minnow. This was cast down and across in the conventional manner, but when the bait has swum three-quarters of the way back across the river Chris swings his rod upstream. This action puts a pronounced curve in the final few yards of the minnow's progress and is a tempting moment for salmon.

Having covered the water above the Bunny Bridge we walked downstream through a wood to fish the further three-quarters of a mile of the Bindon Beat. The pools are: The Run-in to the Railway, Bindon Rush, The Mayfly (a fine pool for spinning), The Return, The Potholes (re-christened The Feathers because the present Prince of Wales caught a salmon there).

In the fishing hut, which we visited after lunch, are paper cut-outs of salmon weighing over 30lb which came from The Run-in to the Railway. Chris: 'Before the line was electrified people used to fish a pool from the middle of the railway bridge. This was dangerous, and on one occasion a rod had to jump into the river to avoid being squashed. Rail strikes were popular with anglers!'

To a stranger these pools are hard to discern, for the river is spring fed and flows in stately uninterrupted fashion through meadows. There are no man-made groynes or rocky places. One stretch resembles the next, and thus one needs an habitué of the river to point out the lies. Chris has gained this knowledge over the seasons. 'I look for places where there is a bit of choke in the river forming a channel — salmon lie in the middle of those narrow places. They like the outside of a bend at the top of a pool, and just above the tail. Sometimes, if there is a back current on the inside bank they face into that current but are, of course, pointing down the river.'

In spring, salmon tend to move in stately fashion slowly up the river. One has to be lucky to place a fly in front of a passing fish, but on the Frome, if you do he will probably take, or at any rate have a look. It is normal to believe that running fish do not take, but this is more applicable to a spate river where a salmon is in a hurry to take advantage of the short-lived extra water.

We came to a place where a chunk of bank had collapsed into the river, forming the equivalent of a man-made groyne. We discussed where salmon would lie in relation to this protrusion. The conclusion reached was that fish would rest about 6ft downstream of the obstruction and as far out from the bank as the protrusion extended. We agreed that fish would not lie in the turbulence to the rear of the obstruction: 'Such places can be productive. But, as soon as one has learned the secret of the site, the floods of next winter carry the lie away.'

The narrowness of the river can cause problems where the two banks are fished by different teams. An angler preceding you down the river on the far bank will put down fish in advance of your arrival, thus spoiling your chance. He, of course, might feel you pressing on his back. The answer is to give him a wide berth and go further down the beat.

Chris started to fish, casting his fly down and across to the far bank. The advantage of a long rod was apparent in that, unlike the almost straight retrieve of a spinning bait, the fly could be manoeuvred. As the tube came into the 'dangle' position directly downstream he moved the rod out over the river; this caused the fly to move away from the bank and prolong those vital final seconds for the cast. I asked whether he stripped his fly fast across the river:

'I don't strip at this time of year when there is plenty of current, I am using a slow sinking line, and I want a deep slow movement. At the end of each cast I draw in a couple of yards. Having said that, I have a friend who fishes the river with a fast sinking line in March and April. He strips fast and takes many fish.

'In summer one needs to induce extra movement. I don't strip or back-up the fly, but I like to impart little jerky movements. Sometimes, when I have moved or pulled a fish, I hook one 20yds downstream. I think this is the same salmon.'

This idea of a pulled salmon moving back has been illustrated to me on the Test where twice I have seen a salmon pricked, and then taken from a lower position. One cannot be sure that they were the same salmon, but one has that belief.

Natural baits

Delaying his use of natural bait until July or August, Chris spins the prawn, obtaining them from the local fishmonger. The mount has a swivel at the head, two transparent plastic fins, a central spike and two trebles, one of which has a spike to press into the body of the prawn instead of a third hook. The mounted prawn is then wrapped around with a length of red elasticated cotton. Adding a $1/4$oz Wye weight 3ft above the bait he casts across the river and spins the prawn back in a slow retrieve. 'The prawn must be used with discretion. People who are not used to the bait may frighten the fish. They then think it is excited and going to take. They continue until the pool is in a turmoil. Those salmon then remain uncatchable for many days.'

There is an NRA bye-law which prohibits the use of prawn, shrimp and worm before 15 May. This is sensible, for the river fishes well with the fly until weed growth becomes heavy in summer — the prawn then becomes a useful bait.

'There are often deep channels between banks of weed. Salmon lie in those places. I cast beyond the channel, draw the bait quickly across the weed and then let it drop into the channel. If a salmon takes, all is well. If not, the problem is then to recover the bait from the deep sluice without hooking the ranunculus between you and the prawn. A long rod would be a help, but I rely on my 9ft Dorchester.'

'Do you rub your hands in earth to disguise the human smell before mounting the prawn?'

'No, but I have a habit which is individual to me. When I mount a new prawn I break up the old one into little pieces and throw them into the river. I believe salmon are attracted by the smell. After all, they can find a prawn in muddy water, and must do so by the aroma and not by sight.'

He continued:

'There seem to be two ways in which a fish takes a prawn. The first is like a little boy tugging at your sleeve to attract attention. There are usually two tugs at first. If followed by a third pull the rod goes down and you've got him. If there are only two tugs he has gone away. That is the way in the late season. Early on they attack with a great surge and hook themselves.'

In summer the water is often completely clear, enabling salmon to be seen through polarized spectacles. A prawn dangled in front of their mouths is tempting.

Time of day to fish

In March, April and the first half of May Chris finds the morning is better than the afternoon, although an early start is not necessary. When June is reached, and during July and August, the best times are early morning and late evening. He will then fish from 6am to 9am, and from 6pm until dusk. 'In the last two seasons of summer drought and hot water, the best time has been at dusk. Then, an apparently deserted river becomes alive with leaping salmon.'

Weed cutting

As we walked the river I counted 35 Mute Swans. These create problems for anglers by pulling up ranunculus. Chris:

'There is nothing more annoying than when one has seen a fish move, and are about to cover it with the fly fished off a floating line, and drifting weed catches on the line. The fly is then skidded away, frightening the salmon.'

Weed is cut by a paddle boat with a reciprocating mowing blade mounted in the bows. This is done by the flood defences department of the NRA to prevent flooding of the adjoining agricultural land. This has taken place for so many years that, although the Authority has no statutory duty to take angling interests into account, the anglers now feel they have a right to expect weed to be cut. This right is now acknowledged. Weed will be cut with angling interests in mind if the riparian owner visits the scene to make his suggestions known. His wishes, in the formation of weed bars and channels, will be taken into account provided they do not impinge upon the major duty of flood prevention.

Sea trout

There is a reasonable run into the Frome, and a catch of between 75-100 fish for the season. Large specimens arrive in spring, and sometimes may be seen taking mayfly of which there is a substantial hatch at the end of May and in early June. The main run of smaller sea trout enter from July onwards.

Unlike most West Country rivers, where fishing for sea trout is a night-time pursuit, this is not effective. Chris has fished for them many times in the dark, but without much success. The key is to fish by day with a small wet fly on a fine leader, searching out lies in shady places under bushes. Flies should have a jungle cock cheek and be dressed on No 10 or No 12 hooks. The Teal & Silver Blue is a fine attractor cast upstream and pulled back fast, as also is a small No 1 Mepp spoon.

The Fishing Hut

The hut is at the bottom of the Bindon Beat. On the walls are paper outlines of heavy salmon, with their descriptions:

'14 March 1959. C. Cecil. Potholes. 31lbs on a plug.'
'1 March 1950. Aylmer Tryon. Railway Pool. 30lbs. Fly.'
'21 March 1951. 33$^{1}/_{2}$lbs. Return Pool. Devon minnow.'
'11 June 1955. 30lbs. R. Heywood-Lonsdale. Corfe's Pool. Shrimp Fly.'

There was also a colour photograph of Aylmer Tryon holding a spring balance from which was suspended a very clean fish of over 20lb.

Extracts from Chris Rothwell's fishing diary

'1986 May 3. Frome. Salmon 12lb 8oz. Kelt Alley on a 2in. Black & Yellow tube fly. Small fish for time of year. Heard of 3 other fish being caught this week.
'1986. May 6. Frome. Salmon 28lb. (Biggest so far). Same 2in. Black & Yellow tube. Very fresh. Cock. 41in. Fish played from Railway Bridge to narrows.
'1986. May 13. Frome. Salmon 17$^{1}/_{2}$lb. Again same as above, below narrows on same fly. Dressed in suit after Common Rights case in Dorchester. Very lively fish. Net marks.

'1989 season. Opened by losing a fish (approx 14lb) in Kelt Alley on a 2^1/$_2$in Black & Yellow tube in mid April. Lost it bringing it to the gaff (short 3 stage gaff) for 2nd time; difficult to reach with 15ft fly rod.

'1989. April 29. Salmon 13^1/$_2$lb. Fishing as Aylmer's guest. 2^1/$_2$in Black & Yellow tube. Kelt Alley. Sunk line.

'1989. May 9. 2 salmon: 12^1/$_2$lb and 10lb. 12^1/$_2$lb fish at Bunny 7.45am on Shrimp fly. Walked up three times. 10lb fish in hole run out of Mill Pool. Rose on fly then took No 4 Mepp ^{1}/$_2$ hour later. First fish missed fly, jumped, then took 4 casts later further down pool.

'1989. June 27. Salmon. 11^1/$_2$lb. Prawn. New piles pool by hut. Too much weed. Lost another. End of long dry spell.'

Remarkable incident

Chris:

'In the days of long ago when I was fish hungry I used to go to the river early in the morning on my day. I wore office clothes and would leave the water at 8.50am for a rush to the office. As sure as fate I hooked a salmon at 8.45am. It weeded me, but could be seen tethered by the line. I jumped in and gaffed him, but couldn't lift him out. The river then swept me away, my antics, no doubt, delighting the passengers in a passing train. I threw my rod ashore but held on to the fish. I landed him, knocked him on the head, found my rod 30yds downstream and went home to change. I was late at the office, having been delayed, as I remarked, by some business on the estate.'

16 April 1991

The River Piddle

(See map, page 149)

Trout and Salmon Fishing

Richard Slocock — Wessex Fly Fishing, Tolpuddle, Dorset

Richard is the owner of a game fishing school which has fishing on the rivers Piddle and Frome, and three lakes stocked with rainbow trout. Lawrences Farm, his angling complex, has three letting cottages for the convenience of fishing pupils and those who come to fish his lakes and rivers. He has long experience of the Piddle and knows the river well from the source near Alton Pancras north of Dorchester to the mouth at Wareham.

Description of the river
The game fishing seasons on the Piddle are:
- Trout: 1 April-15 October
- Sea Trout: 15 April-31 October
- Salmon: 1 March-30 September

The river arose in a marsh area just north of Alton Pancras, but this land has dried due to water abstraction. A small rivulet is apparent in that village and flows quite vigorously through Piddletrenthide until it reaches Piddlehinton where it disappears beneath the ground in a dry summer. The stream reappears at Puddletown. Between Puddletown and Tolpuddle the river is joined from the north by the Devil's Brook. From this junction downstream the river is of a lettable size, and passes through Affpuddle, Briantspuddle and Turners Puddle where it turns south and the Army has a beat. It next passes through Culeaze Farm where Richard rents the fishing. It winds on through part of the Drax Estate where it is fished by a Royal Navy syndicate. The river is then joined from the north by the stable-flowing Bere Stream. The Hyde House water of 1 miles is next and there, below the house, is a fine waterfall. Richard held this water for a number of seasons and cleared the neglected banks to reveal many deep pools. On one occasion, 'without moving a foot in any direction I took, on mayfly, three wild brown trout in three casts, and each exceeded 2lb in weight. It was quite a revelation to me that a river left to itself often produces better wild trout than one where keepers toil away on various improvement schemes.'

In this area the course is through acid heathland where the water becomes tea stained in colour. Below Hyde House is Budden's Farm where gravel is extracted and superb scenery has been obliterated. The river then flows over a weir to the Trigon Farm and Carey Estates once owned by brothers of Richard's grandfather, and today owned by his cousins. At Trigon the river divides into two streams, which rejoin at Carey, and are fished by two small salmon and trout syndicates.

The salmon fishing at Trigon used to be good, with a catch of 30 or 40 fish a year. On 1 March in the mid-1980s Richard went to the lower Piddle, and at the top of the Carey beat saw an enormous salmon with a huge tail, as well as several other fresh fish. He walked upstream to the Trigon fishing hut. There he met members of the salmon syndicate whom he told of the fish. They hurried to the bottom of their water, hoping the salmon had moved upstream. This proved to be the case. The fish was hooked, took eight minutes to land, being tired after a journey straight from the sea, and weighed 35¾lb. There is a tracing of this fish on the floor of the fishing hut. As Richard said: 'This was really the fag-end of the heavy Frome and Piddle fish. The final wag of the tail.'

After Carey the river passes through Wareham where there is a little salmon syndicate run by the Water Authority in the tidal area.

Richard is on the Conservation and Water Resources Committee of the Salmon and Trout Association, and is also Branch Organiser for Dorset. He serves on the Water Committee of the Country Landowners' Association. These positions stem from the attack he made in 1985 on Wessex Water over a proposal to increase abstraction at Alton Pancras in addition to their major abstraction at Briantspuddle. The application to increase pumping was seen advertised in *The Western Gazette* by a most experienced angler, Robert Belgrave who, with Richard, spearheaded the opposition to this proposal. Robert became Chairman of the Frome, Piddle and West Dorset Fisheries Association into which has been absorbed The River Piddle Protection Association.

Richard's personal fishing history

His fishing career started at the age of six years when he suspended a mackerel line over the bridge near the mouth of the river Otter. The first rod was of solid glass and on this, and a Butcher, he hooked and hand-lined in a ½lb brown trout. Fishing holidays followed in the West Country on many rivers. The Otter, with its villages carrying the splendid names of Newton Poppleford and Tipton St Johns, became his hunting ground in the early 1960s for both trout and sea trout.

Salmon came next in the river Brora in Scotland where he purchased his tackle from Rob Wilson's shop. At the age of nine years he passed 10 blank days on the river in April. On the 11th morning he took two salmon of 6lb and 8lb on a Hairy Mary. Following an interlude in farming he came, in 1976, through a family connection, into possession of a length of the river Piddle at Tolpuddle.

The fishing business

In 1979 he established the fishing, tuition and holiday business, creating a lake and two pools to add to his river.

The Piddle is remarkable. Although small it is not unusual to connect with a wild brown trout of 3lb or even 4lb. At Lawrences Farm, his headquarters, he refers to the Piddle as a stream where, in the low water of summer, he maintains water levels and fishing spaces by cutting pockets in the weed rather than making channels and bars of weed. Lower down the river near Bere Regis he has an additional beat of two-thirds of a mile and there the water is of a reasonable width. Fishing is also taken on the upper Frome and on some excellent water on the Wrackleford Estate a short distance above Dorchester. He would like the NRA to be alert to who owns the river Frome sections and to advise and help with weed cutting problems rather than requesting, as at present, that owners give a week's notice of their intention to cut, this time lag being impractical at crucial times in the season, particularly May.

Richard does not let any salmon fishing. Ten or 15 years ago heavy fish were quite common on the lower Piddle, and I have, myself, gaffed a fish of 22lb for a friend at Carey, not far above the tide. For a while Richard fished there for salmon, using a map on which the lies had been marked by Hugo Wood Homer (*see page 152 — Godfrey Gallia, rivers Frome and Cerne*). In that area the river is narrow, being suited to the flicking-out of a Mepp spoon in the restricted spaces rather than casting a fly. Fish have been caught on fly and I have risen one or two where the river flows through open fields, but the flow is slow and there is much weed to obstruct the fly. In 1959 Hugo caught four salmon with 10 casts above the Carey weir. He described the event to me by letter:

> '*The four salmon on the Piddle were caught on 8 May 1959, on a spinner. In fact they were lying "shoulder-to-shoulder" in a small pool and could easily have been caught with four casts, but after each fish was landed I started a few yards further up and had two blank casts before hooking the next fish. They were therefore caught in 10 casts. The weights were 23½lb, 12lb, 11¾lb, and 9¾lb.*'

The catch then reduced to about half-a-dozen a season in the mid-1980s. One must hope that if efforts to reduce the abstraction of water succeed and flows increase, salmon will again enter in spring and summer. Fish still run the river in considerable numbers in the fuller water of autumn and winter. Spawning is successful as far up as Puddletown where they arrive by Christmas and depart by the third week of January. If the winter is markedly dry salmon may be unable to spawn above Cecily Bridge near Bere Regis.

The Piddle produces a few large sea trout which are usually caught accidentally by salmon anglers by day. Richard has a photograph of an outstanding specimen weighing 14lb which was caught at Carey. Due to prolific beds of ranunculus it is almost impossible to fish for sea trout by fly at night, and this style of angling is rarely pursued.

Trout fishing
When Richard started his fishing enterprise in 1981 some of the anglers caught beautiful wild brown trout from the Piddle weighing above ¾lb and brought them in — dead! He realized that so small a river could not sustain a commercial pressure without becoming 'put and take' which he thought undesirable. 'From that day forward, in my first season, I banned killing completely. Barbless hooks are the rule, or barbs pressed in by snipe-nosed pliers.'

Catch and release works well in April and May, but by June the trout have become crafty and rarely fall to other than the most skilled rods. 'At this time a few new faces may be stocked!'

There has been no problem with disease. Some trout grow old, reaching 3lb in weight and some lose condition. These residents will be removed.

'I'll tell you why the system works better on the Piddle than on other rivers. It is because, in truth, the river becomes low, weeded and almost unfishable by July. Our trout have a total rest until the following season; they only have to work for two or three months of the year.'

To release trout it is suggested that the fish be netted, placed on the bank in the net, held with wet hands through the meshes with little pressure whilst the hook is withdrawn, and then the net is turned inside out under water. Up to 10 fish may be caught and released in a day by each rod. There are no grayling in the water, but pike are present and have to be controlled. There is a steady population of crayfish.

Natural and artificial flies

The seasons starts with grannom. Large dark olives also hatch at the same time and are imitated by Greenwell's Glory or Beacon Beige. In early May, small spurwings and medium olives are represented by an Adam's. The mayfly follows and trout fall to Grey Wulff and the French Partridge hackled mayfly. Sedges come next; popular patterns being the little Red Sedge and small deer hair Goddard's. From the middle of June Richard suggests his anglers fish small flies on fine leaders, a No 18 Light Hendrickson being a good example.

Lawrences Farm is ideal for those wishing to learn the craft of chalk stream trout fishing on the smaller river, or take a relaxing fishing holiday in rural Dorset. For those in this latter category Richard is able to offer six days river trouting with a different beat on each day. There is also the chance of taking a rod to the lakes in the evening.
24 June 1991

The Grayling Society

Dr Ronald Broughton — Chairman

History

The Grayling Society was formed in the winter of 1977-78 at the instigation of R.V. (Reg) Righyni. He was an authority on salmon fishing on many rivers, including the Hampshire Avon, and wrote *Salmon Taking Times* and *Advanced Salmon Fishing,* both books being published by Macdonald & Co. Righyni resented the tendency of the era, still prevalent on some Southern chalk streams, that the fish be regarded as vermin and, in consequence, be persecuted in chalk rivers. He gathered his friends together and The Society was formed with Dr Ronald Broughton as Chairman of the original group which formed the Committee. The first Meeting, attended by about 15 persons, took place in Eccles. There are now in the region of 700 members spread internationally.

The fish is widely distributed in the British Isles, from the river Tay in the north to the Tamar in the south-west of England. In addition to some spate rivers, limestone waters, and rivers in Wales, the chalk streams of North Yorkshire also hold grayling.

The fish was introduced to the Test in 1816. It is recorded in the *Chronicles* of The Houghton Club that:

> *'About the year 1816 Mr Tate and Mr Snow of Longstock sent John Haines their fisherman to Heron Court to fetch 25 brace of grayling given to them by Lord Malmesbury. Haines brought the fish in a water cart, and rested them in the miller's trunk at Romsey. One fish only died, and the survivors were put into the river Test at Longstock. They were small, not more than 3 or 4oz each.'*

That they prospered is evident. The *Chronicles* record that in 1846 there were caught in the Test waters of The Houghton Club 73 grayling at an average weight of 1lb 11oz.

The natural distribution, since the last Ice Age, percolated through river systems from the Danube, the Rhine and the North Sea river, through various connections which have been lost over the millennia. The rivers of England and South East Scotland, bordering on the North Sea, were the original grayling waters, from the river Thames northwards.

The Society does not have its own waters, but is comprised, in the British Isles, of local area member groups with a regional Secretary. These areas arrange their own fishing. In the South, on the chalk streams, members usually fish trout rivers after the season for that fish has closed. There is a central Committee which meets two or three times a year. This body concerns itself with wider ranging matters. These include the preservation of grayling in a pure genetic condition which is usually related to the individual river in which certain strains reside.

Grayling flies

The season usually starts in July. By that time fish are well mended after spawning during the close season from mid-March to mid-June. It is of interest that trout spawn before the coldest weeks, and grayling after the frostiest. Thereafter, in past seasons with Reg Righyni, Ron has taken grayling on fly from July until February. Dry fly, nymph, upstream wet fly, and in particular his own invention, the Broughton Pupa, all take a toll.

Broughton's Pupa
- Hook: Size 16, Partridge J1A
- Silk: Purple
- Body: One strand of dark heron herl substitute
- Hackle: Two turns of dark starling neck
- Wing: From a jay wing feather, with dark root and pale tip

With this wide variety of methods one may cope with most situations: if fish are feeding on the top there is no point in fishing underneath; if they are feeding underneath there is no point in fishing on the top.

In winter, although fly hatch in warm conditions, fish are more likely to be taken on a sub-surface offering than a dry fly. As Ron points out, one has not only to match the hatch, and life cycle stage of the food, but to observe the depth at which grayling are foraging. He notes that fish often feed in the very skin of the water surface. There he pursues them with soft hackled flies such as the Waterhen Bloa which may be taken as an insect in eclosion.

Waterhen Bloa
- Hook: Size 14, Partridge J1A
- Silk: Yellow Pearsall Gossamer No 4; palish yellow
- Body: Just a haze of water vole, dubbed on the silk, the yellow to show through. The body should be short, covering two-thirds of the hook shank
- Hackle: Two turns of an under covert feather of a moorhen. His soft hackled wet flies are not only effective in the water skin, but work well 6-8in below the surface. The essential characteristic is that the hackles must be soft to provide movement — this is not an attribute of the Pheasant Tail Nymph. In addition to his wet flies, the dry patterns of the trout angler are acceptable.

In April 1991 Ron took a 3½lb grayling on a No 14 Blue Dun. This ancient fly, described by Charles Cotton, may be recommended to the chalk stream angler as a general imitation of both the iron blue and dark olive duns. It would need, to encompass these two insects of different size, to be carried on No 18 and No 14 hooks.

In autumn the Apple Green, a Pale Olive with ginger hackle, is an effective representation of those olives which hatch at that time. Ron strongly recommends that general imitation dry flies used in September and October should have ginger hackles.

If his dry fly, nymph, and wet fly armoury were severely restricted, the choice would be as follows:

- **Skues' Rusty Dun**

This has a dark blue hackle with ruddy brown, or mahogany, seals fur body. The two tail whisks should also be dark blue, and the tying silk orange. A No 14 Partridge Capt. Hamilton hook is ideal.

- **Red Spinner, Blue Dun, Goddard's Last Hope**

These three each find a place.

- Then there is the **Adjutant,** a Halford fly, of which the Master's dressing is taken from his book *Floating Flies and How to Dress Them* (1886):

- Wings: Medium starling or pale coot
- Body: A strand from the pinion or tail feather of an Adjutant
- Hackle and Whisk: Blue Andalusian
- Hook: 00 or 000.

Halford writes: *'The strand of Adjutant is stripped on one edge only, by tearing down the longer flue with the thumb and forefinger of the left hand. If not procurable, a strip of quill from the pinion feather of an oldish starling can be substituted, although not so good an imitation as the Adjutant. This is the October tint of iron blue.'*

Ron finds the Adjutant takes grayling in imitation of both iron blue and black gnat.

On the dressing of wet flies, Ron is adamant that they be tied sparse. There should be only two turns of hackle or, if possible, one and a half turns. The hackle should be tied facing forward to allow the fibres to kick and move as they press against the water flow. The hook should be short. Considering nymphs, Ron finds the Pheasant Tail as attractive as the Grayling Bug. The Bug is the best imitation he has seen of a maggot — 'although he would not have mentioned the fact to Frank Sawyer!'

Ronald uses a floating fly line, but does not always cast upstream. Although up-river casting is the method generally used, a downstream cast is made from time to time, provided the nymph or fly is able to drift without drag.

Where grayling lie

Finding fish is a priority. They tend to lie lower down a pool than trout, and below, rather than above a set of hatches or other waterfall. The sides of currents should be searched, rather than the centre of the flow which tends to be the habitat of small trout. Such hints have value in winter. In summer, when there may be low levels and flows, grayling are sometimes found in the turbulence at the head of a pool. They lie deeper than trout. It is the subject of controversy whether they rise to a position 'on the fin' as is the case with feeding trout taking floating flies. The majority opinion is that they remain close to the river bed, shooting up at speed to take an insect. It follows that grayling cannot feed on surface food if the water is discoloured, because they are unable to discern an insect from their river bed position. One is therefore unlikely to be successful if a river is turbid after heavy rain. With this opinion Ronald is in agreement. If you ask him the best time of day to fish in clear water, the succinct reply will be: 'When there is a hatch of fly.' In his desire not to be tied down on this aspect of the sport he follows an earlier authority: The Marquis of Granby in his book *The Trout* (Longmans, Green, and Co 1898): *'As to what hours of the day are the best for catching grayling, it is obvious that, as they are in season from August to December, they rise at very different times during these months.'*

There are plenty of grayling in the chalk streams. I am grateful that this wild fish extends our season almost throughout the winter. He is game. Izaak Walton had this to say: 'He is very gamesome at the fly and much simpler, and therefore bolder than the trout, for he will rise 20 times at a fly if you miss him and yet rise again.'
29 November 1991

Applications for membership of The Grayling Society may be made to:
Membership Secretary, Clare Pickover,
The Grayling Society, 20 Somersall Lane, Chesterfield S40 3LA
Tel: (0246) 568078

Epilogue

5 October 1991

When Lara and I go to Bossington for grayling in October the wind blows downstream from the north. There ought to be a law against the north wind, and against cold rain which hamper my efforts. It didn't hamper Lara who started off with a 3lb rainbow, below the bridge, by the single willow, under the far bank. Brian, the Head Keeper, told her where to cast, and the rainbow's fate was sealed. I am used to being outshone. How she does it I don't know, casting to the far distant bank, with a tree to the rear, a weed bed in front, and an 8ft split cane rod. Last year it was the same: for me a blank, for Lara a fat fish. But I didn't really go for rainbow, or so I said, grayling were my quarry.

There are wild brown at Bossington: golden fish, full finned, red spotted and fine of tail. These we returned after removing the hook with artery forceps and wet hands. They were not our prey. Grayling we might take, and a rainbow, said Brian.

By lunchtime two grayling had taken the No 14 Pheasant Tail Nymph, the one with the twist of copper wire. I cannot claim skill. They helped themselves deep down and just appeared, wriggling and twisting in silver flashes as is the way of grayling. The wind still blew, and the rain slanted down, and not a trout or grayling rose. Flies were sensible. They stayed below. Not a dun hatched, and if one had been brave he would have been blown off the water.

It changed after lunch. The wind ceased. There was a moment of warmth. I could cast upstream. A trout rose; grayling followed. The 4X leader was replaced by 5X for flies were coming down. Wading out I caught them as they floated. They washed onto my half-submerged fingers, like eels on a grid. A pale watery, almost primrose of wing, with a body as fine as a barley whisker and the colour of the grain. From my submerged hand the dun floated off and sailed on.

Then they appeared. Dark flies with iron blue wings. Stark, erect and tiny on the sky-reflecting water they floated down, one at a time, and the grayling fed. Dimples were everywhere. Grayling dimple; trout roll. There were one or two rolls with the dimples, and they were upstream of me on the mirror and I couldn't fail. Standing there, with the water swirling about my thighs, I hooked them, and played them, and tweaked them free. Four, five or six took the No 18 Iron Blue. There was no time to change. I just blew out his crumpled hackles, shook him in the Supafloat and false cast him dry. In half an hour they came no more. It was over. The rise complete; the water still. Partridge creaked in the meadow as the sky darkened, and a cock pheasant clattered in the wood. I hooked up the fly and walked back to the hut.

Glossary of Angling Terms

Adipose fin — small fin on the back of a game fish between the dorsal fin and the tail
AFTM scale — defines the weight of a fly line
Alevin — the minute fish which hatches from an ova
Aquifer — chalk stratum underlying the hills and valley of a chalk stream
Arlesley Bomb — a weight incorporating a swivel

Backing — an additional length of strong, thin line joined to, and beneath, the fly line on a reel
Backing up — a method of fishing a salmon fly whilst moving from the tail to the head of a pool
Baggot — a hen salmon swollen with eggs which it cannot extrude
Bail arm — the part of a fixed spool reel which gathers and winds the line onto the spool
Bank — (of a river) looking downstream, the right bank is to your right, the left bank to your left
Beetle — mallet or sledge hammer
Butt — (of leader) the thickest part of a tapered leader where it joins the fly line
Butt — (of rod) the handle end of a rod

Caddis — another name for a sedge fly
Carrier — a small stream leaving, and later re-joining, the main river
Chironomid — a midge
Chlorophyll — colouring matter of green parts of a plant
Collar — short length of thick monofilament sometimes placed between the fly line and the leader
Corixa — water beetle
Crane fly — daddy long-legs
Creel — wicker basket carried by angler to hold trout

Dangle — (on the) position of fly, or taking salmon, when straight downstream of the angler
Dropper — a second fly fished on a leader above the point fly (salmon only, single flies are used in chalk stream dry fly fishing)
Drowner — man who regulates the hatches of a water meadow
Dun — first aerial stage of flies of the order Ephemeroptera

Eel trap — metal grid over which river is diverted and on which eels become stranded on their migration down river

Flight — (hook mount) treble hook, wire (sometimes nylon) and swivel passing through hollow centre of body of Devon minnow
Fry — a small young fish (after the alevin stage)

Gaff — a pointed, barbless hook on a shaft for landing salmon
Gape — defines the gap measurement between the point and shank of a hook

Gravid — (hen) fish with well-developed roe
Grilse — a 'one sea winter' salmon
Groyne — a man-made protrusion from river bank to create a salmon lie
Gye net — a large salmon or sea trout net carried on the back

Hackle — cocks neck feather used in dressing dry flies (hen hackle for wet flies and some nymphs)
Halford, Frederic M. (1844–1914) — the doyen of dry fly anglers
Hatch — (see *Sluice*)
Herl — a length of feather quill on which are short fibres. Used when dressing the bodies of some artificial flies
Herling — small sea trout

Jack — a young pike

Kelt — spawned fish
Kype — upward hook on lower jaw of cock fish

Leader — (cast) the length of nylon joining the fly line to the fly or nymph
Ledger — (see *Paternoster*)
Lie — place where fish pause or rest in a river
Lure — wide term embracing spinning baits, artificial flies, plugs, etc

Marrow spoon — a narrow scoop used to withdraw stomach contents of dead trout for examination
Mepps — a revolving spoon bait

Neck — (of a river pool) the narrow entrance where the river runs into a pool
Nymph — underwater stage in life cycle of some insects

'On the fin' — position of feeding river trout close to water surface and waiting to take passing floating natural flies
Ova — egg of a fish

Parr — small fish in early stage of life cycle
Paternoster — (ledger) method of fishing a spinning bait, worm or prawn slowly and close to the river bed
Peal — West Country term for a sea trout
Peal sling — quick-release harness, of leather or webbing, by which a Gye net is carried on the angler's back
pH — a scale defining the acidity/alkalinity of water
Piling — sheets or staves of wood or metal to reinforce the bank of a river
Priest — a short truncheon with which to kill a fish by hitting on the head
Pupa — an immature stage of some flies

Ranunculus — water plant, sometimes called water buttercup
Rapala — a type of plug bait

Redd — depression cut in gravel or small stones by fish in river bed where female deposits ova, which are then fertilized by milt of cock fish

Run-off — the downstream, tail-end of a pool

Schoolie — small sea trout on first return to river in summer from the sea

Scissors — (to be hooked in the) description of the point of the angle between the upper and lower jaws of a fish

Sea lice — suckered lice found on flanks and back of salmon and sea trout when they enter the river from the sea

Sea trout — a migratory brown trout

Shoot — (to) allow extra fly line to be pulled out through the rod rings when casting, to obtain extra distance

Skues, George E.M. (1858–1949) — innovator of fishing the upstream nymph

Sluice — (hatch) boards which may be raised or lowered to control depth or flow of river

Spate — the rise and fall of water level in a river following rain (not applicable to chalk streams)

Spinner — (natural fly) second aerial and final egg-laying stage of flies of the order Ephemeroptera, sometimes called a 'spent'

Spinners — general term covering revolving artificial baits

Split cane — a rod of hexagon cross-section formed of six faced strips of cane bonded or wrapped together with silk

Spoon — a type of artificial bait, sometimes revolving

Spring tide — high tide occurring after full or new moon

Stale fish — a salmon or sea trout which has been in fresh water for some weeks, usually a fish in autumn that is darkish or red

Stew — a pond to hold trout for stocking

Stickle — a shallow section of river between two pools

Tailer — a wire noose to land salmon. Grips at wrist above the tail

Toby — a type of spoon bait

Trace — about a metre of nylon, sometimes wire, between the swivel at the end of spinning line and bait

Walking up — a method of persuading a salmon to move upstream, following the angler

Wye weight — a weight used in salmon and sea trout fishing; metal loop at one end for line attachment, and swivel at the other to which the trace is knotted

Wind knot — a knot formed unintentionally in the leader whilst casting. The knot weakens the leader

Where to Fish and Where to Stay

The River Test

Laverstoke	Fisheries Consultant — Alistair Stobart Portals Property Ltd, Laverstoke Mill, Laverstoke, Whitchurch, Hampshire (0256) 892360
Middleton Estate Longparish	Head Keeper — Jeff Smith Fishery Lodge, Forton, Longparish, Hampshire (0264) 72393
Govett's Estate, Newton Stacey	Head Keeper — Terry Snelgrove, Riverside, Newton Stacey, Nr Andover, Hampshire (0264) 860271
Wherwell Estate	Head Keeper — Bill Hawkins, Antlers Cottage, Church Street, Wherwell, Andover, Hampshire (0264) 74468
Bossington Estate	Head Keeper — Brian Parker, Mill Cottage, Houghton, Stockbridge, Hampshire (0794) 388530
Kimbridge Estate	Ian Veal (Sporting Manager), 2 Meadow Cottage, Kimbridge, Romsey, Hampshire (0794) 40428
Timsbury Fishery	Knight Frank & Rutley (Managing Agents), 10a High Street, Hungerford, Berkshire (0488) 682726
Broadlands Estate	Head of Fishing Dept — Bernard Aldrich, Lee Lodge, Broadlands, Romsey, Hampshire (0703) 513052
Nursling Fishery	Head Keeper — Vic Foot, Nursling Fishery, Nr Totton, Southampton, Hampshire (0703) 732880
Testwood Fishery	Head Keeper — Graham Purbrick, The Fishing Lodge, Testwood, Southampton, Hampshire (0703) 867508
The Orvis Co has a beat at Kimbridge	Bridge House, High Street, Stockbridge, Hampshire (0264) 810017
The Rod Box has a beat at Longparish	London Road, Kings Worthy, Winchester, Hampshire (0962) 883600

Where to stay

- The Grosvenor Hotel, High Street, Stockbridge, Hampshire (0264) 810606
- The Old Three Cups, High Street, Stockbridge, Hampshire (0264) 810527
- Danebury Hotel, High Street, Andover, Hampshire (0264) 23332

The River Itchen

The Orvis Co has a beat at Kings Worthy	High Street, Stockbridge, Hampshire (0264) 810017
The Rod Box many beats	London Road, Kings Worthy, Winchester, Hampshire (0962) 883600
Lower Itchen Fishery	Lindsay Farmiloe, Embley Ridge, Gardners Lane, East Wellow, Nr Romsey, Hampshire (0703) 812599

| *Woodmill Fishery* | G.O. Roberts, Woodmill Fishery, Swaythling, Southampton, Hampshire |

Where to stay
- The Bugle Inn, Twyford, Hampshire (0962) 713070
- The Royal Hotel, St Peter Street, Winchester, Hampshire (0962) 840840
- Lainston House, Sparsholt, Winchester, Hampshire (0962) 63588
  (see also Stockbridge hotels)

The River Meon

Portsmouth Services Fly Fishing Association	Hon Sec — Dick Stacey, Willow Mead, (opp Otterbourne PO), Nr Winchester, Hampshire (0962) 713806
	Membership restricted to personnel serving or who have served in the Armed Services
Park Gate & District Royal British Legion	Hon Sec (fly fishing section) — W.E. James, 4 Norman Road, Gosport, Hampshire (0705) 527156

Where to stay
- Little Uplands Country Hotel, Garrison Hill, Droxford, Hampshire (0489) 878507 — also has small stocked lake and 500yds river.
- The Bugle Hotel, Titchfield, Hampshire (0329) 41888

The River Avon

The Services Dry Fly Fishing Association at Netheravon	Hon Sec — Col D.A.N.C. Miers, East Farmhouse, Wylye, Warminster, Wiltshire (09885) 219; Head Keeper — Allan Cook, 620 Thorn Road, Netheravon, Wiltshire (0980) 70288
Salisbury & District Angling Club has many waters.	Hon Gen Sec — R.W. Hillier, 29 New Zealand Avenue, Salisbury, Wiltshire (0722) 21164
The Piscatorial Society	Hon Sec — James Hunt, 26 High Street, Market Lavington, Devizes, Wiltshire (0380) 813357
Trafalgar & Longford Estates	Head Keeper — Mike Trowbridge, Waterways, Chapel Lane, Charlton All Saints, Salisbury, Wiltshire (0725) 21167
The Somerley Fishery	Head Keeper — John E. Levell, 4 Forestside Gardens, Poulner, Ringwood, Hampshire (0425) 477827
The Royalty Fishery	Fishery Manager — David Ransly, Watersmeet, Mill Road, Christchurch, Dorset (0202) 485262

Where to stay
- Head Keeper Allan Cook of Netheravon, can arrange B&B (0980) 70288
- Antrobus Arms, 15 Church Street, Amesbury, Wiltshire (0980) 623163

- Hayburn Wyke Guest House, 72 Castle Road, Salisbury, Wiltshire (0722) 412627
- The Red Lion, Milford Street, Salisbury, Wiltshire (0722) 23334
- Struan Hotel, Horton Road, Ringwood, Hampshire (0425) 473553
- Fisherman's Haunt, Salisbury Road, Winkton, Christchurch, Dorset (0202) 477283

The River Wylye

The Piscatorial Society	Head Keeper — George Maich, 5 Sherrington, Warminster, Wiltshire (0985) 50272
Bapton	The Farm Manager, Bapton Farms, Nr Wylye, Wiltshire (0985) 6268
Wilton Fly Fishers	Hon Sec — E.J. Hunt, Lee Mill Cottage, Leegomery, Telford, Shropshire (0952) 252374 Head Keeper — Norman Smith, Keepers Cottage, Manor Farm Lane, Wishford, Salisbury, Wiltshire (0722) 790231

Where to stay
- The Swan Inn, Stoford, Nr Salisbury, Wiltshire (0722) 790236
- Peter Biscoe, Newton Cottage, South Newton, Salisbury, Wiltshire (0722) 743111

The River Nadder

Compton Chamberlayne Estate (also from Rod Box)	Head Keeper — Charles Patrick, Dinton Mill, Dinton, Near Wilton, Wiltshire (0722) 716445
The Burcombe Fly Fishing Club	Maj Christopher Perkins, Baverstock, Nr Wilton, Wiltshire (0722) 716383
Teffont Fly Fishing Club	Col J.N.D. Lucas, Chilmark, Nr Wilton, Wiltshire (0722) 716463

Where to stay
- The Lamb Inn, Hindon, Salisbury, Wiltshire (0747) 789573
- The Bell Inn, South Newton, Salisbury, Wiltshire (0722) 743336
- Newton Cottage, South Newton (0722) 743111

The Rivers Kennet and Lambourn

The Chilton Estate	Head Keeper — Stephen Jones, The Fishing Cottage, Chilton Estate, Leverton, Hungerford, Berkshire (0488) 682327 (Estate office — (0488) 682581)
The Hungerford Fishery	Hon Sec & Gen Manager — Col D. Macey, 100 High Street, Hungerford, Berkshire (0488) 682770

The following are possible sources of trout fishing in the Kennet area:
- *Savernake Fly fishers* — John Hounslow (0672) 512607
- *Eastridge Estate (Littlecote water)* — Eastridge, Ramsbury
- *Rupert Wilson,* The Coach House, Lower Denford, Hungerford, Berkshire (0488) 683758
- *Estate Office,* Hungerford Park Estate, Berkshire
- *Barton Court Fishery* — E.D. Hill, Barton Court Fishery, Spinney House, Kintbury, Berkshire (0488) 58226
- *The Sutton Estate,* Estate Office, Nr Newbury, Berkshire (0635) 40036
- *The Eddington Estate (The Craven water),* Hungerford, Berkshire.
- *Roxton Sporting Ltd* — manager Ian Abbot, 10 Bridge Street, Hungerford (0488) 84943

Where to stay
- The Bell, Lambourn Road, Boxford, Nr Newbury, Berkshire (0488) 38253
- The Bear Hotel, Charnham Street, Hungerford, Berkshire (0488) 82512
- The Three Swans Hotel, High Street, Hungerford (0488) 682721

The River Allen

Upper Allen Fishery	Shaftesbury Estates, The Estate Office, Wimborne St Giles, Dorset (07254) 214
	River Manager — H.J. Teasdale, Woodlands Gate, Woodlands, Wimborne, Dorset (0202) 822325

Where to stay
- The Horton Inn, Nr Wimborne, Dorset (0258) 840252
- The Bull Inn, Wimborne St Giles, Dorset (07254) 284

The Rivers Frome and Piddle

Wrackleford House (also day tickets)	C.J.R. Pope, Wrackleford House, Dorchester, Dorset (0305) 262900
Dorchester Fishing Club	J.J. Fisher, Rew Hollow, Godmanstone, Dorchester
The Weld Estate	Agent — C. Rothwell, Lulworth Castle, Wareham, Dorset (Estate Office: 092 941 352)
The Moreton Estate	arranged by Humberts of Blandford
The East Holme Estate	arranged by Humberts of Blandford (0258) 452 343
East Stoke River Laboratory	East Stoke, Wareham, Dorset.
Tolpuddle Trout Fishery Piddle only.	Richard Slocock, Lawrences Farm, Tolpuddle, Dorcester, Dorset (0305) 848460
Trigon Estate	G. Sturdy, Trigon House, Nr Wareham, Dorset (0929) 55 2097

Where to stay
- The Priory Hotel, Wareham, Dorset (0929) 551666
- Kemps Hotel, East Stoke, Wareham (0929) 462 563
- Worgret Manor Hotel, Wareham (0929) 552957
- King's Arms Hotel, 30 High Street East, Dorchester (0305) 265353
- Wessex Fly Fishing, Lawrences Farm, Tolpuddle, Dorset (0305) 848460

Game Fishing Instruction

Charles Bingham, West Down, Warrens Cross, Whitchurch, Tavistock, Devon (0822) 613899

The Orvis Co, Bridge House, High Street, Stockbridge, Hampshire (0264) 810017

The Rod Box, London Road, Kings Worthy, Winchester, Hampshire (0962) 883600

Wessex Fly Fishing, Lawrences Farm, Tolpuddle, Dorset (0305) 848460